More than a left foot

More than a left foot

Bob Williams-Findlay

Resistance Books
London

© Bob Williams-Findlay

Cover design by Keith Dodds

ISBN 978-0-902869-72-1

Published May 2020 by Resistance Books
PO Box 62732, London, SW2 9GQ
info@resistancebooks.org
www.resistancebooks.org

Contents

Preface by Marian Brooks-Sardinha   1
Introduction: I am that I am   12
Background story: Coming to terms with disability   19

Part One: A life apart   39
    1. In the beginning   40
    2. First steps   54
    3. My teenage years   72
    4. Love, death and crazy talk   89

Part Two: Mainstreaming my life   109
    5. The art of living   110
    6. When two worlds collide   127
    7. A sense of self   145
    8. Glory days   158
    9. On the barricade   177
    10. The aftermath   199
    11. New beginning   216
    12. Going down the Brummie road   226

Part Three: More than a left foot   251
    13. I'm gonna try and change the world 252
    14. From both sides now   270
    15. Dreams, schemes and other things 289
    16. Make your mind up   305
    17. The wilderness years   324
    18. Into the light   342

References   355
About Resistance Books   369

Preface

Marian Brooks-Sardinha

Bob Williams-Findlay, the well-known disability activist, has written this book as a personal memoir and as an explanation of his development as a thinker and doer in his field. My only claim to be qualified to write this preface is that I became friends with Bob at a very important period in his life, when he enrolled at Essex University.

When I first met Bob, I had little appreciation of the way in which disabled people were marginalised from the mainstream of society. While I had a basic conception of unfairness and exclusion, it was limited by a lack of experience and by the fact that I was a child of my time. To do justice to the impact that meeting Bob had on me and my other friends, I will first try to describe briefly some of my own encounters with disability, growing up in the Fifties and Sixties.

As a child, I was quite severely asthmatic. I was prescribed amphetamine-based drugs, common at the time. I did not know that the drugs were almost certainly responsible for making me anxious and very thin. Even if my parents had known this, what choice did they have? Treatments were limited and there were no alternatives. I was seen as 'delicate', and advised not to take up a wind instrument or over-exert myself. I was also prescribed breathing exercises every day which must have helped, because by twelve or so, the asthma had resolved to the extent that I could cope with most things except school runs. As I grew into my teens, I retained a residual idea of being 'delicate', which didn't stop me getting into the usual things like smoking, staying up all night, dancing frenetically and so on. The point to this is that at no time did I consider myself disabled, and nor did my family. A long-term condition that cannot be seen might make you 'delicate', but not *disabled*. Disability was 'other'.

Educational practice in the nineteen-fifties and early sixties dictated that 'impaired' and 'able-bodied' children rarely crossed paths. I remember no child at my primary school with major physical impairments. In the Fifties my rural school had three class teachers, including the head, who catered for over one hundred pupils. There were no teaching assistants. Consequently, if you had achieved your goals and were at a loose end, it was usual to help out other children with reading and writing. I do recollect 'helping' a little boy a couple of years younger than me. He had what I suppose professionals would call mild intellectual impairment and struggled with the basics of reading. I got the impression from things adults whispered that his inclusion in a mainstream school was a bit unusual for the time. He had siblings at the school and no doubt his family fought to have him enrolled there. Nowadays, with rigorous attainment targets for schools, he might well have been 'off-rolled'. I don't think I was much help as an eight-year-old teaching assistant, and although his reading didn't improve a lot, he learnt a valuable life lesson in dealing effectively with bossy people! I lost touch with this boy when I changed schools, but I imagine that at the end of the primary stage, he would have been wrenched from his family and his supportive village environment, to be sent to a special school, possibly as a boarder.

Talking of boarding, my next school was a girls' direct grant foundation, a Methodist school that also functioned as a public sector grammar school for local girls who passed the Eleven-Plus. Consequently, it had an unusual selection of students, including quite a number of international and armed forces children. The boarding facility ensured that parents whose jobs precluded their daughters going to a day school were catered for. While most of these parents were genuinely upset at having to choose boarding, there were a few who effectively 'dumped' their daughters there. As my Mum taught at the school, we sometimes had these girls to stay for part of the holidays, as did other staff, or they would have had to stay in the boarding houses all year without a break. One or two were the illegitimate children of prominent members of the upper classes, others the collaterally damaged daughters of parents caught up in 'scandalous' divorces. A few were disabled, though there were no wheelchair users, given the labyrinthine, twisting corridors, different levels and gothic staircases. I particularly remember a girl with dwarfism, who spent a lot of her holiday time with one of the house-mistresses, who eventually became like a second mother to her. She seemed happy enough at the school. She was well liked, though sometimes treated with a kind of schmaltzy patronisation by one or two of the staff. The general opinion amongst her peers was that her family must be ashamed of her. To be fair, no-one at the school approved of this. She must have been resilient, and I believe she went on to have an independent life, in spite of being so cloistered in her formative years. Many years later I saw her, well-dressed and confident, standing across the platform at a London train station. I waved tentatively, not thinking she'd recognise me, but she didn't see me.

In the sixth form, having switched to a co-educational school, I became used to the casual use of terms like 'mong' and 'spazzer' used mainly by the boys to describe people with impairments, and frequent mocking of misfit students by the use of these labels, often accompanied by gestures and mimicry. This, of course, goes on today, though it is a bit more likely to be challenged by teachers, and occasionally other students. I did observe at the time that girls, in an all-girls environment, seemed less cruel than boys. I'm not sure whether that remains true now, but with the exception of the odd bully, the female environment was kinder, less posturing and dismissive than one dominated by young teenage males.

To fast-forward now, I went to Essex University at the end of 1969, and did a language year in Spanish, followed by a degree in Government, graduating in 1973. During my undergraduate years, I got involved in the 1972 miners' strike when students hosted striking miners from Yorkshire NUM, putting them up on campus to help them picket incoming coal shipments that were being brought in. It was an exhilarating time and a genuinely novel co-operation. Unlike a lot of people, we cheered every time the lights went out during the three-day week crisis. I also joined the International Marxist Group, so I became a card-carrying Trotskyist, engaged in movements like Troops Out of Ireland, feminist campaigns and a lot of theoretical discussion, on which the IMG placed great importance. The IMG and I weren't always a good fit. I was keen and passionate about the political work and the theory, but often had a sneaking suspicion that I was more frivolous and ill-disciplined than some of my fellow comrades, which left me with feelings of guilt and inferiority. I was getting depressed and my life and my studies suffered, so I took a temporary leave of absence from the group, re-joining but finally resigning over differences in around 1976. I had friends, some very good ones, but I was badly in need of a friend on the same political wavelength. Bob proved to be that friend.

During his years at Essex from 1973-77, Bob's politics and later direction were formed in the crucible of the student 'Troubles'. My timeline of these events has blurred, and now I remember specific moments, vignettes and scenes rather than having a cogent, reliable memory of the order of things. The dates I ascribe here may not be entirely accurate, but the narrative is, I hope, true.

I'd heard of Bob before I met him, probably during the academic year 1972-3. He was described by comrades in the IMG and other friends as a poet with cerebral palsy living in Wivenhoe, a pretty and bohemian village near the university. I also knew he was a friend of Bernard Brett, a disabled activist with whom I was acquainted. Not having met Bob at that stage, I had the impression of a folk poet, someone reading his work in a corner of a pub. That was only part of the story.

When Bob started at the university and joined the International Marxist Group, I got to know him better. There were a few disabled students at Essex by this time. The university maintained that it was a disability-friendly place, to use a term that hadn't yet been invented. A new, brutalist campus, it had lifts and ramps, and it was possible for students with limited mobility to live on the ground floors of the residential towers. Bob's account of this environment shows that it was, at most, partially accessible by today's standards. However, Bob didn't choose Essex because of this; he chose it because it was there, and so was he.

Bob says in his memoir that he was not very motivated by disability politics at this time. We did talk about it quite a lot, but mostly in terms of the effects of institutionalisation, which he had recently escaped from. I remember, as he confirms in this book, that he came out of institutional care unable to cook, or really handle much in the way of housework, but he would not have been the only student in this plight at the time. We were mostly pretty relaxed about these things. We talked, more seriously, about the psychological effects of institutional care, and even at this time he was articulate about the social oppression of people with impairments. Apart from having to listen carefully to get used to his speech, I think most of his new friends accepted him without taking his impairment that much into account. I remember at the end of a night in the pub, Bob, being pretty sober, offered to get fish and chips for everyone. Some older people came up, horrified, and said, 'You're not really going to let him do that, are you?' We replied something to the effect that

Bob was probably more capable of doing the chip run than anyone else in the pub. I think this incident is telling, in that although the people in the pub were clearly wrong, it's probably fair to say that most of Bob's university friends didn't take Bob's struggles with his impairment into much account. We didn't really think about those issues very much, except, perhaps, in terms of worrying about Bob's safety when we were in potentially dangerous actions like those at Grunwick.

Bob's circumstances occasionally conveyed minor advantages. For example, he always evaded the police in his 'Noddy car', a small disability vehicle not unlike a Reliant Robin, but with one seat. (Why, the thinking went, would a disabled driver need to carry passengers? The Noddy car was standard issue. Getting a bigger adapted vehicle was complex.) This was where patronising attitudes sometimes worked in Bob's favour. He mentions that a small person could crouch down in the car unseen by the cops. That small person was often me, usually clutching a few beers as he gave me a lift home! On one occasion, two of us got a lift, one crouched down on each side. The police never stopped us.

Bob goes into detail in this book about the series of protests at Essex known as the 'Troubles', between 1974-77. I was also involved in those events. In 1973-4 I was taking a year out prior to doing my master's degree, and working locally, so I had to be a bit discreet about it at the beginning, but was heavily involved in the later stages. Reading Bob's account of these days, a number of things occur to me with hindsight. The university authorities really handled the situation very poorly. I think, like Bob, that the events of 1974-77 were a different type of political action from the earlier events of 1968. I don't believe that 1968 bothered them too much, but they were really concerned about the use of picketing and tactics evolved from the 1972 miners' strike. Of course, during the earlier 1974 picketing phase, there were striking miners again on campus. I think that really scared the university. Essex was new, its reputation high but precarious, and it was getting hammered in the right-wing press. Essex had also been home to some of the Angry Brigade, an anarcho-situationist group, some of whom were convicted of terrorism offences in 1972. We, of course, had little in common with them, but the press coverage blurred the distinction. By 1974 I think that the university leadership was very afraid.

Bob explains this in his chapter on the Essex Troubles, in particular, how the Annan Report on the events upheld the idea that students were being directed by an elite band of dedicated 'reds under the bed'. Flattering, perhaps, but this was an exaggeration. Bob is right when he says we stumbled into it after getting involved in a perfectly respectable campaign on student grants and later on fees. However, this Cold War hangover in thinking shows us why the university authorities were so punitive against the students in general, and a few in particular. It is tempting to think that Bob, Will and Ronnie were singled out for extremely harsh treatment because they were all in, or close to the International Marxist Group. Possibly, but the irony is that for the IMG this was a bit of a sideshow in some respects. Student activism was important, yes, but the branch wanted to do other work; there was Ireland, there were women's campaigns, supporting the UCATT Shrewsbury 24, going to the early Rock against Racism events and other anti-fascist initiatives. Towards the end of this period, we spent a lot of time supporting the Grunwick strikers at Willesden. These are just samples of the things Bob and I did, in addition to trying to give some attention to our studies and other commitments. It was exciting, but sometimes you felt your life was on hold.

Looking back on this frenetic time, I can't help feeling that Bob *was* singled out because of his perceived disability. The university unwisely adopted a legalistic route to overcome the protests, even in the face of opposition from many staff. By now a post-graduate student from 1974 until I left in 1977, I was quite aware of intense staff debates over what was going on. There was even a case of fisticuffs between two lecturers, which was kept hush-hush at the time. However, once the authorities went down the disciplinary route, they embarked upon a quasi-legal process of evidence gathering. Bob was at a disadvantage because he was more noticeable, and could not hide as others might do. A lot of the evidence against him and others was slapdash and inaccurate at the least, and included some downright lies. The standard of evidence for a university disciplinary procedure was lower than that required for a criminal case. For example, the university fined me for participation in the 1976 occupations, and I pointed out at the hearing that the Proctor could only have identified me within the banned area by peeping through a hole in the brown paper we had hastily put up on the glass doors to prevent being overlooked! He had not, of course, mentioned this in his statement. Much more seriously for Bob, there was interplay between the evidence gathered against him for internal purposes, and evidence put forward for his criminal trials. Somehow, against his intentions and against his nature, Bob had become the biggest, baddest red under the bed. This is especially ironic as, to my certain knowledge, he spent time and effort dissuading some impatiently naive students from taking revenge actions.

The things I remember most about Bob at Essex University are the long discussions we had at 5, Gladstone Road, a large and run-down Edwardian student house in the Hythe area of Colchester. I moved in in 1975, and stayed two years. A number of students came and went, some of them very politicised, others not. My brother, a trainee social worker, arrived a year later, and we all got along pretty well. The house was in a bad state of repair, but unusually for leftist students, we didn't make much fuss about it because the landlord was a mature student himself who had no money for renovations. I recently revisited the area and saw that the house has now been impeccably done up in an elegant style, no longer a student rental. In addition to the old residential towers, students now live in a large number of commercially-run, indentikit cubes with bright cladding, situated on the floodplain under the university.

Like me, Bob was finding IMG membership a two-edged sword. He had a poetic streak in his nature that didn't take easily to direction! There were a number of tendencies in the organisation, inevitably in a group that took a Leninist democratic centralist line, meaning, amongst other things, that you had to abide by the majority decision and defend it publicly. By the mid-Seventies there was rising interest in notions such as 'the personal is political.' Neither of us liked what is now called identity politics, but we were uneasy about the organisation's practice in many areas. Bob has gone into this in the book in greater detail, so I'll just say we spent a lot of time talking, reading and thinking about the Marxist concept of base and superstructure, cultural autonomy, and we were becoming more and more interested in the role of the arts within politics. During some of the period at Gladstone Road, I was painfully writing up my MA dissertation, so I had time to think. Both Bob and I became interested in a group, the Revolutionary Marxist Current, some of whose members eventually joined Big Flame. I started spending more time in London, where I contributed to Wedge, a short-lived but hopefully ground-breaking 'Revolutionary Magazine of Cultural Practice and Theory.' Probably our biggest claim to fame was that our name was pinched by Red Wedge, part of the 1970's anti-racist music scene! There is, indeed, another, modern online magazine of the same name. El Lissitsky has a lot to answer for.

I hope this account of our days at Gladstone Road doesn't sound too worthy. Bob remembers a lot of university gigs in his account of this period, and so do I, including going to see the Stranglers and the Damned, where the third band on the bill was a promising outfit called the Police. We went to local pubs, especially the Artilleryman in Colchester, then a rather charming, dusty old pub frequented more by students than soldiers, now a spruced-up, fashionable venue with a nice beer garden. We didn't really go clubbing, because, odd as it may seem to younger readers, the commercial night-time economy didn't really exist outside major cities in the 1970s. Some of us cooked in the house, which I enjoyed. Bob may remember the authentic Boston pork'n beans I made that took eleven hours to prepare!

Inevitably, our time at Essex was coming to an end. Bob got into the Centre for Contemporary Cultural Studies at Birmingham. This was another important milestone in Bob's development, and it was run very much as a co-operative effort under the late Stewart Hall. I went to Bradford to do another course. Our paths diverged, but in the following years we had a similar beginning to our entry into permanent employment. In the early years of the Thatcher government, it was difficult to secure permanent gainful, 'proper' employment, even if you had post-graduate qualifications. While Bob was taking his first steps via insecure and frustrating work with YOP trainees, I was working on similar temporary contracts in colleges, often working with the same kind of students and dealing with their external management companies.

Eventually, both of us found our way into more permanent career paths, but it was even harder for Bob than me. Bob's desire, when I first met him, was to break away from the disabling constraints of institutionalisation and the dispiritingly narrow options in life available to a disabled person at the time. And, boy, how he did it! He did it because he grabs at everything life has to offer, and because he has true grit. It is to Bob's huge credit that he has used his own experiences to deepen his knowledge and commitment to disability work and to politics in general, while still having a rich personal life. Describing him as a disability activist is hopelessly inadequate; Bob's distinctive approach is that everything he does is grounded in a historical, materialist vision. He always looks at a problem contextually, marking him out from others, and giving him the edge over those whose lack of such an analysis leads them into static identity politics. He does, to some extent, thank his time at Essex and Birmingham for this way of thinking. He has contributed a vast amount, and now that he is 'retired', he continues to inspire and encourage another generation. I therefore commend this book to anyone who wants to find out more about his life and thoughts.

Marian Brooks-Sardinha
Saltaire, September 2019

Introduction

I am that I am

This is why introductions are important – because in the beginning, despite the fact that we already believe we know what it means, there's a chance that over time the definition will change from one thing to another.

Andrew Kendall

I, a disabled person

In this introduction to *More Than A Left Foot*, I'm going to touch upon its core elements and provide context to my journey's path. If you've chose this book expecting one of those stories that details one person's triumph over tragedy, then you're likely to be sadly disappointed. This book isn't about an individual who's bravely battled against all odds in order to succeed. No doubt some people might choose to read my account of the things that have happened to me in this way; however this book is more about placing one individual's life's journey within the context of British society's treatment of people with significant impairments. In case you're not familiar with this term, I'm starting from the understanding that an impairment could be 'an injury, illness, or congenital condition that causes or is likely to cause a loss or difference of physiological or psychological function.' (Northern Officers Group, 1999; unpaged)

It's often said everyone has a story within them and, since I was a teenager, I've had the desire to write about my experiences in life. My starting point, of course, is to acknowledge that like almost every other human being there's an unquestionable uniqueness which has played a major role in shaping my life. My uniqueness is due to a cocktail of genes, experiences and influences which are both known and unknown. Nevertheless there's one aspect of my make up that has especially helped create the type of human being that I am. From the moment I was dragged into existence by a pair of forceps, my relationship with the world has been largely informed by the fact I was born with cerebral palsy (CP). Again, before anyone jumps to the wrong conclusion, I want to stress that in this book I'm not going to be talking so much about the impact of my medical condition on my life, but rather about the social and political consequences of being a person with a physical impairment living in a society I see as actively working against the interests of people like me. Another way of expressing this is to recognise that a significant part of my personal journey has been shaped, not by the impact of the CP itself, but as a result of how as a person with an impairment I've been impacted upon by the economic and social nature of our existing society which helps determine its structures, systems, values and differing cultures. This way of looking at the relationships between people with impairments and capitalist societies is explained in a stand-alone theoretically based chapter entitled, *Background story – Coming to terms with Disability*, which you're welcome to read when it suits you.

Why a piece of life-writing?

More Than A Left Foot isn't so much an autobiography but rather an attempt to develop a piece of life-writing which involves a personal account alongside historical events with the introduction of some political, sociological and psychological analysis along the way. Recognising my position within society as a person with cerebral palsy began when I was a teenager and can be linked to my desire to be a writer. Above I spoke briefly about my unquestionable uniqueness, but to a certain extent there are also any number of commonalities which have played a crucial part in my life story. There is one individual who had an early influence of my life and subsequently helped me to decide how to name this book. When asked to select a book by my teacher as a school leaving present, I chose the recently published Down All the Days by Irish poet and writer, Christy Brown. This was Brown's second book published sixteen years after the first which was called, *My Left Foot*. Christy Brown was born with CP in 1932 into a large Irish working-class family. He had learned to both write and draw with the only limb he could control, namely, his left foot. I enjoyed Down All the Days, but it was his first book that caught my imagination because there were large parts of his story, I felt I could identify with.

Is cerebral palsy a neurological disorder?

I feel it's necessary to speak briefly about cerebral palsy in terms of it being viewed as both a medical condition and an impairment. The term cerebral palsy (CP) refers to any one of a number of neurological disorders that appear in infancy or early childhood and permanently affects body movement and muscle coordination but don't worsen over time. Even though cerebral palsy affects muscle movement, it isn't caused by problems in the muscles or nerves. (A.A.N, 2018; unpaged) CP is considered the most common movement disorder in children. It occurs in about 2.1 per 1,000 live births. Cerebral palsy has been documented throughout history with the first known descriptions occurring in the work of Hippocrates in the 5th century BCE. (Wikipedia, unpaged) No two people are affected by CP in the same way however it is generally described as a disorder that affects muscle tone, movement, and motor skills (the ability to move in a coordinated and purposeful way). Cerebral palsy usually is caused by brain damage that happens before or during a baby's birth, or during the first 3 to 5 years of a child's life.

There are numerous forms of CP depending upon the cause and location of the brain injury. In my case it was always said that I had athetoid cerebral palsy, although many of the descriptions don't seem to match my experience. So, what goes on with my body? Dr Ananya Mandal (2018; unpaged) comes closest to explaining it for me:

> The thought areas of the brain trigger or stimulate the motor area to send signals to the muscles that finally carry out the action.
>
> Throughout the action there is a constant to and from of information between the brain and the muscles via nerves of the spinal cord. This regulates the power, speed, coordination and balance necessary for a smooth action. Gait or normal locomotion or walking, running etc. is another complex area of movement that in addition requires maintenance of posture and balance.

My speech and facial movement are also affected. How I move, and my dexterity, are governed by both my conscious and unconscious thoughts interacting with the social environment or the situations I find myself in. Living with the condition for over sixty years has given me this knowledge and understanding, but it also means I find myself often in conflict with how professionals view me, and people like me. This is a common criticism coming from a wide range of people with impairments. At no time in my life have I denied the fact that my brain was damaged at birth and as a consequence my body doesn't function in the way a 'standard body' (sic) does. Where it becomes complicated is that this 'reality' becomes subjected to interpretation and ways of seeing it that have been constructed over the years. Cerebral palsy has existed for centuries however it wasn't until the 19th century did it become part of medical pathology. We should note that pathology is the study of disease and that 'it bridges science and medicine'. (The RCP, 2018) From my point of view these conflicts largely arise from the dominant ideologies which construct disability as an individualised 'problem' and this focus has informed how social and cultural practice has steadily developed since the rise of capitalism. The impact of how society views and treats disabled people is a major theme in this book.

The structure of More Than A Left Foot

More Than A Left Foot is divided into three parts and covers the majority of my life. There are themes, issues and anecdotes I could've and wanted to include but in the end decided to leave out for various reasons. I've also spoken about certain people and events within specific contexts and made selective choices about talking about both personal and political issues. Constructing the book in this way means I've not attempted to reveal all the differing aspects of my character, breadth of interests or lay myself completely bare; warts and all. Some might argue, of course, I've revealed too much, others will say I've concealed things which needed to be out in the open, but there's a need to recognise I've certain responsibilities which include respecting the rights of others. I also accept changing the style of writing within chapters might displease.

Within part one, A Life Apart I explore my early life growing up with cerebral palsy (CP) and how it led to me being placed within segregated education. This early section of the book has a fairly straight forward narrative with an exploration and reflection on my experiences and relationships. There's a dual purpose in calling this part A Life Apart. Not only does it refer to my time in segregated education, it also introduces a book with the same title written by the researchers, Miller and Gwynne (1972). By coincidence I was outraged by this book as a young adult along with other disabled people and this reaction led to the first steps in our liberation struggle.

In the second part of the book, Mainstreaming My Life, the style of writing shifts with the introduction of a more academic feel as I employ theoretical concepts to address some of the social and political issues I was dealing with as I came increasingly into contact with nondisabled people and differing social situations. Similarly, this section will see the inclusion of some quotations and references. A core element of this middle part of the book centres upon what is chronologically a short space of time. I've devoted a significant length of the book to my time at the University of Essex because it had such a profound impact upon my life in terms of shaping the person I became.

The final part of the book, More Than A Left Foot, covers the substantial period of my adult life and offers an insight into the development of the Disabled People's Movement, my involvement in mainstream politics, an introduction to people I worked with, as well as featuring aspects of my personal journey.

Is calling the book, More Than A Left Foot, just a tribute to Christy Brown? As a socialist with cerebral palsy, I've always found it ironic to be called a 'Lefty' because of my left-wing politics. When thinking about writing this book one of the things I considered was the desire to show that I was more than just a person with CP or someone driven by politics; so it seemed logical to choose this title. Given this, the title and final part of the book are therefore a deliberate play on words; words that are hugely significant to me. By taking this approach within the book I believe I'm challenging the traditional idea that there's something wrong with me and that all my life I've struggled to overcome or come to terms with my abnormality or disability (sic), and to show instead how my life journey has been shaped by the whole of who I am, as I am.

Background story

Coming to terms with disability

I have often seen expressions of fear, pity and contempt in people's faces when they look at me. Some have told me, they would rather kill themselves than live like me - without knowing anything about me. Being part of and growing up in our society we often internalize these attitudes and suffer from low self-esteem and self-respect. We become our own worst enemies.

Dr Adolf Ratzka, 2007

Approaches towards disability

The aim of this chapter is to provide some insights into the development and decline of disability politics in the United Kingdom and their connection with the global struggle by disabled people. The chapter will also consider the changing nature of disablement over time, therefore, it'll focus on how disablement is understood, defined and acted upon. The language or terminology associated with 'disability' has always been problematic not only because words are given alternative meanings, but also because of the overlap in meanings given to particular words. It's common within disability politics to refer to two broad approaches towards disablement. I'm using the term disablement to refer to: 'the process of becoming disabled'. Later in this chapter I'll explain how disabled academic Mike Oliver developed two models of disability – the individual tragedy model and the social model – to capture the essence of how societies relate to 'the disability problem'. (Oliver, 1990) Other theoretical approaches towards disablement do exist however I'm of the opinion they've made very little impact on disabled people's political activities or understanding of their social situations.

The dominant approach sees disability as arising from the loss or reduction in bodily functioning caused by an individual's impairment. Disablement within this approach is generally thought to include biological, functional, and social components. The second approach is offered as a radical alternative. In this approach, developed by disabled people, disability is seen not as a characteristic of an individual or being caused by an impairment, but instead it's indentified as arising from imposed social restrictions created by the social organisation of a given society.

These social restrictions or disabling barriers may be encountered at a micro level through, for example, attitudes, inaccessible environments or they can result from the structures, systems and values that can be located at the macro level of that society. This approach has produced what are called 'social models of disability'. (Priestley, 1998) In both approaches towards disability, cerebral palsy is viewed as an impairment.

Before going any further I need to put the record straight. In Chapter Five I'll talk about coming into contact with Paul Hunt and the beginnings of Union of the Physically Impaired Against Segregation (UPIAS). At the time I struggled with the proposed name of the organisation because I kicked against the description of being described as 'impaired'. The young Robert wasn't able to decouple the material reality of having a dysfunctional body from the oppressive ideological framing of that body. The word impairment has it's linguistical roots in the verb: to impair, and it means 'to make or cause to become worse; diminish in ability, value, excellence'. In my eyes using the word impairment permitted people to consider me and other disabled people as being 'flawed' or 'abnormal' and this seemed wholly judgemental to me at the time. I find it interesting that even today I come across disabled people who are not familiar with the ideas within disability politics and therefore still feel the need to reject being referred to as being impaired due to the negative associations. These days I do accept that cerebral palsy is an impairment, however, I still reject how it's socially evaluated.

An important influence on my theoretical thinking has been disabled academic Paul Abberley and I agree with Paul's assertion that:

> For disabled people the body is the site of oppression, both in form, and in what is done with it. (Abberley, 1997a; 173)

In order to understand this comment and my take on disability, it's necessary to provide some historical context and to also present some of the theoretical arguments that have helped to inform or influenced both my politics and my thinking on life in general.

Making the links between Capitalism and Disablement

There have always been people who, because of injury, disease or genetic makeup, haven't had bodies which are been fully functional. The place of people with impairments in both history and societies is very much open to debate because attitudes, perceptions and the responses to them vary so greatly. According to Borsay (2005) there are currently three main approaches to studying the history of disability. First is the biographical approach which looks at great reformers and their institutions. Second is the empirical approach which evaluates different care strategies and the development of rehabilitation and orthopaedics. The third approach which both Borsay and I take is a materialist one. The materialist view locates past experiences of disability within the political, social and cultural organisation of society. It examines how society creates disablement.

A number of disabled academics, for example, Finkelstein, (1980; 1981); Oliver, (1990), Gleeson, (1997); Russell and Malhotra, (2002) employ a historical materialist approach towards disability. Approaches using this methodology look for the causes of developments and changes in human society in the means by which humans collectively produce the necessities of life. Social classes and the relationship between them, along with the political structures and ways of thinking in society are founded on and reflect contemporary economic activity. (Fromm, 1961)

The central argument recognises that people with impairments have had specific social relations in given societies however it was with the introduction of the capitalist mode of production that we see a systematic approach towards people who we unable to fulfil their assumed social roles as human beings. Russell and Malhotra (2002) outline the material conditions that brought about the creation of 'disabled people' and their social exclusion:

Industrial capitalism thus created not only a class of proletarians but also a new class of 'disabled' who did not conform to the standard worker's body and whose labour-power was effectively erased, excluded from paid work. As a result, disabled persons came to be regarded as a social problem and a justification emerged for segregating them out of mainstream life and into a variety of institutions, including workhouses, asylums, prisons, colonies and special schools.

This returns us to Oliver's two models of disability –

the individual tragedy model and the social model. It's important to recognise that a model is a 'schematic description of a system, theory, or phenomenon that accounts for its known or inferred properties and may be used for further study of its characteristics.' Oliver used the 'individual tragedy model' to explore how dominant ideologies and practice around 'disability' came into existence and the oppressive impact they've had upon disabled people's lives. Gleeson, (1997: 196) offers a summary of the 'materialist' or 'radical' social model which he sees as understanding:

> ...disability to be a logical outcome of the capitalist mode of production. Using the insights of this model, an important critique has been developed of the root cause of disablement - the capitalist system. Disability in its current form is said to have emerged at the time of the industrial revolution, with the growth of the commodity labour market a key factor in the process of disablement.

Scheer and Groce (1988) argued that before European industrialisation the majority of people with impairments were integrated into community roles and that family connections offered protection. This way of life also enabled them to participate in wider social networks. Stone (1985) puts forward the view that with the increase in urbanisation, many of these people became detached from traditional support networks and thus became objects of social control In terms of people with impairments encountering social restrictions (disability). There's some evidence of particular forms of social restriction existing throughout history for individuals with impairments, but disablement as a systematic form of social oppression was created by capitalist societies. (Oliver, 1990) This has led to the view that disability is *historically specific*. In stating the historical specificity of disability, I believe it's necessary to acknowledge that ideas and beliefs from previous times can be deposited within the thinking of newer forms of ideology and cultural practice. Stuart Hall (1980; 342) applied this approach to 'racisms' and I take a similar stance on explaining disability.

By the middle of the nineteenth century British society had felt the impact of the Industrial Revolution. Fredrick Engels in 1845 published, *The Condition of the Working Class in England*, based on personal observations and research in Manchester which detailed the brutal nature of industrial capitalism and how prevalent impairment was during to working and living conditions. There were also a series of moral panics around urbanisation, ill health and depravity; taken together they fed into the clamour for standardisation and control which led to contours being drawn around what was considered to be '*normal*'. The increased usage of institutionalisation, the birth of the eugenics movement and the proliferation of charities contributed towards 'cleansing' society of its 'mad and hapless cripples'. Non-conformity was unacceptable, and those people deemed incapable of keeping standards associated with 'normal activities' – productive and reproductive – had to be 'taken care of' in more senses than one. (Foucault, 1977)

These processes firmly established people with significant impairments as being 'outside' mainstream society both in terms of how they were seen and also via institutionalisation. My own research shows that the term 'able-bodied' was introduced not in the first instance as a medical category but within the Poor Laws when there was a moral panic over armies of unemployed men roaming the countryside. The 'able-bodied poor' were deemed as social problems and laws were introduced to control them. The original meaning attached to able-bodied referred to the 'ability to labour' and it was employed long before 'disabled' was viewed as a particular recognised category. In the 14th century disability simply meant to be 'unable' therefore as capitalist social relations developed, the focus or gaze fell upon bodies that weren't considered able to be productive; however it was the Poor Law Amendment Act (1834) which began the categorisation process. (Finkelstein, 1980; Stone, 1985)

Oliver outlines how pathologising the body underpinned the institutionalisation of disabled people and why the rationale behind this was based upon the simple idea that 'placing people in institutions was not only good for the health of individuals; it was also good for the health of society'. (Oliver, 1994; unpaged) Medical practice since that time has focused firmly on how the body 'functions' vis-à-vis social tasks and doctors along with other professionals were concerned with the impact of impairments on people's capabilities. In crude terms, the *less* someone functioned 'like a normal person' (sic), the *more* 'disabled' they were judged to be. Key ideologies such as individualism and normality contributed to the process of identifying 'disability' as the negative outcome of a loss of functionality caused by an individual's impairment. I'm nevertheless convinced that it took the First World War to shape and establish the dominance of the approaches that view disability as 'an individualised personal tragedy'. (Findlay, 1994) This remained largely unchallenged for the next fifty years.

The battle lines were drawn

The distinction between impairment, disability and handicap never registered with most people and I'd argue that in Britain within every day usage and the development of social policy these terms were used interchangeably for decades. When a challenge did come to how impairment, disability and handicap were *made sense of*, it came from within the ranks of disabled people. It was a campaign led by disabled people, for example, that resulted in the word 'handicap' being phased out of usage; although some of the arguments employed – there wss an association between 'cap-in-hand' and begging – is highly questionable. (Snopes, 2011)

Oliver's social model of disability developed the basic premise put forward by UPIAS that the focus of professional intervention ought to be not on attempting to manage 'impaired bodies', but rather to transform the social environments in which they exist. Oliver (2004; 23) said:

> In the broadest sense, the social model of disability is about nothing more complicated than a clear focus on the economic, environmental and cultural barriers encountered by people who are viewed by others as having some form of impairment – whether physical, sensory or intellectual.

When using the radical social model of disability we are suggesting that 'the fundamental relationships of capitalist society are implicated in the social oppression of disabled people'. Logically then, 'the elimination of disablement...requires a *radical transformation*, rather than a reform of capitalism'. (Gleeson, 1997; 196) Mike Oliver (1994; unpaged) also developed a set of criteria for identifying who might be considered to be disabled people from a social approach perspective. Thus:

1. they have an impairment;
2. they experience oppression as a consequence; and
3. they identify themselves as a disabled person.

However he went onto say something quite challenging for most people because it goes against how we have been encouraged to view things:

> Using the generic term [disabled people] does not mean that I do not recognise differences in experience within the group but that in exploring this we should start from the ways oppression differentially impacts

on different groups of people rather than with differences in experience among individuals with different impairments.

Paul Abberley had issues with how some disabled academics and activists failed to articulate what they mean by 'the oppression of disabled people'. (1997a; 161) Terms such as exploitation, institutional discrimination and social exclusion are all associated with disabled people's 'oppression'. (Davies, 1993; Barnes and Mercer, 2003) In my opinion the lack of clarity around what is understood as 'the oppression of disabled people' stems back to how UPIAS spoke of disability (imposed social restriction) as a 'social situation'. UPIAS described the situation for people with physical impairments in the following manner:

> The disadvantage or restriction of activity caused by a contemporary social organisation *which takes little or no account of people who have impairments* and thus excludes them from the mainstream of social activities.' (1976: 14) (Emphasis added)

What I want to argue is that whilst this isn't wrong; it *is* imprecise because there's a vital element missing. The central reason capitalist societies take *'little or no account of people who have impairments'* is that historically, they've subjected people who have impairments to 'negative evaluations' and viewed them as being dependent, contributing very little, and with little social worth as a result. It's therefore *how* people with impairments were 'taken into account' which ultimately meant they weren't seen as beyond being a 'problem'. (Findlay, 1994)

Our bodies are a central feature in our social oppression as Abberley argued. As we have seen the medicalisation of people with impairments' bodies has been a key feature in our social oppression. To fully appreciate disabled people's social situation as oppression, I believe it's crucial to acknowledge the power that lies behind seeing disability as an 'individualised problem' understood through the medicalisation of the body.

Oliver (1996; 30) informs us there were various attempts from the 1960s onwards to provide 'a conceptual schema to describe and explain the complex relationships between illness, impairment, disability and handicap.' The World Health Organisation (WHO) finally accepted a classification system developed by Philip Wood (1980), a Briton who was an epidemiologist in public health. The adoption of the International Classification of Impairments, Disabilities and Handicaps (ICIDH) met a mixed reception. Maria Barile (2003; 211) cites a literature survey reviewing the definition of disability conducted by Solomon in 1993 and states that:

> In the community at large, the ICIDH terminology reinforces the fear of impairment and the medical perception of disability.

Opposition to the ICIDH steadily increased among disabled people's organisations and disquiet had been mounting from professional circles as well (Pfeiffer;1992). Much of this criticism came from how the classification system was being employed. Abberley (1991:4) wrote a critique of the Office of Population Censuses and Surveys' disabiliy surveys and said:

> ... the notion that functional limitation can be investigated without regard to the different social and environmental contexts of people's lives, as the standardised OPCS questions attempt to do, is a dubious one.

Feeling under increased pressure the WHO in 2001 adopted the International Classification of Functioning, Disability and Health (ICF). Within the World Health

Organisation's ICF the word 'disabilities' is used as an umbrella term '....covering impairments, activity limitations, and participation restrictions'. Thus:

- an impairment is a problem in body function or structure;
- an activity limitation is a difficulty encountered by an individual in executing a task or action;
- while a restriction is a problem experienced by an individual (due to having an impairment) in involvement in life situations. (WHO, unpaged)

Is this fundamentally different from the concepts with the ICIDH? In a paper on the ICF, Rob Imire (2004) refers to a number of claimed differences existing between the two classification systems. The ICIDH was considered problematical because it fails to 'acknowledge the presence of social barriers' in influencing disability. (Bickenbach et al, 1999: 1177) By contrast, Imire cites Marks (1999; 25) who argued that the ICF:

....seeks to develop the conception that 'mind, body, and environment are not easily separable but rather mutually constitute each other in complex ways'.

The upshot of this shift is that whereas within the ICIDH 'social barriers' were reduced to simply being the consequence of the impact of an impairment, including the loss or reduction of functionality, what the ICF does, according to Bickenbach et al, (1999: 1177) is to conceive disability as being 'a compound phenomenon to which individual and social elements are both integral'. I was a member of the UK consultation team and we continued to raise concerns about how these 'interactions' were being viewed and would be subsequently applied. Maria Barile (Barile, 2003; 214) picked this up when she argued:

... by framing impairments as negative, and functional and structural integrity as positive (p. 11), the classification is making shaky assumptions about how these standards will be used by the primary users of the classification. How will professionals use it to classify and assess individuals with disabilities? And will professionals keep the new definition in mind? or will they apply the old ones, which have been internalised by the majority of people?

Individualism, Neoliberalism and Disablement

Over the last twenty five years disabled activists in the UK and worldwide have criticised how the ICF and approaches based upon it have been used by governments to construct bio-psycho-social models to determine Neoliberal welfare policies (Jolly, 2012; Grover & Karen Soldatic, 2013; Symeonidou, 2014).

The introduction of the ICF therefore needs to be understood from within the context of its impact upon socio-economic policies. Marta Russell and Ravi Malhotra (2002) wrote:

> It is also evident that the definition of disability is not static but fundamentally linked to the needs of capital accumulation. Hence, when the welfare state entered into 'crisis', governments attempted to narrow the definition of disablement and to cut entitlement levels.

In Britain the lives of many disabled people are dependent on the welfare state and social policies that underpinning it. The Disabled People's Movement for the bulk of its existence had to address the economic and social policies of a Conservative government led by Margaret Thatcher. John Hills (1998; 4) noted:

> Taking the period of Conservative Government from

1979 to 1997 as a whole, four themes stand out as central to policies towards the welfare state:
- Attempts to control public spending
- Privatisation
- Targeting
- Rising inequality

All of these areas had a profound impact upon disabled people, especially through various welfare reform programmes, however I would go further and argue the underpinning ideologies eventually affected aspects of disability politics. Sutcliffe-Braithwaite (2013; unpaged) informs us that:

> Thatcher wanted to re-establish an economic and legal framework and a cultural ethos which rewarded what she saw as the 'Victorian' or 'bourgeois' values of thrift, self-reliance and charity among all classes.

She goes on to point out that Thatcher's aim wasn't to 'abolish the welfare state entirely, but to chip away at it, leaving social security as a last resort for the very poorest minority'. Two core elements of Thatcherism which are also present within global Neoliberalism are: individualism and self-reliance. It's perhaps paradoxical that the birth of the Disabled People's Movement coincided with the beginning of the largest ideological and material attack upon them since the Victorian era. Gareth Millward offered an insightful response to article by the Voluntary Action History Society (2013, unpaged) called, *Margaret Thatcher and the Voluntary Sector*, in which he says:

> Thatcher's Victorian legacy is really important, I think, because it's vital to realise that the 'neo' in neo-liberalism harks back to a supposed golden age.

She also tried to formalise such ideas in quasi-autonomous structures. While the Department of Health had been supporting charities via grants under Callaghan, she ramped things to the next level. The creation of the Independent Living Fund for disabled people in 1988 is a good example. Cash limited and with half its trustees appointed by the Department of Health, the other half were appointed by the Disablement Income Group. All the money came from the state – but rather than giving social security as a right, it gave discretionary grants like an old fashioned charity or foundation. Bizarre mix of Victorian era alms for the deserving poor and late C20 concepts of social welfare.

The old Poor Law concepts of 'deserving' and 'undeserving' were to strike back with force at the end of the 20th century and the beginning of the 21st. This 'bizarre mix' as Millward called it, characterised much of the 1980s with the development of Community Care and wave after wave of welfare reform. Bob Sapey (2010; 4) characterises it in the following way:

> One of the UPIAS strategies was to campaign for independent living as a right. However, by the mid 1980s the main concern of the British government was the spiralling costs of social welfare brought about by prime minister Margaret Thatcher's attempts to encourage the privatisation of social care. Her government had been funding private care providers to the point where the funding mechanism was out of control and furthermore, virtually all the increase in expenditure was for segregated care. Their aim through the NHS and Community Care Act 1990 was to control expenditure through the mechanisms of the marketplace which they tried to achieve by giving yet more authority to local councils and their social care administrators. Social workers became care managers and disabled people became service users as the language of welfare adapted to the ways

of the market.

Sapey's paper explores the shiftts within social policy towards disabled people with a particular emphasis from the mid-1990s when New Labour introduced its neoliberal 'third-way' policies which focused upon 'rights with responsibilities'. In practical terms what this meant was:

> [It's]....responsible for the introduction of social policy packages such as direct payments which enable people to pay directly for their own care. While a policy such as this appears to place the individual in a position of control, in its delivery it is not entirely what it seems, as for example a package such as direct payments is subject to fiscal restraints which are managed by social service departments.

In 2015 I wrote a paper called, *Personalisation and self-determination: the same difference?* In it I questioned the extent to which direct payments, independent living and personalisation employed the dynamic meaning of disability as understood by Finkelstein and UPIAS. What I went on to suggest is that we have seen is a set of accommodating 'interpretations' of the social model of disability employed by more liberal and reformist disabled activists and sections of the disabled community, which in turn has allowed service providers and the state to exploit this situation. This is a sharper critique than the conclusion reached by Sapey five years earlier when he wrote:

> The government discourse is about change and citizenship, but their critics from within the disabled people's movement suggest that the policy of personalisation may in fact be a compliance approach, designed to appease disabled people but in reality following an individualised understanding of disablement. (Sapey, 2010; 5)

My harsh words stem from the belief that within social policy and other pieces of legislation since the middle of the 1990s, we have witnessed a whole catalogue of concepts and language use being 'absorbed' by the state, charities and service providers. Jenny Morris (2011: 3) makes this point when she wrote:

> [T]here are aspects of the arguments made by disability organisations which have been capitalised on by the politics and ideology driving recent and current policies in ways that are significantly to the disadvantage of disabled people. These concern, in particular, the social model of disability and the concepts of 'independent living', and 'user involvement' or 'co-production'.

It's been quite common over the last twenty years to hear local authorities speak about supporting the social model or implementing what's called 'independent living' however any close scrutiny of their policies and practices reveal their approaches are a million miles from those developed by the Disabled People's Movement.

The failure of the Disabled People's Movement to address this issue and the unwillingness to discuss divisions within our own ranks has produced an unhealthy situation where disabled people are witnessing conflicting approaches towards defending what is referred to as 'disability rights' and many activists themselves aren't fully understanding or appreciating what lies behind these conflicts. There is not a single factor which has led to these divisions. Tensions existed prior to and after the defeat of the Civil Rights Bill and the passing of the Disability Discrimination Act (DDA).

Vic Finkelstein, a founding member of the Disabled People's Movement, was highly critical of focus on obtaining 'anti-discrimination legislation'. In 2001 he delivered a presentation in which he said:

Civil Rights are about individual people or groups of people – this is a legalistic approach to emancipation. [...] the campaign for 'disability rights' does not depend on, nor is it a reflection of, the social model [or, to avoid confusion, the radical UPIAS *interpretation*] of disability'. In the 'rights' approach parliament grants legal rights to those *it defines* as 'disabled'. The focus is on identifying characteristics of the individual, rather than the nature of society, and then making selected 'concessions' to those so defined. ....It's not just that the liberal right wants to inherit the ideological underpinnings of the social model of disability, but they want also want to rewrite (reclaim) the past. The left may lose this battle, but at least let's be clear about what is being done to the social model of disability.

In my opinion the strengething of individualism, both as an ideology and within practice underpinned by Neoliberal policies, has changed vital aspects of how disablement is encountered in Britain and globally. I stated earlier that I held the view that the underpinning ideologies of Neoliberalism eventually affected aspects of disability politics. Disabled people brought into the language of rights, citizenship and social inclusion and this has come back to bite them hard.

The Age of Austerity: disabled people under attack

The current situation disabled people in the United Kingdom find themselves is without a doubt one of the most oppressive in living memory. Many disabled people are experiencing cuts to services and social security benefits which they rely upon to live independent lives; whilst others fear that the reduction in services will ultimately lead to them being forced back into residential care. The Blair Labour government set the framework that the coalition government of Conservatives and Liberal Democrats and then the Cameron and May governments have built upon this during the so called, 'Age of Austerity'.

The contours around who is and who is not regarded to be a 'disabled person' are changing as the Government attempts to dismantle the welfare state. Within the field of social policy making and reports from the mass media there's almost a 'common sense' understanding that 'disabled people are dependent creatures who are unemployed and on benefits'. I'm of the view that this attack isn't just about reducing the welfare bill; it's also about making 'disabled people disappear' and therefore no longer a concern for the State. Clearly, they can't make disabled people disappear in reality, but the Government can and is re-defining who fits within the labels that are being thrust upon them. On the one hand we have an ever decreasing number of disabled people who are being presented as 'dependent', 'deserving' or 'vulnerable', yet on the other, a growing number of disabled people who are finding out they aren't really 'disabled' after all! Suddenly, the inability to walk isn't a 'disability' (sic) any longer where a wheelchair provides mobility. This shift isn't just about moving disabled people off benefits as I've already stated, it is about reducing disabled people reliance on a whole raft of welfare services including social care. As Grover and Soldatic (2012; unpaged) argue:

> Both Australia and the UK are witnessing the emergence of a more restricted 'disability category' which can be explained through reference to the neoliberal turn in which the relief of the financial needs of disabled people are being subverted to productivist concerns with labour flexibility, growth in part-time, casualised labour markets and low wages related to international economic competition. What this means for working age disabled people is that they are now experiencing a diminishing

citizenship as previous entitlements are reduced in value and made more precarious through their link to employment-related conditionality.

Many people talk about a return to Victorian times, but inadequately discuss how charities and institutions were employed to remove disabled people from the public gaze. Today, the emphasis is on getting disabled people into the labour market and being self-reliant; however, just as with the personalisation agenda, this rhetoric isn't supported by structures or financial changes that would make it a reality.

Despite the emergence of organisations such as Disabled People Against Cuts a strong case can be made for arguing that the understanding of disability politics by disabled people is at one of its lowest points since the first faltering steps in the 1970s and it's evident that the British Disabled People's Movement hardly exists as a social movement currently.

Within *More Than A Left Foot* both the highs and the lows of the UK Disabled People's Movement will be spoken about. I'm hoping this book will contribute towards addressing the need for disabled people to offer an appraisal of our past in order to contribute towards building a fresh perspective on understanding *disability politics*.

Crucially, there's an urgent need to politically assist disabled activists to build bridges between the past and present with the aim of influencing our futures. In truth, it's likely we'll have more questions than answers; but by opening up a dialogue and considering the central questions that brought us politically together in the first place, we can start the process of piecing together a national strategy to both defend our people and extend our liberation struggle.

It's time to acknowledge that many of today's disabled activists have either lost sight of, or have never been introduced to, the Disabled People's Movement's key components and as a result huge differences of opinion exist on what we are seeking to achieve and how best to resist our oppressors. Just at the time when people with impairments are living disabled lives in the age of austerity, there appears to be a lack of joined up thinking at a strategic level and an absence of collective political leadership coming from within the ranks of disabled people.

There's without a doubt a struggle taking place, however we need to ask if, as disabled people, we are adequately equipped to defend ourselves from the further onslaught or aligned enough to take disabled politics into the mainstream arena? This isn't to deny the importance of the activism of groups such as DPAC and others; however, we are entering a new political phase which suggests campaigning against austerity measures will prove inadequate because in a sense it's presently little more than a form of fire-fighting. The type of campaigning currently taking place is a part of a resistance movement; nevertheless, it is not an adequate base upon which to try and re-build the type of *disability politics* required by disabled people in their struggle for social and political emancipation. To be in a position where we can begin to articulate the type of *disability politics* required, it's necessary to remind ourselves of how the Disabled People's Movement came into being and what established it as a 'social movement'.

Part One

A life apart

Most great accomplishments do not look promising in the beginning. If you give up on a big dream too early, you have probably stepped on gold and mistook it for a rock.

Israelmore Ayivor

Chapter 1

In the beginning

I was born at the Royal Buckinghamshire Hospital in Aylesbury late into the night of the 25 January 1951. Among the team of medical staff involved was a Scotsman who wore a kilt under his surgical grown having rushed from a Burns' Night do. My birth was far from planned as you will see, however, whatever the circumstances leading up to my mother being driven at full speed down wet country roads on that winter's night; the day I was born was without a doubt the one I would've chosen for myself. I often ponder over my stubbornness; refusing to enter the world as a Capricorn.

January 25 was right for so many reasons. I don't really believe in Astrology any more than I do a divine being; but anyone that knows me will tell you, I've all the traits of an Aquarian: artistic, distant, visionary, and there's no mistaking my perverse sense of humour. Another reason this date makes perfect sense is that when my Dad was born he had a full head of dark curly hair along with a pair of sideburns. A neighbour on seeing the child said, 'That's wee Robbie' – a reference to Scotland's best known poet – so my father was named Robert Burns. Rumour has it that my parents were going to call me John, after my grandfather, but once I had arrived on the bard's birthday, there was only one name suitable.

Telling you how I came to have my name is jumping the gun a little. So let me go back and explain how my fateful journey had begun by introducing you to my parents, Bob and Sally. My Dad's family were crofters. Mum's father had had a rough childhood being an orphan. There were many stories she told me about how he could've have been a champion runner, but he ran for money at Powder Hall where he had to throw races from time to time. When Bob and Sally met, he was working among boiler makers in a shipyard on the Clyde and her father was the Works manager.

My mother's name was Sarah Mac Scott, but she didn't like the way people said 'Sarah', (thought it sounded too common), so she called herself 'Sally' instead. From her own accounts she sounded like a tomboy who was full of life; perhaps too much so for her father's liking which might explain why she was reined in to help her own mother look after the smaller children. Both the Scott and Findlay families were fairly large, though Dad rarely spoke about his childhood, Mum was the complete opposite. I'm surprised I developed an interest in oral history considering the amount of times she retold the stories about her growing up! No, to be fair, it was interesting most of the time and I can see how it influenced my own journey to a certain extent.

The Scott family were very musical with most of them able to either sing or play at least one instrument; Mum sang in a church choir and her father played in a Scottish band. Putting together the pieces of personal history I've gleamed down the years, my parents' upbringing was very different and as a consequence contributed to my father's inability to express himself and my mother's frustration at his lack of ambition.

My knowledge of what happened before I was born is very patchy. I know, for example, during the 1926 General Strike my Mum was a seventeen year old shop assistant working in Glasgow and was sent back home to Paisley for her own safety. However on New Year's Eve, 1938 my parents wed. Like many women of her generation, she wanted children, so it came as a bitter blow when she was told she might not be able to have any. As it happens, she fell almost immediately. My eldest sister Jean came along and six years later Mary arrived. During this time the family had moved to England and had lived in various parts of the country.

By the late 1940s Mum and the two young girls were living in Kent whilst my Dad worked away. Again, from what I've pieced together from what Mum and my sister Mary told me, it was a period in Mum's life where she had felt lonely and resentful; having a sense of abandonment. To all sense and purposes she was more or less living the life of a single mother; a very difficult position to be in during post war Britain. It would seem that after a visit she had given my Dad an ultimatum: unite the family or face the consequences. There's little doubt that I've traits that come from both of my parents; I certainly have my Mum's forthrightness and the sharpness of both wit and tongue! She arrived in Leighton Buzzard full of determination to get the marriage back on track. The year 1950 saw my Dad working as a bulldozer driver whilst my Mum ran a small shop. Part of the process of renewing their relationship resulted in my Mum, at the age of forty, becoming pregnant. Well, how else did you expect me to put it?

The events leading up to my birth are unclear because my sister Mary's account of what happened differs to the version told me by my mother. I was under the impression that, given my mother's age, past experiences in labour and her general well-being, the local doctor wanted her to undergo a caesarean section. Exactly what went wrong I'll probably never know now but the bottom line is: someone, somewhere, cocked up. Through the vagueness there has always been this idea that I should've been born on or around Christmas. According to Mary the neighbours were convinced Mum had gone into labour on Christmas Eve, but the midwife sent her home again.

Now, having much in common with my namesake is one thing, but making comparisons with that other guy? I'm not sure I really want to go there!

Thankfully, I didn't become a Christmas baby however why I had to wait another month before making my entry into this world remains a mystery. In those days pregnant women went into a nursing home to have a baby and in my Mum's version of events the midwife running the place had become annoyed because Mum was in there taking up a bed and wasn't showing signs of giving birth. This is a matter of conjecture, but it could well be that the doctor may have told my Mum later, that it was at this stage she should've had the caesarean. In many ways this would've made a certain degree of sense. What I do know is that instead of consulting the doctor, the midwife took it upon herself to induce my Mum and quickly discovered she was out of her depth.

It was somewhere between fifteen and twenty miles to the main hospital and once there the priority was to try and save my mother's life. Weeks later the senior nurse confided in my mother that there was a sense of panic in the operating theatre and that she had never seen so much blood; not even as a result of a major car accident. As a result of using forceps to deliver me I experienced severe brain damage which caused cerebral palsy.

For the first week or so it was uncertain as to whether or not I would survive the brain trauma. My mother was a small woman and I'd weighed in at ten pounds; which had, of course, added further complications to the birth. I was placed in an incubator under the watchful eye of a paediatrician called Mr McCarthy. How unusual it was, I don't know, but he sat with me through the nights until it was certain I would survive. They knew I had cerebral palsy quite early on, but what they didn't know was the extent of the damage for quite a considerable time afterwards. The early years of my life couldn't have been easy for my family. Jean and Mary were still quite young and Mum had the shop to run as well as looking after us all. However it was quite a while before I was allowed home, but apparently on the day Mum brought me from the hospital Mary had run all the way home to see me.

Of course I've no real memories of the early years therefore this picture I'm painting is coloured by what others have told me. I do recall, however, the curtain that hung between the shop and the living area and going for walks along Plantation Road towards the firs. On one occasion Mary, I think it was, gave me a fir cone to play with and, being a typical baby, I'd deliberately dropped it over the side. Because I hadn't pestered her to pick it up, she had just carried on walking, however on the homeward journey when we reached the exact spot that I'd dispatched the cone, I began making noises and pointing downwards. Another story, rather than a memory, is Mum's dread at taking me shopping in Woolworths. After one near miss she would always frisk the pram before going to the till; it would seem I was an artful shoplifter who was extremely skilful at hiding small soldiers and cars under the blankets. It's not surprising that on an early hospital visit my mother reacted badly when a misguided doctor dared to question my intelligence! Parents are bound to be over protective, but Mum knew this guy was talking through his hat.

In the early Fifties the medical profession saw cerebral palsy as being very much connected to having learning difficulties, as we would call that type of impairment today. Mum came across two schools of thought; there were the doctors who told her not to expect too much of me, and I think I'm right in saying one doctor actually implied that if my parents did want to leave me there in the hospital then the doctors would understand; in other words, it would be perfectly acceptable for them to want to get on with their lives. The other school saw me as a guinea pig; therefore, I was paraded up and down in front of hundreds of doctors and had almost as many naked photos taken of me as a porn star has. I think it's important to stress that it wasn't the fear of me having learning difficulties that drove my Mum to argue with the doctors who said I was 'probably retarded', but rather the fear that these ignorant views might hold me back. There's no doubt in my mind she would've loved me no matter what the nature of my condition had been.

What about my father? There's little doubt he blamed the family doctor for failing to order the caesarean section; but I think there was more to it than that. Without wishing to stereotype all men, especially Scottish ones, there seems to be this romantic notion of producing 'an heir' as an embodiment of one's manhood. Dad had had two daughters, but I question the extent he saw himself as a good family man; could he have viewed my up and coming arrival as an opportunity to put things right, placing a cherry on top of the cake at the same time? And look what happened. I'm trying to see things from where he was at the time. Perhaps I am being harsh, but I always saw my father as a man full of guilt; a man always on the run from himself. His involvement with me early on was more on a personal level and that it was Mum who dealt with the army of medical experts I had to see. Even if Dad had been disappointed by the fact that I was born the way I was, unlike many fathers, he didn't reject me. According to Mum on my arrival at home it was Dad, rather than her, who would tend to me in the middle of the night.

What were those early years like for my family? I think Mum struggled to balance things because it wasn't simply a matter of running the shop, managing a family and bringing up a small baby. Most of the time I was content to sleep in my cot or pram when she was serving, but there were the times when I wouldn't settle and then she really did have a balancing act on her hands. There she would be, behind the counter in her apron, with a product in one arm and with me tucked under the other. I'd better explain the reason I was under her arm; I was unable to sit upright for a considerable length of the time. Mum's involvement in the shop was limited during the first year of my life because there were almost daily trips to and from the hospitals in Aylesbury. It was a punishing and brutal regime for the both of us. She was expected to ensure the girls were ready for school as well as washing, feeding and dressing me before going to the hospital. When I became too heavy, they did provide an ambulance. Sometimes it would arrive unexpectedly early, other times it would be exceedingly late or fail to arrive at all.

Neighbours had to be paid to look after the shop while Mum took me to the hospital and often stock went missing. In the early Fifties State aid didn't really exist, meaning that most families had to manage the best they could. Looking back I'm still surprised by the support given to my parents by the very young NHS. I do however temper this with a little down to earth cynicism; after all both the local GP and the hospital knew my birth had been a medical cock-up, so rather than own up to what mistakes had been made, they tried to compensate in other ways, for example, by taking me into hospital for a week at a time to give my mother a break. Today this would be classed as respite care. No one ever suggested that my parents ought to seek legal advice and from time to time as I grew up there were stories in the media about cases of medical negligence where people were awarded thousands of pounds for situations similar to mine.

Perhaps the most ironic part of this story is that I discovered I'd as much right to claim compensation as my parents did; this was in 1972, which just happened to be a year too late! When I asked Mum why they hadn't done anything about what had happened, she explained they had been too busy trying to cope, which made perfect sense, until she added 'they,' (meaning the State,) 'had at least provided me with a decent education'. It's enough for me to say that I've never shared my Mum's point of view on this subject. The nursing home had to change its client base as a result of my birth, but in many ways the midwife was made a scapegoat and I'm of the opinion it was my family more than me who lost out. The extra money from any compensation would've have made life easier, especially for Mum.

There are some funny stories relating to my 'respite' periods. I don't believe my Mum made the most of the time she was given because she would frequently hop on a bus and visit me with new toys. She said she felt guilty each time she left me; however, I didn't help because after she had gone home, I would scream and shout the place down. The only problem was, it wasn't my Mum or even my Dad, I screamed out for; it was my sister, 'Hairy'. In those days I couldn't formulate the letter 'M'. I would become upset for other reasons during my stay. First, there were the guinea pigs they would bring round for the children to hold; unfortunately, they had to stop giving them to me because the spasticity in my hands meant I was in danger of squeezing the life out of them. Then there was the routine cleaning problem I caused. The nurses would move all the beds down one end of the Ward in order to sweep the other, but this necessitated pushing the beds together. They had to isolate my bed, especially from those of the little girls, due to the fact I'd climb into theirs and the nurses were scared I'd end up squeezing them to death like the guinea pigs!

In the local community my family also had a little bit of 'respite care' offered by a childless couple called Ethel and Bert who lived across the street from the shop; they were more than happy to take me off Mum's hands. There was a photograph taken with me wrapped in a huge nappy hanging from a washing-line and Ethel and Bert standing proudly either side of me. Not quite sure what today's child protection or health and safety would make of that, nor of one of my everlasting memories of Ethel's nails, caked with brown snuff. I really loved them both and often visited from time to time into my late teens when I went home during the summer break.

Talking about love, in my eleventh month an incredibly important event took place in my life. In the run up to Christmas and Mum, being a typical doting mother, wanted to buy me something special for my first one. It still makes me smile when I think about it, but she decided to ask me what I would like! According to her, I simply said, 'bow wow'. By some strange coincidence, a few days later, a lad popped into the shop to buy some sweets and as Mum was serving him, she noticed there was something wriggling under his jacket. Apparently, he was heading down to the firs because his Dad had told him to abandon a puppy there. It wasn't a small bag of sweets that the boy left the shop with, but rather a huge box of chocolates from the top shelf. Mum had done a swap. Later, a tiny mongrel bitch called Ming lay at the bottom of my pram, licking my toes as I lay sleeping.

Running a shop and looking after me was taking its toll on my Mum's health. The shop was sold, and my parents bought instead a three bedroom house half a mile down the road. The next four years were made up of regular trips to the hospital for physiotherapy and check-ups. I'm not really sure of the background as to why on one visit to Stoke Mandeville Hospital I met the famous neurologist, Ludwig Guttmann, who founded the Paralympic Games, but I did. He told my Mum and Mary not to worry because I would eventually learn to walk. A little later I would attend physiotherapy in a small village just outside of what's now Milton Keynes. It was here that I began to learn how to walk with support. Mary and Mum would link arms and I'd walk between them. These early years saw a punishing regime for my Mum and me however there were lighter moments. Apparently, I would entertain the Ambulance passengers by singing around Christmas, 'Away in a manger', provided I was paid to do so.

And talking of money, there was one incident where I managed to embarrass my Mum in front of Mr McCarthy. On one visit, Mr McCarthy had some coins and he put a sixpence down and asked, 'Robert, what's this?' So I said, 'It's a tanner.' And my mother said, sounding utterly shocked, 'Oh, no Robert, that's a sixpence.' The paediatrician smiled and said calmly, 'No mum, if Robert wants to call it a tanner, it's a tanner.' Mum always blamed Bert and Ethel for my common language.

This wasn't the last time I demonstrated my knowledge to the medical profession. The local GP paid an unsuspected visit to the house, barely surviving Ming's protection of me. Once inside he noticed the television was on and made some comment about the programme. It was me, not Mum, who responded. I told him bold as brass that it was Richard Dimbleby, a well-known broadcaster, on the television. Mum thought she was going to have to scrape him off the floor because he couldn't believe someone so young, and with a 'profound physical impairment, was able to recognise individuals, especially those off the goggle box. It would probably be frowned upon now, but I would watch a fair amount of television.

I believe Dad was reasonably well paid for a manual worker, exactly how much that was, remained a bone of contention till the day he retired. Each Friday he would disappear into the outside toilet and then re-emerge to stuff the 'housekeeping' behind the clock in the living room. When the shop had been sold, my family moved into a house without an inside toilet or bathroom; Dad began to convert the old kitchen into a bathroom with an inside toilet when I was around-about four years old, and it was fully completed as I entered secondary school. Do-it-yourself was never one of his hobbies! So, we might've lived with an incomplete bathroom for eight years, but at least we were one of the first families to own a television. Mary, and her best friend Celia, would join in the fun when Mum would stop work for a while and sit with me to watch, Watch with Mother. Andy Pandy, Bill and Ben, the Wooden Tops and Muffin the Mule all left a lasting impression on me. I can remember having a toy version of Muffin the Mule like so many other kids of the 1950s.

As I grew older, I would also watch some adult programmes too; mainly documentaries such as The

World at War. Did they give me nightmares? Not half as much as a TV drama did in 1956 during the Suez Crisis. This drama was in the style of a 'news flash' about a pending nuclear attack on the UK; but as a five year old, I had no idea that it was 'fiction' and my parents had no idea their son was taking it all in. When they dragged me upstairs halfway through it, I hung on tightly around my Dad's neck, believing with all my heart that this was going to be the last time I was going up the stairs to (or should that be in) Bedfordshire? Waking up the next morning was such a relief, but I never told anyone what I had thought. Despite this, I'm convinced my interest in documentaries provided me with a very sound background into history, a subject which I've studied all my life.

When I wasn't watching television, I would play like any other child. I had a huge round wooden box made of balsa wood, full of toys. My favourite three toys were a huge red tractor I imagined was like the machine my Dad drove, a fort he had made for me and a big fire engine I would peddle up and down in the back garden. Mum would play with me some of the time, but looking back I don't think she had the patience to do it for long; she always complained she had too much housework to do. Throughout my childhood this was the pattern, I was left to entertain myself. There were only three times in my life when I went home to Leighton Buzzard and played with any other kids.

I'm not sure how old I was, but around the age of four or five I had a home tutor who began teaching me the three Rs. I think my Mum was more than happy with situation until one afternoon her friend Violet – who had a horrid son called Graham – overheard my tutor explaining 'the birds and the bees'. Dad wasn't impressed by her either. One night, whilst in his care, and after a pitch battle where I attempted to stop Mum and Mary going to the cinema, he tried to distract me by reading from an exercise book. It was a poem she had written, which began: 'Robert is a naughty boy...' I immediately burst into tears. Dad hurled the book away and picked me up instead; the only thing he ever taught me after that was how to play dominoes!

I've not spoken much about Jean because I only have one or two recollections of her. The clearest one being shortly before I was packed off to boarding school and it left a lasting impression on me. It was early evening and I was playing on the floor by the fire with Mum and Dad sat each side when the living room door opened, and Jean entered with a tall American G.I. called Charles. Young as I was, I could sense the tension in the air, and I remember Dad turning his face to the wall when Charles asked permission to marry his seventeen year old daughter. After a short stay in Bedford, the young couple along with their first son, Charles Jr. flew to Crete and then in the early 1960s onto Berlin. Mum and Mary, visited them out there. I can only remember seeing Jean again four times after she was married; once when Charles was born and about six years later when she paid one of her three trips home with Stephen and baby Cindy.

One trip home was with another daughter, Lynne during the 1970s and we spent about an hour sat talking to each other at Mary's dinner table. Being in my 20s, politically active and at University enabled me to talk quite confidently to this sister I didn't really know. It soon became apparent that the only things we had in common were biological; the blood, genes and a long thick neck. In recent years, through Facebook, I've had more contact with my 'big sister'.

Trying to piece together what happened over fifty years ago is quite difficult and I'm forced to rely much of the time on hearsay or past memories. Although my Mum wasn't very good at playing with me, I've always had the impression Doctor James raised concerns about her physical and mental health in relation to looking after me. She had shown signs of stress and had collapsed; on the other side of the evaluation, he regarded her as a 'possessive mother' and therefore wasn't quite sure how she would take to the idea of me attending a boarding school. Looking back, I can imagine the 'professionals' holding what would be called a 'case conference' to determine the best way of convincing my parents that it was 'in my best interest' to attend the John Greenwood Shipman Home in Northampton.

This might seem strange, but I only discovered who John Greenwood Shipman was quite recently when undertaking research for this book. Dr John Greenwood Shipman (1848 – 1918) was an English barrister and Liberal Party politician who went to school in Northampton and then in 1900 was elected MP for the town. It was his wife Clara, twelve years after his death, who presented their former home in Dallington to the Manfield Hospital, Northampton for use as a convalescent home in the memory of her late husband. In 1932, it was visited by the then Duke and Duchess of York the future King George VI and Queen Elizabeth, the Queen Mother on their official visit to Northampton.

Twenty four years after this Royal visit, a very small boy still unable to walk without holding onto furniture or without two sticks held together with wood, made his first visit to this grand old house. The external features of this house were unmistakeable; a mixture of redbrick and sandstone. Inside the solid structure was held together by stained wooden panels. I've no idea how many rooms there were as parts of the building were off limits to the pupils. The grounds of the house were magnificent. The house was served by a large patio where most of the children played during fine weather. Beyond this was a huge lawn area that was circled by a wide path which was capable of allowing wheelchairs and tricycles to pass one another. In the far right corner of the garden was a large white shed where all the bikes were stored. Children would ride around the gardens on the bikes and have races.

The gardens were well sheltered by large walls, huge

trees and dense foliage. Children were discouraged from playing between the trees and thick bushes, but when I was about nine or ten years old, I'd love wondering around in there. Two spots in particular drew me towards them; the first was along the back wall where there were produce growing and I would imagine this was like a secret garden, clearly influenced by the children's book. By the main gates the wall was slightly lower than elsewhere and there was no need to climb up the trees to look over it. I'd often stand there and watch the rest of the world go by and wonder whether or not I'd ever become a part of it. The grounds also had a small summer house which may have been used as a storeroom by the gardener. How many times I saw inside it, I'm not sure, because all I can remember is it having wooden planked floor and walls with light streaming in from cracks in the shutters.

Like many other special schools down the years the John Greenwood Shipman Home had three kinds of staff members; there were the domestic staff who did the cooking and cleaning, two teachers who taught the juniors and seniors, and finally the care staff. In my secondary school the care staff were called Housemothers, but I don't recall this school using a grand title. There was a Matron, a tall slender woman in her thirties, who was known as Sister Pickerskill and I imagine this was because she had a nursing qualification. The other carers were divided into day and night shifts. There were around twelve boarders aged between five years and eighteen.

In this chapter I've sought to offer briefly an insight into my background and now I want to move on and try and present a reflective account of what life was like for me. I hope the glimpses of the past I can offer you will enable you to piece together a sense of history in the making and a better understanding of the journey I've taken as a person born with cerebral palsy.

Chapter 2

First steps

The first step, my son, which one makes in the world, is the one on which depends the rest of our days.

Voltaire

Not surprisingly, my recollections of what life was like for me at my first school are very hazy and limited to either strongly negative or positive memories. I doubt my feelings about being bundled off to a boarding school and away from your family at the age of five and a half are that much different to any other person who went through a similar experience. Someone that age isn't really going to understand why their parents were willing to let them go. Did I resent being 'sent away'? I don't ever recall seeing being sent away from home as a punishment; what hurt the most was being 'absent', not knowing what was going on at home and having a sense of being 'pushed out'. It was only years later when Mum spoke about how awful it had been for Dad, Mary and her, was I able to fully come to terms with the experience.

I believe I spent the first school term at the school, including weekends, and if I can remember correctly there were only two or three pupils who lodged full-time. My only memory of those days was being taken into town with another boy. I've no idea how we got there, and I think the reason I cling onto this is the fact it was the first time I had ever gone out in public in a wheelchair. At home my parents had carried me everywhere, so I hadn't a wheelchair of my own. During the school days I either used my two sticks, which meant very slow progress, or I crawled everywhere on my hands and knees. The staff would always complain about how dirty my hands and knees got! I'm not sure, but I think I wasn't only being encouraged to walk, there was also part recognition that I've never found pushing myself around in a wheelchair easy.

Things changed during the second term and my Mum would come by train on a Friday afternoon and take me home for the weekend. On one of these occasions she had the surprise of her life. In truth I'd developed my walking skills shortly before going to school, however, as I've already indicated I found it easier to hold onto the furniture to travel around the house. At the school there were wide open spaces, so I needed to use my sticks. The trouble was, not only did I find this slow going, but my balance was still not very good and often I would trip myself up.

This memory remains clear as day: it was mid-week and I was returning to my classroom by walking through the dining room. Half way across I'd caught the board that lay between the sticks with my foot and went down with a thud. No one else was in the room to help me up and my knee hurt like hell, so I hurled these sticks across the room, hauled myself up and then just walked away! So, on the Friday, my Mum was asked to take a seat and wait for me in the dining room; normally she would've fetched me out of the class. She said later she wasn't sure what was happening, but then the door on the far side of the room opened and she saw her son, for the first time, walk in unaided. The look on her face remains indescribable.

The routine of Mum picking me up on a Friday and Dad returning me late Sunday afternoon lasted for the next five years. I always hated Sunday evenings because I'd arrive back at school just in time for tea and then shortly afterwards it would be time for bed. Who knows how many of those Sunday nights I spent buried under the covers crying myself to sleep. Thankfully for me the night nurse on Sunday and Monday nights was a lovely Polish woman who was probably in her late fifties. She was extremely motherly and often came to comfort me if she heard me sobbing. It would seem that I'd tell her everything, even my darkest secrets! I said, 'thankfully', because the night nurse who worked the rest of the week was the complete opposite. She too was foreign, and I'd convinced myself she was not only German, but probably Hitler's half-sister! I lived in terror when she was on duty. I remember one time accidently wetting the bed because I'd held the urine bottle wrongly; she was very rough with me as she changed both the bed and my pyjamas. However the real terror, especially in winter, took place a few years later when she 'taught' me to dress.

Her idea of teaching me to dress consisted on her getting me out of bed an hour before anyone else, stripping off my pyjamas and then dumping me and my clothes onto a cold wooden floor. At the time I was sharing a room with another boy called Roger, who wasn't significantly impaired, and he was allowed to stay in bed until seven o'clock. We were expected to go down to breakfast at eight, so what this meant was that I was pulled out of bed at six and then left to struggle into my clothes. I wasn't able to do up buttons at the time so I just had to sit there until about quarter to eight waiting for her to come back and finish off dressing me.

Another horror at the school was the food. Each child was expected to bring back from home each week a brown bag of fruit. This was given to us daily however the problem was the kitchen staff would prepare the fruit around four but by the time we eat it at six, the mixed juices and air had started turning it brown. Not sure if this doesn't partly explain my lack of interest in fruit as I grew up. There was one terrible incident when we were served white fish in milk – even today I can't stomach the stuff. That day I point blank refused to eat it. The first threat I had was that if I didn't eat it, they would simply serve it up until I did. Well the adamant seven year old told them in no uncertain terms that he'd rather starve. This of course led to the guilt trip of starving children in Africa. Again, I retorted, I was quite happy for them to parcel it up and send it to the children! This produced the final threat which was to send for the Matron. I looked up and calmly said, 'You can send for the Queen of England for all I care, I'm not eating it!' Just in case you're thinking things couldn't get worse for me, they did.

As I sat staring at the plate, another boy kicked a toy dumper truck over in my direction and I was eventually caught dropping the fish into it. I think the plan was to fill the truck and kick it away till after the meal. I can't remember how this little episode ended but in recalling it I've just remembered a time probably a little later when I stopped eating and drinking altogether and became seriously ill through dehydration.

What this story does illustrate is that from an early age I was quick witted and able to express myself. There's another story where I think I took my Mum's breath away. We were on our way to visit a friend of my Mum's when we were approached by this complete stranger who said right out of the blue: 'I'm sorry dear, is he mental?' Of course, my mum just didn't know what to say or do. Me, on the other hand, just looked at the woman and said, 'No, but you are!' Mum didn't know where to put herself. As for the woman, she beat a hasty retreat.

These are among the only vivid memories I have of my early years at the school which don't involve a small curly haired blonde girl called Gillian. Our first day and my last day at the school began and ended the same way; with a kiss. Over a five year period Gillian was my 'girlfriend' off and on; I still chuckle over some of our exploits. When did this 'romance' begin? After the first lesson of the day there was always a milk break around twenty to eleven and each child was given a small bottle of milk. By the way, this was years before Maggie put a stop to all that! Anyhow, I had been given my milk and then taken over to the physiotherapy room and placed upon a very large the carpet. The only other person in the room, sat in the opposite corner of the carpet, was this beautiful doll like little girl. We both ignored each other for a couple of minutes and then suddenly out of the blue she rushed over and kissed me on the cheek! Not for the last time by any means, I immediately raced after her to repay her kindness, only to be foiled by the returning therapists.

A few months later Gillian and I were in trouble again during the school's Christmas party. Shortly before the party began, I spied a man being met at the door by the Matron and then led to her office. I didn't say anything to anyone about this until he appeared before the young children in a red robe and carrying a sack. At this point I spilt the beans to Gillian and we began to laugh. Unhappy with our behaviour the Matron asked us why we were being so disrespectful to Father Christmas. In unison we both proclaimed in indignant voices that he wasn't the real Father Christmas.

With two children under six years old about to ruin the centre piece of the party, I suspect the Matron thought she could face us down by challenging our disbelief. I didn't want to admit to spying, so I was struggling to explain why he wasn't real; it was at this point Gillian came to my aid and said in a matter of fact way, 'He hasn't got a white beard!' See, even in the mid-50s, disabled children weren't prepared to have cotton wool pulled over their eyes!

The fact the children were all different ages didn't seem to present too much of a problem, nor the fact there were children at the school with a wide range of impairments. Looking back, I now realise that apart from those who had cerebral palsy like me, I remained utterly ignorant of the other children's medical conditions. Many will no doubt argue that there were practical and sensible reasons for keeping the children in the dark, and I can understand this, but this protection also had a number of down sides too.

Having gone to the school at an early age and with two older non-impaired sisters, the idea of being with disabled children wasn't an issue. Well, I say that it wasn't an issue but there was one incident which has stuck in my mind ever since and probably explains why I remember the bathroom so vividly! I was probably eight years old when a younger boy arrived at the school mid-term and the care staff treated him as if he was really delicate. Although he was younger by a couple of years, the rest of us boys couldn't understand why he still wore nappies, and the staff members weren't forthcoming in telling us either. It was therefore a complete shock when two of us were in the bathroom and this kid was lifted off the toilet and we saw he had an extra penis coming from his back region. I think the staff member had forgotten we were there and there was a sense of panic because this 'secret' was out.

I'm speaking about this for a number of reasons because it relates to issues that'll come up again later. The immediate question relates to how children are 'protected' from the realities of illness and impairment; so, at what age should children be made aware? I was only nine when I returned from the Summer Holiday and so eager to team up again with the boy who sat next to me in the classroom. We all filed into class and I assumed he was late or had missed the school bus because his desk remained empty. Wisely, the teacher came over to me first because she knew we were the best of friends, and broke the news that Paul had died of pneumonia. It was the first time I had encountered death and I found it so difficult to comprehend. Only after being told a little more about his condition was I able to understand how this illness had led to his death.

I get quite annoyed when parents refuse to address questions children have about people who are ill or impaired. In my opinion, this notion of 'protection' has more to do with the fear and ignorance of adults rather than causing harm to the children. Clearly, there needs to be a balance, however, I'd argue most western societies' cultural attitudes towards illness, impairment and death are socially oppressive and deeply harmful. For people with impairments from my era as we grew up, we were expected by non-disabled adults to 'deal with' the consequences of being impaired, but rarely did they attempt to discuss issues surrounding our actual impairments.

Looking back, it wasn't until I was around ten or eleven that I became really self-conscious about being impaired; one could say that even then it had more to do with the social restrictions I experienced than having the impairment itself. As a child having an impairment was 'normalised' in the sense that it was no big deal among ourselves, however, it was the behaviour of adults that disrupted this and made it 'problematic'.

Going back to the bathroom incident, the staff made my companion and I swear not to tell anyone else what we had seen. I remember talking to him later in hushed whispers about not really 'understanding' what we had seen, but nevertheless sharing a greater empathy with the kid we had viewed as 'odd', but until then hadn't any idea why. In my opinion this story is almost allegorical because to me it captures the essence of how fear and ignorance helps fuel prejudice and discrimination thereby socially producing disabled people as 'Other'. (Engelund, 2012) As an eight year old, I was far from understanding these complex ideas.

I had other friends apart from Gillian and Paul with whom I mixed with most of the time. There are some things which are impossible to explain and for me my preferred friendship with females rather than males is such an example. Down the years, as you will see, I've had some good male mates and at my second school I spent lots of the free time in sporting activities with boys. Despite this, and especially at my Northampton school, I enjoyed female company more. The majority of the boys with whom I got on with were day pupils, and apart from Gillian, the girls were boarders.

Three girls in particular were part of my 'gang'; Christine, Mary and Laura. All three had cerebral palsy and were wheelchair users; however, Mary had athetoid cerebral palsy which disrupts the control of muscles and results in spontaneous, irregular writhing movements. It also meant she had no speech and communicated through the use of a 'letters board'. This process was extremely slow and extremely frustrating for her because she was without a doubt an extremely intelligent young woman. Both Christine and Laura had spastic cerebral palsy which meant their limbs were extremely stiff. Laura was the quiet one of the three and usually spent her time listening and watching everyone else. With hindsight, it is quite likely that Christine had mild learning difficulties; if this was the case, they didn't have much impact upon our friendship.

Due to the nature of our impairments and the disabling barriers we encountered, the social activities we could engage in were quite restricted. Much of time we played board games, with Christine moving all the pieces, or we listened to music. Christine and I wrote a letter to a pop star called Helen Shapiro in 1961 after she charted with, 'Don't Treat Me Like A Child' and 'You Don't Know'. I think it was because she was only five years or so older than us that prompted us to write, but I doubt either of us imagined we'd get a reply, but young Helen wrote a letter back which Christine kept. Talking about disabled children's social activities is rather complex because on the one hand they have the same interests as their non-disabled counterparts, yet on the other hand, they have to negotiate a 'different' reality brought about by the limitations of impairment, social restrictions caused by disabling barriers and often their experience of segregation. I've explained how our activities were limited, but this doesn't really tell the whole story.

Having a school full of disabled children with a variety of needs and only a handful of staff meant that the older children and those facing less significant barriers were often 'left to their own devices' or were expected to care for one another. I've a specific story to illustrate this point. There was a Scottish member of staff called Mrs Senior and to a certain extent, she reminded me of my Mum. One afternoon Mrs Senior was present when a group of junior pupils, including me, were having a 'rough and tumble' and I was on the wrong end of it all. I yelled out, 'You ****, that really hurt!' A shocked Mrs Senior said, 'Robert, what did you just call him?' So, innocently, I repeated it! Fortunately for me, she quickly realised I hadn't a clue what the word meant and that I'd learnt it from an older boy. This didn't prevent me from getting a severe ear bashing either!

As far as I'm aware there weren't too many problems with younger and older children mixing, but not everything came to the surface or was public knowledge. I'd a negative incident involving a senior boy called Tony who lured me into the Summer House hoping to interfere with me. Nothing serious happened, but he pounced from behind and I could feel his cold wet dribble on the back of my neck. As he touched the zip on my shorts, I froze rigid and after a minute or so he let me go and left. I never said anything to anyone about what happened as he never approached me again.

My schooling between the ages of six and nine was fairly typical for children of my age. To be honest I have no actual memories about this time in relation to the classroom. The only thing I know for certain was that due to my home schooling I had the reading age of a seven year old when I first went there. The year 1959 does however stand out for two distinct reasons, both of which seem hard to believe considering they relate to an eight year old, but I'd argue they cast a light on the person I grew up to be. I remember going back to school on the train one Sunday with my Dad and seeing a young man wearing a CND badge. Despite my tender years I felt drawn towards him with what I now know was a sense of solidarity. Where had that sprung from? Later the same year, I sensed a darkness descend when the Tories won a second term in office under Harold Macmillan. Could this simply be put down to my parents' influence? I've always argued my ideas were in advance of my years for most of my childhood.

It may well have been this fact that led to a number of negative incidents developing in the last couple of years at the school, especially after my transition from the junior into the senior class. Alongside my friends who were boarders I also had a group of friends who were day pupils. My best friend was called Barry and he was extremely bright. During the lunch period we would make up stories together based on comic book characters. I carried on doing this long after I swapped schools and most of my ideas were based upon super heroes out of DC comics or my own ideas for super heroes. Alongside the Justice League of America, I came up with my own super heroes called, The Purple Thirteen; not that I can remember too much about them now. It's however true to say that similar characters with identical powers did emerge over time.

As an aside, I'm pleased that one of my favourite DC heroes, The Green Lantern has finally made it to the big screen.

Barry did save my neck once when there was a craze among the boys at the school to buy 'caps' for toy guns and money went missing from the teacher's desk. I honestly can't remember if we were responsible or not, I think we may have been, because the teacher gave the class a week to return the money. Barry said we should put the money back and brought the money in from home; but it was me who was charged with the dirty deed of sneaking it back. There was also another incident involving money and 'caps' which involved Roger and me. The school was collecting money for charity – Children in Africa or something like that – and typical of me, I took the moral high ground and argued we should donate our money to charity instead of buying 'caps'. Roger refused so we had a row and he hit me in the mouth with his gun and my lip went up like a balloon. Roger got into trouble for hitting me, though I think he didn't mean to hit me, and the incident helped me raise lots of money for 'the good cause'.

With the class having mixed ability there was times when the teacher had to spend more time in one-to-one situations with the others than being in front of the whole class. This meant I was given set pieces of work to do and if I finished it, I had to wait until the Teacher had time for me. I became bored and frustrated. The teacher realised I'd outgrown what the school could offer me and there was a real risk I could start going backwards or develop bad behaviour. To be fair this teacher did encourage me to write and she 'helped' me win a book prize in a competition with the grand title of: The Brooke Bond National Travel Scholarships And Educational Awards. It was first prize for secondary essay. I still have the book which is called, Worlds in Space. The details of the award are on the first page and I'm struck by the fact that under 'school' it simply says: 'Spastic Northampton' with the date of March 1963.

Perhaps it wasn't just my school work that led her to conclude I was in the wrong environment. One morning she arrived in the classroom to find me jumping up and down with joy. I'd misunderstood the news that Harold Wilson had beaten George Brown in the Labour Party leadership race, and thought he had been elected Prime Minister. This strange child then went on to write an allegorical story about three different creatures who were always fighting each other until something terrible happened to the river bank and they were presented with a choice – either work together in common good or further their own interests and risk everything. I think it was this that led to her contacting the education authorities about me.

The issue of being 'left to our own devices' in the classroom was only part of the story; it also impacted upon after school activities as well. I was growing up fast and despite popular myths, boys and girls in the late 1950s and early 1960s weren't totally 'innocent'. Sexuality, like impairment and death, is another taboo subject in relation to young people, especially disabled ones. Today there are many heated debates around the 'sexualising' of young girls but the fifties were on the eve of the so called, 'Permissive Society' and everything was so different back then. Personally, I believe it was extremely naïve of the authorities and the staff not to take account of the fact that in a co-ed school there would be a certain amount of curiosity. Being male, I accept my relationship with my own body is going to be different to how females feel about theirs and the differing social pressures that exist, therefore what I'm about to say comes from personal feelings rather than some grand theory. I'm in no position to say that a boarding school environment created greater opportunities for young people to explore their bodies, but I do believe there was a closeness of interaction which is unlike mainstream settings. In some ways it's this 'closeness' that makes this subject area so complex.

Having been 'left to our own devices' I believe my little 'gang' grew tired of playing the same old games and sought different ways of entertaining ourselves. I've no idea when or why it happened, but I do know we progressed onto 'role play' activities that were called playing 'doctors and nurses', (in real terms it should've been called 'doctors and patients'; however, that would open up a whole new can of worms and I'm not prepared to go there!) We clearly understood we were crossing boundaries, even if we didn't fully understand why, so these games were kept secret and took place 'out-of-sight'. Having separate toilets for boys and girls was a clue in terms of 'difference' and boundaries, however there was a mixed dormitory up to the age of nine, but I'm guessing the staff didn't expect disabled children during light summer nights to practice 'medicine'! In many ways I'm not convinced this exploration of each other's bodies should even come under the heading of 'exploring sexuality'; for the most part it was innocent, mere curiosity, but at the same time knowing it was taboo made it into something else. For me, these games became more sexual as we grew older and gained more knowledge from the outside world.

My early 'education' came from two specific sources. The first was when I was around about ten years old and involved Roger again, the boy I shared a room with, and a French girl who came for a single term but during which time she caused utter havoc! Looking back, she must have been older than us and certainly more knowledgeable and experienced! I was still very naïve and extremely shocked by this girl's account of her relationship with her brother. I stumbled across this girl and Roger in the bushes one day and therefore wasn't surprised when I heard the pair of them and been called in 'to see Matron' a week or so later. What I hadn't accounted for was the girl's attitude towards me.

One morning, the 'nasty Nazi' (sic) didn't just haul me out of bed at the crack of dawn in her usual fashion, but she woke Roger too and told him not to talk to me. When ask why, she said that I knew what I had done. Over the next hour or so I was left to ponder this and I finally realised it was to do with me visiting Christine in her room before I went to bed. The French girl may have decided that if she was going to get into trouble with Roger, then my liaison with Christine ought to be public knowledge too. What happened next is hard to describe. Roger and I dressed in relative silence, though we did have a few whispered exchanges, and when the time came to go to breakfast, we were told the silence had to continue. Once downstairs we found all the others were already there with the tables arranged so that Christine and I had to sit together in the middle of the room. When a child broke the silence to ask why we were being collectively punished, they were told it was because of what Christine and I had done. After breakfast it was our turn 'to see Matron' and I'm not sure if was due to guilt or fear, but I don't recall being asked about what had taken place.

All I remember is being told off for behaving badly and informed that if I hadn't been in my last year at the school, I would've been asked to leave. Christine told me she hadn't been threatened in the same way, so I think the threat was to deter me from any other 'wrong doing'. It worked in so far as to say it scared me to the extent that I must have bottled it all up inside so that when I went home the following weekend I was extremely upset, nevertheless, couldn't tell my parents what was wrong.

The other 'education' in terms of sexuality came via the News of the World and their coverage of the Profumo Affair. In reporting the scandal of the Secretary of War's affair with a London 'model' who was also said to be a mistress of a Russian spy, the Sunday carried a number of photos of Christine Keeler. So before returning to school I 'borrowed' the newspaper in order to 'read' it during the week in the bike shed. The photo I remember vividly is one taken by Lewis Morley and has Keeler sat provocatively on a chair; however it wasn't actually explicit in any way; but to a young lad the imagination was enough. It wasn't until a couple of years later that I encountered magazines such as Playboy and Razzle, so my knowledge of the female form was limited to a few grained photos and a fumble with a few class mates.

Towards the end of my time at the school, despite what had happened with Christine, my relationship with Gillian began to develop into something deeper. It wasn't a particularly physical relationship, but it was a caring one that transcended a simple school friendship. Despite the first day kiss, I've the feeling that it wasn't until she had a week as a boarder whilst her mother had a baby that we really became close friends. Anyway, what is significant is the fact that I wasn't happy just seeing Gillian in the classroom during the day, so we asked permission to speak on the telephone in the evening. Whilst the matron thought this was an odd request as we had only seen each other hours before, she did allow us to talk and how we talked! Then in the summer of 1963 I had to leave both the school and Gillian behind. The final act before leaving was to find her and give her a last kiss. We both knew we wouldn't stay in touch so that was a real good bye kiss.

I did visit the school once after that, but I don't think Gillian was there at the time. This visit had been brought about because of different school holiday dates and it was my first experience of how things can quickly change. School has a big impact upon most children's lives, however, for children like me it had been our homes for six years and therefore a lot of our personal growth was cemented with the bricks and the people who were there with us. So, when I saw my friend Barry, I was extremely excited and began to tell him plans I had for stories we could work on together. He smiled politely, but his eyes told the real story; although a small length of time had gone past; the truth was we had gone our different ways and we were no longer the small boys we once were. This wasn't the last time I was to find myself in this type of situation.

I mentioned earlier that my teacher had contacted the educational authorities and unknown to my family discussions took place with the National Spastics Society with regards to me attending one of their schools. Out of the blue a letter came inviting my parents and me up to the Spastics Society headquarters in London in order for me to do various tests, including an IQ test. I remember arriving at this impressive building in Park Crescent.

Having completed the tests, we were asked to wait while they discussed the results. Finally, we were called back in to talk about my educational future. I must have been so anxious about what was going on, I actually went deaf for an hour. Once we got outside, I said, 'Well, what's happening? Am I going to a new school or not?' My results were so impressive that the Spastics Society invited me to attend their 'grammar school' for children with cerebral palsy.

This was a new start, but the down side to it was that the new school was even further away from home; it was in Tonbridge in Kent. Unlike my first school it had its own school uniform, so we had to go to London and try on this school uniform which was a maroon blazer, grey trousers, grey shirt and a maroon tie. At the time I can remember thinking 'Oh boy! Am I going to be able to cope here?' I was already questioning my ability even before I entered the school on 19 September 1963. Despite my own inner doubts, I went straight into the A stream. Most of the pupils who went to Delarue never forget the school motto: 'There is no failure other than ceasing to try'. The irony of this being that according to my Mum as a youngster my favourite saying was: 'I can't...' As I grew older, I realised that for the majority of disabled people often we had little choice but to battle on against the odds.

Before looking at my teenage years at Delarue I want to end this chapter with a brief look at family life before my great upheaval. Going home at weekends and long holiday did give me a taste for 'family life' but for the most part it was a fairly lonely existence. Jean had long since flown the nest and Mary had her own life. I think it was roughly around this time that Mary met David who became her husband. I can remember Mary going to the cinema with me a couple of times to see Elvis Presley and a film called The Village of the Damned which was very scary. However my childhood memories of Mary really centre around two particular activities. It was a ritual that on a Saturday morning Mum would disappear up town 'shopping' and leave Mary to do the housework and keep an eye on me. Mum would be gone three or four hours, where the shopping would end up with a lunchtime drink with a female friend. Needless to say Mary resented being put on in this way and my sister could be quite moody when upset; so I spent as much of Saturday morning in bed as I could.

Mum's shopping trips were always a sore point with me; it wasn't just Saturday mornings. During my school holidays she would go 'up the street' quite regularly and I'd have no idea when to expect her back. A few years ago, I realised that by today's standards Mum's treatment might be regarded as child abuse. As I grew older these hours I spent alone saw me progress from playing with toys to playing and singing along to records. An older boy at my first school helped select the first half dozen records I brought. At first, I played my records on a small red portable player and then later, Mum and Dad brought me a big stereogram. I was more into Elvis than Cliff but brought records by both of them. Often, I would 'borrow' records from Mary and I think I've still a couple of them!

I started to go and watch the local football team Leighton Town and for many years I had a trike and would ride everywhere on that. Mum would accompany me to the game and Dad would pick me up when he finished work. Quite often he would watch most of the second half with me. I know for certain Dad and I watched a couple of games in the First Division in 1965-66 when Northampton Town reached those dizzy heights. After the journey home on the trike we had another ritual to contend with.

When Mary was courting David, he would come around for Saturday tea which consisted of cold meats and cakes. I understood, initially anyway, that as 'our guest' it was an act of etiquette to invite David to choose first which cake he wanted. The problem was that he'd always go for the one I wanted. After a while I found this etiquette a little tiresome because by this time Mary had her hooks in him and he was virtually a member of the family! Was I resentful? Sure I was; I wouldn't say it was really towards David, who has been like a 'real' brother to me almost from the beginning, I felt my parents made more fuss of him than me. I was the one who they rarely saw after all.

So it was against this type of background that I swapped schools and swapped from seeing my family every weekend to just seeing them for chunks of time during school holidays. In the following chapter I'll write a little more about school holidays and the alienation I felt. Re-reading this account of my early life I'm not quite sure what kind of child I've painted myself to be. Perhaps this will become a little clearer in the next chapter.

Chapter 3

My teenage years

Old enough to see that it's wrong, young enough to do it anyway!

Abhishek Tiwari

In the final year or so at my Northampton school I had outgrown what they had to offer me; I was like a big fish in a very small pond. Transferring to The Thomas Delarue School in Tonbridge brought me back to earth with a bump because it was a huge culture shock to my system; I was small fry once more. What made moving to this new school unusual was the fact that it was a 'new school' for everyone. Delarue had been opened in 1955 in a big house situated on a large estate called Dene Park which had been owned by John Hollom. Hollom was High Sheriff of Kent in 1917 and his estate had 682 acres of land, out buildings, stables and a farm. The estate was eventually split up and is currently run by the Forestry Authority.

The new purpose-built school was further down the hill just off the Shipbourne Road. In 1965 Delarue won a Civic Trust Award which were given 'to recognise outstanding architecture, planning and design in the built environment.' The school's architecture was very 'functional' with most of it being designed around quadrangles and long corridors. The British Medical Journal, in June 1955, hailed Delarue as 'Britain's first secondary school for spastics' although the National Spastics Society viewed it as having both a grammar and secondary stream. If anyone is interested in the early history of the Spastics Society, a charity established primarily by parents, I would recommend the book by Richard Dimbleby (1964) called, Every Eight Hours, as it neatly captures of how disabled people were both seen and treated in the 1950s and 1960s.

Not surprisingly then, an early memory of Delarue was of Mr Davis, the headmaster, addressing assembly and telling us that as pupils of Delarue we were the crème de la crème and that it was our duty to be proud of being there. I had already convinced myself I'd been placed in the wrong stream; so, this unsettled me even further.

On 9 June 1964 a red helicopter landed on the lush green playing field behind the school to mark the beginning of the Royal visit by HRH Prince Philip, the President of the Society, who came to formally open it. For days before the visit the pupils had had to rehearse their roles and as luck would have it, I was stuck in a double period of maths!

When the Duke did his walk-about he stuck his head around the door and asked what activity was taking place. Being informed it was 'elementary maths' he just laughed; which didn't go down well with me or the other poor sods who hated the subject. Upon a given signal, once the visit was over, we all had to rush around the edge of the school and form a guard of honour at the foot of some steps. I once had a photo of a small group of year 1A boys quashed at the front of the line with Robert, hair in a mess, clapping as the Duke came down the steps. Clearly, my Republican sympathies hadn't formed by then.

The majority of the first years placed in the A stream stayed together throughout their schooling although we were joined by a couple of others in subsequent years. My best friend was Steve, although we called him 'Titch', on the account of his size. I'm not keen on being descriptive about an individual's impairment unless it's relevant to a particular issue or storyline; however, in Steve's case, the fact he had spastic hemiplegia was significant in the development of our friendship. In our early days we would walk the grounds together and talk, however my gait was such that I would at times lean to the left. Steve's right hand and my left hand for differing reasons would from time to time 'lock' onto any object they came into contact with and so, from time to time, we would accidently 'hold hands' before breaking free again. At the time I was still unaware of what homosexuality was, so when the Matron called us in to talk about 'our special friendship' after spying us out and about I hadn't a clue to what she was referring to. Steve said later, that he almost wet himself as neither of us could afford to explain that as our hands linked, we were busily discussing the fact that there was a loose panel between the boys' and girls' toilets!

In many ways the relationship Steve and I had contained less boundaries than the one we both had with Richard. I'm probably not in the best position to talk about Richard aka 'Dick' and I certainly don't want to speak ill of the dead; but over the seven years at Delarue, Richard was the person I clashed with the most. He was certainly closer to Steve than me, though in terms of sporting activities Dick and I did more together. Dick taught me to play chess and encouraged me to join the school's chess team. In the early days at Delarue the three of us got on together fairly well though I always felt old 'Dickie' suited the 'crème de la crème' image more than I ever would. If he hadn't been a disabled person, I sense that Dick would've probably made a name for himself and looking back, even in the first year, it was obvious that he was destined to become Head boy. A few years ago, I heard that he had died, but there was little said on the cause of his death. Just like the small boy at my previous school there were supposed to be 'medical issues' that the rest of us weren't aware of. There weren't many physical fights at school, but those that involved Dick were treated slightly more seriously than the rest and at least four of these were to also involve me! The others who formed the backbone of our class were Ann, Sharon, Hugh and Jean. Ann, like Richard, died quite young and left a daughter behind. She used both arm crutches as well as a wheelchair. My first and probably biggest bust up with Steve was over Ann during our first year. We both liked her, but I beat him to the punch by asking her out on a Saturday afternoon. After going to the cinema, I thought it would be romantic to go for a walk in the local park, unfortunately I hadn't checked the time the main gates were shut. We had to walk miles to find a way out and were late getting to the café we had all agreed to meet up. Neither Steve nor Ann were impressed by my behaviour; it was another four years before I took her out again! Ann and Steve were regarded as a couple for a number of years off and on, but Ann's best friend without a doubt was Sharon.

Despite spending countless hours in the classroom with Sharon we never socialised a great deal outside of a 'group' situation. Sharon Hughes being a Catholic, didn't have the same Sunday ritual I had, she wasn't into sport and so we didn't really have any cause to socialise outside of the classroom. This shouldn't be read as me saying I didn't like or get on with her; we just weren't close. I doubt there was more than half a dozen times where we crossed swords, and these were over specific issues. One of the biggest arguments was between Ann and Sharon on the one side, and the boys on the other, was all to do with the school uniform. The boys had to wear grey long sleeved shirts, black trousers and a maroon tie all year round; whereas the girls had a summer uniform which consisted of light cotton blue skirt and an open necked top. Only if the temperature reached a certain height were the boys allowed to remove their ties. In the boys' opinion this was sexist and unjust, but the girls argued it had to do with personal care and hygiene. Clearly then, it was okay for males to stink! Even today I look at schoolboys with their shirt tails hanging out and ties adrift and wonder why society hangs onto this brainless tradition of making boys feel uncomfortable.

It might sound strange that with only forty odd pupils together in an enclosed space there were close friendships made rather than whole group engagement, but this needs to be placed in some kind of context. Boarding schools like Delarue had tight regimes which left little time for socialising. An ordinary week consisted of a variety of daily routines. The first routine consisted of getting up and going for breakfast. The second routine, which I seriously considered leaving out of this account, involved the 'constitutionals' – moving one's bowels! Like clock-work people lined up at various toilets to 'do their business'.

Because Steve, Dick and I were independent and didn't require support from the Housemothers, we all went to a loo far from the queuing throng of desperate faces. Oddly, the twenty minutes or so before Assembly became as much a 'social occasion' as it was a functional necessity. Perhaps this was a young male thing; none of us felt uncomfortable with this arrangement. It was a good way to catch up with news or prepare for the day ahead.

The school routine begun at a quarter to nine and finished the first part at four. There was a fifteen-minute break in the mid-morning and an hour for lunch. For the first few years we three boys sat together in Assembly and during the second year our 'team' was joined by an older boy called Cliff. On more than one occasion we were chastised from the stage for our unruly behaviour. Two particular incidents stick in my mind and both involve the use, or should I say misuse, of language. At beginning of the second year the Headmaster announced the names of the fresh in-take and without failure two of the girls' names were always said together from that moment on. Looking back, I believe it's the movement in the names –

Mary Lee and Amanda Dee – that tickled us. We all burst out laughing, which didn't go down too well. It might also in part explain why Cliff, despite months of effort, made no headway with Mary!

The other incident also directly involved Cliff as well. Cliff had found a small animal skull in the grounds and he kept it in a box which he carried around with him. Probably as a corruption of: 'Alas! Poor Yorick', Cliff nicknamed the damn skull, 'Horace'. This one morning Cliff placed 'Horace' under the chair in front of him. At the end of Assembly, the Headmaster announced that Cliff had lost a Swiss watch and he asked the assembled throng to keep their eyes open for his 'Oris'. I said in a large whisper, 'It's okay, Cliff; Horace is down there!'

The period between four and five saw me engaging in some kind of physical sporting activity; I could add slightly tongue-in-cheek, unless I was in some kind of 'relationship' which wasn't too often! I preferred team games which were seasonal with football being played two thirds of the year and cricket the other third. The weather only determined whether the games were in or outdoors.

There were two tarmac areas where we played games. From year three until I left, I was the school's goalkeeper. A couple of times we had sporting events at weekends against the Surrey Amateur Football Coaches Association. The first time we played five-a-side they begun by trying to 'pass' the ball into the net but towards the end of the game they were 'shooting' and still only beat me once or twice. This resulted in me gaining the nickname: 'the Cat' after the Chelsea and England star, Peter Bonnetti.

The truth was I modelled my goalkeeping style on the Northern Ireland 'keeper, Pat Jennings. He was my hero from the first live match I ever watched – Watford versus Swindon Town – heady days for a twelve-year-old! When not kicking, saving or hitting a ball, I would ride around the grounds on a Trike. My other past-times would include snooker and as I've already indicated, chess or draughts. This period before the evening meal and the time between eight and when he had to go to bed, were the only time we had to socialise with people outside of our own class during the week.

Between six o'clock and eight we were back in our classrooms doing set homework. It was a long day for five days a week. The weekends were also regimented with Saturday mornings being taken up with homework and writing home and Sunday morning being herded off to Church. When I was sixteen, I asked my Dad to write and ask for me to be excused from going to Church, but he refused. During my last two years I visited various 'alternatives' to the Church of England, including the Salvation Army. Going to the Army almost had repercussions because they sold 'The War Cry' in the local pubs and one Saturday night they visited a pub where a small gang of us would 'sneak' into before returning to school. They said nothing fortunately. During the summer months a Welsh Baptist, called Di Davies, would join me in another 'alternative church' which was the park in the centre of Tonbridge. It was such a farce and a feat of planned engineering each week. Coach loads of pupils dragged off to Church and a smaller group of Catholics attended Mass via a mini bus. The majority of the pupils hated it.

I suppose my relationship with Jean was similar to the one I had with Sharon although there were different circumstances involved. Jean had come from mainstream schooling and belonged, in the early days, to 'the school of hard knocks' which meant she was very threatening during the first year. Whether or not it was just an act or a phase Jean went through I'll probably never know, but she caused the class to shun her in our first term because of her ongoing fight with Hugh. Hugh and Jean both had hearing impairments as well as having mild cerebral palsy, but this common feature was blown away by the fact that Hugh was Jewish, and Jean's idol was Adolf Hitler! Our classroom during this period was like a re-run of the Second World War with insults reigning down like bombs. Over time Jean mellowed and became one of the most caring people I've known. Hugh, on the other hand, did feel restricted by the lack of accommodation made for his hearing loss but, just like the usual stereotype says, he didn't use this as an excuse and went on to achieve good exam results.

My relationship with Hugh turned on the fact that he too played a lot of sports and we were in the same dormitory for a while. I've talked about the core group of pupils I spent the majority of my time with over the years at Delarue to show what a diverse bunch of people they were. In a while I'll recount specific stories which include pupils from other classes and backgrounds, but for now I want to reinforce the idea that in a way it didn't matter whether I got on with Sharon or Richard outside the classroom, the fact we were together learning and exchanging ideas for seven years means they were instrumental in helping to shape me into the type of person I became.

I've often said I've mixed feelings about my time at Delarue. The fact it was a boarding school where I was months at a time means it was both a school and 'my home'. If I divide the two, then for most of the time I would share the views of many others who attended Delarue that the academic side was of a high quality. I would argue that it was only during my last two years when I was doing 'A' levels did this side of the schooling let me down. This said, I also hold the view that this too was partly down to non-academic issues; my history teacher was going through severe personal difficulties which affected his ability to teach. He was losing his sight, and no one picked up on the fact he withdrew into himself to the extent that for the majority of the 'A' level syllabus, we weren't actually being 'taught'. We weren't given guidance on how to write an essay to the standard required at that level and most of my 'studies' were reduced to looking up historical events in Encyclopaedias.

I failed the exam and I know it wasn't down to a lack of interest in the subject; it was a case of being ill-equipped to deal with the type of questions that were asked.

I also had a problem in my 'A' level Geography exam as well however in order to explain what went wrong, I want to first say something about my academic ability and support needs. It's no secret that I wasn't the best pupil in the class by a long way; Ann, Sharon and Steve were good at English Literature and Language, Richard and Steve shone at Maths and I just held my own at History and Geography.

Our English teacher, Jane Elsdon-Smith, had been on the Japanese 'most wanted list' and wasn't someone you messed with. She was an interesting character who would defy being pigeon-holed. She took us by surprise one day in November 1963 when she spoke about a new BBC drama series called Dr Who in which her daughter, Jacqueline Hill, was going to play the role of the school teacher Barbara Wright. Another time, when she was our sixth form class teacher, she called me into her office to look at a small marble statue she had. In a non-plus voice, she explained that she had been doing some research and she thought the piece I was holding was by Rodin. I immediately felt the blood drain from my face as I pleaded with her to take it out of my trembling hands!

The most remarkable story about this upright conservative lady relates to how she sought to teach me grammar. We were doing nouns, verbs and adjectives. She explained that, 'verbs were doing words' and then proceeded to go around the class giving each of us a letter from which we had to come up with a suitable verb. I sat there in sheer panic as I waited for my turn, and when it did come, I was presented with the letter 'F'. First there was silence and then my eyes widened with horror as only one word loomed large in front of me. At that moment her laugh broke the silence and she said, 'By Jove! I think he's got it.' To me that will remain a moment of pure genius on her part because she managed to win my confidence by relating to where that young boy was at!

Another subject I wasn't too bad at, although most people who know me double-take when I tell them, was Bible Knowledge! I almost cocked up the 'O' level exam because I rushed through the paper in order to go to a party. On the science side of education, I only ever attended one Physics class because the school decided that the priority for me was to learn to type. So, whilst my other classmates did Physics, Maths, etc. I had two double sessions of typing each week! However, during my 'O' levels I had mainly used two amanuenses – I could be mistaken here, but I think they were married to each other. Both were well educated, middle class people who played golf and did their bit for charity. Despite their backgrounds I found them both fairly down to earth and I was happy to work with them. The role of the amanuensis is simply to follow instructions and write down what people said and in the majority of cases this is what took place.

I had two incidents which weren't strictly by the rules; one positive and the other negative. During one of my 'O' level exams I freaked at the questions and began to panic, but the female amanuensis told me to close the paper and talk to her for five minutes. This did the trick because I returned to the paper and completed it. Unfortunately, the other experience was pure interference and cost me dearly.

In my 'A' level Geography exam one of the questions required making a choice between two methods of collecting data – dot plots or bar graphs. I wasn't sure which one would be the most appropriate, so I spent some time weighing up the options and then finally decided to use the dot plot method. The male amanuensis said that this would take a considerable amount of time and did I really believe they would want this during an exam? He persuaded me to change my mind; speaking to the teacher later it was confirmed that this 'change of heart' meant the difference between gaining an 'A' level and having to settle for an 'O' level pass.

This wasn't my only poor choice I made in terms of studying either. When in the Lower Sixth I began an extra curricula class in music theory. If I wanted to use an excuse, then all I would say is that at that moment in my life I was a seventeen-year-old with low esteem and I wasn't prepared for a teacher who wanted to heap praise on me. I'd spent most of my time at Delarue feeling inferior outside of my sporting adventures and suddenly just after a handful of lessons I was being rushed through a grade one exam because the teacher thought I was capable of doing 'O' level music theory within six months! She kept on about my ability to such an extent that I switched off, didn't study for the exam and not surprisingly, failed it. Of course, I've kicked myself ever since and I've looked at learning music again, but it has never happened.

The first impact of what I had done in terms of the music exam failure came when another English teacher, Mrs Freda Elwood, invited me to help her finish a love song for a school pantomime and I successfully managed to write the second verse to fit her score. I knew from that moment I had probably just buggered up any real chance I had of being a famous song writer! Yes, I did fancy doing this; I had even written to Alan Price a famous song writer at the time and he had offered me a few tips. Having said I wasn't use to having praise, I suppose that isn't strictly true. Mrs Elwood didn't praise me as much as gave me encouragement to write. As I've already said, my use of grammar leaves a great deal to be desired, but she saw something in my writing ability. Her background included being an editor of a literary magazine and she put me in touch with an agent who worked for David Higham Associates.

Looking back, I don't believe I was ready or mature enough to have a sensible relationship with this agent. My poetry remained my first love and I had encouragement from an editor working for Faber and Faber who had worked with Auden. With all this encouragement, what went wrong?

In 1967 I passed 'O' Level English Literature and Language as did everyone in my class so there was no indication that there were going to be any surprises the following year. Most of us took four 'O' levels and mine were History, Geography, Bible Knowledge and Maths. Returning to school in the Autumn of 1968 I was totally unaware of the climate I was walking into. So, I go back thinking everybody had gained four O levels like me. It was only when the headmaster, Mr Mayhew, approached a gathered throng in the dining room and said almost through gritted teeth, 'Oh, well done Bob on passing all your exams', that I had a sense something strange was going on. Shortly after when I met up with Hugh, who explained that we were top of the class. I couldn't believe I'd passed Maths and everybody else had failed. During the mocks, much to Mr Pink's despair, I had regularly finished fourteenth out of fifteen, but I was the one who managed to get through. There was some resentment and I heard rumours that I'd been accused of cheating, but the truth was quite straight forward.

Both Ann and Sharon had studied hard and, in the exam, sought to answer all the questions, whereas I simply did as much as I could before moving on through the paper. I picked up points for demonstrating 'method' as opposed to the others who stuck with trying to answer fewer questions. My feelings of being on cloud nine didn't last long as a series of events brought me back to earth again with a bump.

The school's first Headmaster, Mr Davis saw the change in school buildings through before retiring and being replaced by Mr Tudor who didn't really leave much of a mark on the place. The only major dealings I had with him were in relation to sex education lessons. I've always been too much like my Mum, willing to support the underdog, voice an opinion or step forward to represent others. Of course, in reality, no one really thanks you for being like that. Most of my class would complain or voice opinions behind closed doors but the majority were happy to do what they were told and not ask too many questions. Me, on the other hand, would want to know why this or that happened; how come they'd let A get away with this whereas B can't? So, no guessing as to who agreed at the start of the second year to go to the headmaster and say, 'Isn't it time you put sex education on the curriculum because we're getting older and it's a bit silly that nobody talks to us about what we should and shouldn't know.' Fair play to Mr Tudor he did provide lessons however from that moment onwards I felt as if I had been earmarked as a potential troublemaker; a label that stayed with me all through my time at Delarue.

After Mr Tudor, the brother of Christopher Mayhew who had been a Labour MP but then had crossed the House to become a Liberal MP, became the Headmaster. It's true that I've never really got on with authority figures however in all honesty I can't really explain why Mayhew and I ended up with nothing but contempt for each other. We seemed to clash over a number of things ranging from the length of my hair through to my friendship with a Jewish girl called Nirit. Over the years I had had a couple of girlfriends, but none of these relationships had caused me any grief. Nirit was considerably younger than I was, and she was homesick for her native Israel. So, I decided to befriend her to begin with. Nothing illegal ever happened between us, but my refusal to stop the relationship had dire consequences.

The first sign of trouble was when I had my collection of poetry seized. I had given my folder of poetry to a girl in Nirit's form who had wanted to read it. The next morning the girl came crying to me saying that they'd taken it off her and she was sorry I'd get told off. When I approached the Housemother who had done this, she said the girl had been too young to read such filth and that's why it had been taken off her. I was then called into the

Headmaster's office and told that I had engaged in inappropriate behaviour. Mayhew branded my poetry 'pornographic filth' and banned me from writing it at school. I was informed I could only have my work returned at the end of term when I had to take it home. The offending line was: 'I want to run naked through the long grass/ Feel the warmth of the sun on my skin...' I really didn't see what I had done wrong.

Then one day whilst I was pushing Nirit towards the bridge that linked to the girls' dormitory, the deputy matron pulled me to one side. I remember standing on the bridge with her as she said, 'Doesn't it bother you?' I wasn't following at first, so I asked what it was that should be bothering me. 'She's a Jew and you're a Christian' was the response. I said, 'So?' And she said, 'Well doesn't it bother you that you're likely to go to Hell if you carry on with this relationship?' I said, 'What are you talking about? This is a ridiculous argument to use.' At this point she simply stormed off. Rightly or wrongly, I wasn't going to be bullied into giving up my relationship, even though it was a very difficult one. With all the pressure being placed on us both Nirit would swing between not wanting anything to do with me through to clinging onto me for dear life. In the end I felt trapped, whatever I did seemed to land me in trouble.

My time in the Lower and Upper Sixth Forms was a nightmare. It's hard to recall how the events unfolded, but Steve for some reason decided he was unhappy, so one day around half four he told me he was going to return home; would I cover for him? So, I kept my mouth shut until after tea. When people started asking questions, I thought it best to tell the truth and was the one who got it in the neck! With my best mate gone, I felt really lonely as there were only six of us left doing 'A' Levels. Shortly after Steve left; only to return for the final exams, it was announced through the grapevine that the Headmaster was going to appoint six Prefects that year and people did the maths. One day my classmates were called out from

Prep one by one and returned smiling. Then towards the end of Prep this guy John from the class below bounced in to show everyone his new Prefect's badge. When he left the room fell deathly silent; I can't even begin to explain how I felt that day. Prefects, of course, had their own common room and within weeks of their appointment were invited to a meal at the Headmaster's house. I had to do Prep on my own that day. There I was in humiliating silence for a second time.

I did get support through this difficult time and some of it was from unusual quarters. My classmates were too busy being Prefects to worry too much about the fact that no one had prepared me for what was going to happen; Mayhew left me to stew in my own juice. The class below mine rallied round me, partly I suspect because they couldn't believe that John, who had arrived from a mainstream school, had been given that final position. At no time did I resent John because I knew he wasn't responsible for what Mayhew had done and I'm still friends with him. There was another source of support which I've kept secret until now. A local businessman took an interest in the school because his name was De La Rue.

Every so often he would formally arrange for a couple of pupils to go out for tea with him and his wife. Over the years I think I had been invited twice however towards the end of my time at Delarue the couple would arrive unannounced and take me out. Once he stopped in town one Saturday and offered me a lift back to school. To this day I've no idea why the couple gave me the attention they did, but it was invaluable at the time. On my last afternoon at the school the Deputy Headmaster, Mr Williams, a pipe smoking Welshman took my Mum and me to one side and apologised for what had happened to me. He swore that if he had been in charge many things would've been done differently and openly admitted that I had been victimised for 'being high spirited'.

Memories are funny things and I've been told that

there's a tendency among some people to cling onto painful and negative ones rather than focus on positive events. It should therefore be said that not all my memories of Delarue are dark and depressing. There are those which relate to me being a typical teenage boy; the time my hand shook violently when the young speech therapist asked me to feel her breathing by placing it on her chest! Then there was the staff versus the pupils' football match where I came rushing off my line as Mrs Watkins, a Housemother, bore down on goal. I failed to stop her scoring, but I did collide with which meant that I ended up on top of her. I was ribbed for weeks after that. Another funny goalkeeping incident was when I failed to stop a penalty kick and let out a four-letter word only to hear the voice of Mr Mayhew saying, 'Oh, hard luck, Robert.'

Another lasting memory of mine illustrates the comic side of my personality. One lunch time the noise in the dining room was almost intolerable and this led to the Matron storming in and yelling, 'Quiet!' Unfortunately for me I was looking at a deaf kid called David at the time. David wore hearing aids and just as the Matron hit her highest note, one of his aids popped out! Everywhere instantly fell into silence apart from me; I was crying with laughter. The dining room was the scene of many daring feats involving food, such as the time Steve Burton and I tried to impress a new Housemother by holding a Weetabix eating contest. Another Housemother had to step in and halted proceedings when it had reach fifteen biscuits each.

Many people, whether they are disabled or not, would argue that the teenage years are full of angst and therefore my account of what happened at Delarue wasn't particularly unique. Whilst there's a grain of truth in this, there's a body of opinion among some of us who went to this school that a certain degree of inequality took place. There was an undercurrent that was abusive to those who dared to exert a degree of individuality outside the expectations the school placed on us. In the next chapter I will develop this as a theme because it helps to frame my transition from being a teenager into a young adult.

Chapter 4

Love, death and crazy talk

I have loved to the point of madness
That which is called madness
That which to me
Is the only sensible way to love.

Francoise Sagan

The early 1970s were difficult for me for a whole host of reasons. No matter how much I hated the final few years at Delarue, it nevertheless gave me a sense of security. Reading a number of accounts of pupils leaving Delarue, this appears to be a familiar feeling. The majority of my life up to this point in time had been spent it in segregated educational establishments where school and an organised social life were virtually seamless. Suddenly, both were being taken away from me. At the age of nineteen I was faced with the prospect of returning home to my parent's house in a town where I hardly knew anyone. I had found the long school holidays lonely and boring enough; how would I cope with the possibility of spending the rest of my life under these conditions?

The truth is my parents had very little in common with me. It was okay whilst I was growing up to watch television at night or go with them to the local Working Men's Club to listen to bands and play dominoes in partnership with my father. We made a pretty good team and often thrashed everyone out of sight. I think it was my ability to play dominoes that helped Dad realise how intelligent I was; this was however a double edged sword. On the one hand, Mum would tell me how proud he was of my achievements, yet on the other I always felt he found it difficult to relate to me as I neared adulthood. My brother in law David ended up copping my jealousy and frustration because Dad seemed to find it easier to talk with him about cars than about things going on in my life.

My Dad wasn't very good at showing affection or communicating with other family members and so it was difficult for us all when he would resort to showing generosity towards strangers; usually in the form of buying them drinks. On more than one occasion this activity resulted in me being placed upon public display as my father 'showed me off'. The first incident I have no recollection of but apparently it was shortly after I had learnt to walk. He gathered a crowd to watch me, but I ended up in a bruised heap and my Mum didn't half give him a tongue lashing according to her account. You would've thought he would've learnt, but a few years later I had to entertain a young trainee speech therapist who turned up out-of-the-blue after an encounter with my old man. This however was topped by the arrival at our door one evening by the local league dominoes champion who had been challenged to come and play against me. For the rest of that school holiday I couldn't do anything wrong in my father's eyes having belittled one of Dad's rivals. This may have been a good moment, but I wasn't prepared to spend the rest of my life performing in this way.

I'm often asked about what careers advice I was given, and I usually respond with a snort and a laugh. If I remember rightly, I spoke to the 'careers people' once in an attempt not to get any more hassle from Mayhew. At nineteen, sheltered most of your life from the big wide world, how were you supposed to react to the question: 'So what do you want to do?' I hadn't got a bloody clue to be honest! The closer it came to having to make decisions about my future, the more certain I grew in terms of not wanting to return to Leighton Buzzard and so I decided to go where my heart took me.

One of my school friends called Ken was lined up for an interview at Oakwood Further Education Centre which was also run by the Spastics Society. Ken was a Scot with a cutting sense of humour and someone I'd been friends with for a number of years. He had been extremely supportive during my 'troubles'. It was only after Ken told me Carol Nelson was having an interview there too that my ears pricked up.

Carol and I had a little bit of 'history' between us, however to be truthful, it's a little difficult to describe this history because it has similarities to the teen comedy film, *Gregory's Girl*. I was in my third year when I first saw Carol and found myself smitten. God knows how long I 'worshiped her from a far' and to me she was my Billy Joel's Uptown Girl, although in reality I discovered later that her father was a self-made Londoner who ran a large window cleaning firm which took the shine off this image a little. One of my earliest striking memories involving Carol relates to me being angry at the idea that her current boyfriend had been cheating on her. It was early morning and I was lying in bed thinking about her being hurt. The Tremeloes song, 'Silence Is Golden', was fuelling my emotions when I suddenly discovered the bodily transition from childhood to adulthood had begun.

Like so many other romantic stories this one was destined to be a case of unrequited love. Both Carol and I had various relationships over a three to four year period and, more often not, she was going out with someone that most of the other girls saw as 'the catch' of the school; so what hope had I? As I wrote in the previous chapter my life during the last two years of schooling had been in utter chaos. My relationship with Nirit had caused trouble and when I broke up with her, I also had an army of critics lining up to have a go at me.

Carol at the same time was going through a turbulent relationship with Richard, the Head boy. Neither of us had stable relationships and one early evening it all kicked off. Call this a feeble excuse if you like, but by this time I was more of a friend than a boyfriend to Nirit, and in this role, I was helping her with some homework when all hell broke out in the corridor. Richard and Carol were having a terrible flair up and it was starting to look ugly. Even to this day I can't really explain my actions, but I calmly left the classroom I was in and took hold of Carol's wheelchair and pushed her away from the scene. The following few days saw us spend a considerable amount of free-time together which had tongues wagging in every corner of the school. Not for the last time, the pressure exerted upon us was too much and we both agreed a serious relationship wasn't what either of us needed at that time and so things returned more or less as they were.

Over the next few months, I tried to create distance between both Carol and Nirit as I struggled with preparing for my exams. Despite this effort I just couldn't get Carol out of my mind. To make matters worse Richard and I shared adjacent bedrooms and with my mate Steve back at home, I was feeling utterly alone. The bedroom I had was a ground floor one and subsequently had its own fire door. Around nine o'clock one night I sneaked down the hill to an off licence and brought a small bottle of whiskey. My Dad drank whiskey, in truth I've never liked the stuff, but that night it was the only thing I could afford. By two in the morning I had had enough, but wasn't drunk or incapable; it did however give me enough Dutch courage to enter no man's land. What had sparked this adventure in the first place had been the fact that the school's laundry was stacked near the toilets on our corridor and I had spied one of Carol's nightdresses there. It was probably around three when she woke to find me sitting at the foot of her bed. She wasn't angry or upset to find me there but wisely she coaxed me back to my room and no one else was any the wiser.

This night visit wasn't my only act of stupidity during this period; shortly after the exams were over the fire alarm went off in the middle of the night and everyone had to be evacuated. I remember seeking Carol out and standing in front of her as we waited for the 'all clear' signal. Her look on her face told me that she wasn't convinced it had been an accident and there's every chance my own face had given me away. It was the middle of the night; I was feeling lost, and just had to see her just like before. What I'd done was wrong, there's no denying that, and of course, I was petrified in case anyone discovered the truth. Alarms don't just go off, do they? Imagine my relief when the Fire Brigade the following day discovered a fault in the system.

The result was that no one had their arse fried as a result of my actions. Among my last acts of defiance was to wind the staff up by becoming friends with one of the school's 'sweet hearts'. I doubt many people down the years have openly spoken about this, but in my opinion, which is shared by a few others I've spoken to, there was an undercurrent of class distinction at the school where some of the pupils were held in higher regard than others. According to this girl her mother had taught the Queen how to dance and rather than hold it against her, I thought it would give the staff an even greater reason for not wanting her to associate with an older boy like me. There wasn't anything really going on between us, she was far too nice for me to even consider taking advantage of her, but I did shamefully 'talk up' the prospect of us 'becoming an item'.

I waited for a reaction to come from the staff in connection with my advances however when a reaction did occur it was from an unexpected quarter. It was Carol who pulled me aside and questioned my intentions and wasn't too impressed by my flip explanation that it was 'just a bit of fun'. Not only did she tell me to stop fooling around in this manner, she also reminded me that she was more my age and type, so if I wanted 'a bit of fun', I knew where to go.

It was against this backdrop that I made my decision to seek an interview at Oakwood. I thought why not try and go with her; if anything happens then that would be a bonus. Five of us attended for interview with another male and me undertaking an aptitude test to see if we were suitable for computer programming. The crazy thing was, he failed, and I passed. I can laugh now but I ended up in Kelvedon to train to become a computer programmer for the Ford Motor Company! Can you imagine someone like me who had never set eyes on a computer; someone with a love of writing flowery poetry seriously getting into programming? What on earth was I thinking? And, of course, it didn't work because I wasn't up to it and found the whole thing totally alien. Common Business-Oriented Language – COBOL – is one of the oldest computer programmes around. As the name suggests its usage tends to be in business, finance, and administrative systems for companies and governments. It's a very long winded language and it certainly was in my hands! After floundering for about six months it was finally agreed I could jack it in.

What can I say about Oakwood? It was a small residential college in a village called Kelvedon which lay just off the A12 and fairly near to Colchester. Mr Doughty, who was himself disabled, was the Principal and there were about twelve people from various backgrounds and apart from Ken and Carol there were other men I'd known from my time at Delarue. Although I had a rough time whilst at Oakwood, I still look back on my friendships with most of the people there with fondness. During my time at Oakwood I was in transition; trying to discover who and what I was. At the time I made no distinction between living with an impairment and encountering disablement. I was very naïve and inexperienced, but the year I spent at Oakwood was to be a bridge between my old world and the new one I was about to enter.

Most of my friends up to this moment in time had been forged through the fact we either shared a classroom, bedrooms or because we engaged in the same activities. At Oakwood friendships were made by personal choice even though we shared a confined space. With each person I made friends with at Oakwood there was a specific set of circumstances and each relationship had its own dynamics. Some readers will question why I'm writing about this, but in my opinion, the importance lies in the fact that for many disabled people, institutionalisation determined both who and how they become friends with people. In my opinion Oakwood saw both the restrictive contours of making friendships and a more open-ended approach which was to some degree self-determined.

When Carol and I weren't on good terms in the December of 1970, I would go for walks with Steve and a woman called Sue who was in her last few months at Oakwood. She was about to get married herself but was having doubts; I think having someone to relate to helped her to put things into perspective. Sue and I talked about poetry and music; besides, it was good to be friends with someone not from Delarue! Most of our socialising was not inside Oakwood or as part of its community and so in many ways in was not much different from the type of friendships I made later on in life within mainstream settings.

A very different set of circumstances existed with Trish who came in the January. She had a life threatening condition and found being at Oakwood pretty difficult too which in turn made it difficult to know how to include her. Looking back, it's easy to see how Carol and I unintentionally increase her isolation because we were together often in a shared space with Trish. One weekend, Carol was away at her parents, I went to their room to collect a book and found Trish alone and crying. At first, she refused to tell me what was wrong, but after a while she explained how difficult it was watching Carol in a relationship and knowing no man would want to have her as a lover. What could I say? I gently took her in my arms and hugged her. I told Carol what had happened; we tried to be a little bit more sensitive around her and at the same time, when it was possible, include Trish in activities. Slowly we found she had a personality larger than life and a wicked sense of humour. After I'd left Oakwood, so I was told, Trish became close friends with a nice guy called Neil, who was by her side when she died.

Although Oakwood was called a 'further education college' apart from the programming which had someone from Ford pop in from time to time, the 'learning' was left to the individuals to plan their own activities. All I can remember is Carol starting an A Level Sociology course, Steve, one of the guys I shared with, was studying Law and Gareth painted. What the rest actually did was and remains a mystery. Apart from struggling with the work I was doing, the first six months at Oakwood were fine and I felt accepted by the others. Discounting Dick, who was a loner, the small community mixed well together which was just as well in a confined space. Not surprisingly, especially given my intentions it wasn't long before Carol and I began our relationship anew.

Looking back, there's little doubt that I'd carried with me a considerable amount of baggage from my Delarue days and from time to time this impacted upon our relationship. I know Carol found it hard to deal with my mood swings but at the same time she was helping me to regain some self-esteem by talking me through various outstanding issues. Life at Oakwood wasn't all doom and gloom and I recall Carol and I going out with others to watch Hot Chocolate. At the end of the gig Errol from the band came over and spoke to us.

It's not possible to go into details but shortly before the Christmas break, we had a big falling out and went home to our respective homes without exchanging gifts. I was devastated by what had happened and swore to myself that I would put things right when we returned. I've never liked Christmas at the best of times because the ritual of going to David's parents on Christmas Day and Mary's on Boxing Day only served to intensify my loneliness – three married couples and me. This particular Christmas rates among the absolutely bloody awful ones I'd experienced with me feeling guilty about leaving on bad terms with Carol and seeing Dad in so much agony due to a mystery illness. What happened next, with years of hindsight behind me, can only be classed as the height of stupidity. The Christmas break had made Carol and I realise how much we'd missed each other and so we quickly patched things up between us. At the end of January, it was my twentieth birthday and I chose that moment to ask her to marry me. Much to my pleasure and surprise she agreed. Both of us accepted that this 'engagement' didn't mean we were going to rush into marriage; it was simply meant to be a commitment to each other. This beautiful moment however was quickly soured. Carol told her parents over the phone and within days they paid her a visit.

The Christmas break had also coincided with the arrival of Trish which meant that Carol had given up her single room to share with her. In this double room, along the wall by the door, was a large wardrobe. The entry of Carol's father into her room can't be described as anything other than spectacular. I was placing something in the wardrobe immediately behind the door when it opened with such force, I'm shocked it didn't fly off its hinges! The smack on the back sent me crashing into the wall at the back of the wardrobe and when I managed to recover my senses the glare on his face, coupled with the lack of an apology, told me that the next few hours were going to be tough! The message from Carol's parents was loud and clear: they didn't see me as a suitable partner. To be fair to her mother, who I liked, she did attempt to be a go-between and sought to smooth the waters. The problem was that I had become engaged to 'daddy's little girl' and he was particularly protective of her.

Between the January and April of 1970, despite the hostility of Carol's parents, things did begin to pick up for me. First of all, I began to consider writing about my life, so in many ways it was a forerunner to this book, although it barely left the ground because I lacked the necessary skills of writing at that time. Nevertheless, an opportunity did arise that enabled me to use the skills I did have. The local football team's coach had to submit reports on matches to a Colchester newspaper and these tended to be written in long hand and were very basic and factual. I offered to re-draft them and type them up each week for a very small fee. After a while both he and the newspaper were impressed by my copy. At one time I had considered the possibility of being a sports journalist but quickly realised too many barriers stood in the way. Most of the re-drafting required changing the grammar – a difficult feat for me – and adding a bit of 'spice' to make them interesting as well as factual; it wasn't a case of writing my own material. Steve, one of the guys I shared with, had managed to 'bend the rules' and gained permission to have a large dog called Portia. Another of my 'jobs' was to take Portia for walks around the village and so one week I not only sent off my usual copy about football, I enclosed a short article about the dog. Much to my surprise my reports and the article were printed the following week.

Steve also encouraged me to take an interest in the subject he was studying and lent me a few books on company law. Initially, being the active type, I thought this would prove to be boring however I did find it interesting. Ironically, I found my 'new subject' far more interesting than Carol's books on sociology which led to some heated discussions. At that time, I couldn't see the point of sociology and there wasn't even a hint that I'd eventually study it at University! But that's jumping the gun somewhat. Although I was critical of sociology, the discussions we had did encourage me to think a great deal more about people like myself, living in institutions like Oakwood. My political framework had begun to develop through my teenage years and by the age of twenty I was firmly anti-capitalist in my thinking.

Through what now seems an extremely crude analysis I argued the absence of disabled people from mainstream society was primarily down to the nature of the society in which we lived. Carol said that with such strong convictions I ought to do something about them. This is another good example of Carol trying to get me motivated again. I'm not sure how it happened but the existence of the Disablement Income Group (DIG) was brought to my attention. DIG had been founded in 1965 by two disabled women called Megan Duboisson and Mary Greaves with the aim of promoting the economic and social welfare of disabled people. I discovered much later that quite a number of disabled people who were to be influential in building the Disabled People's Movement, for example Ken Davis and Peter Large, were embarking on a similar journey.

DIG was a campaigning group involving both disabled and non-disabled people however the local group, based in Colchester, was run by a man called Bernard Brett. Bernard was a Quaker who took a keen and active interest in social issues, particularly the homelessness of young people, and he often gave young people shelter if they would act as personal assistants for him. Due to a severe form of spastic cerebral palsy Bernard was only able to use one arm and had no speech so his only communication was through a word-board and a battered old typewriter. His communication might've been laboured, but he had one of the sharpest, organised minds I think I've ever encountered. It wasn't long before I was regularly attending meetings at Bernard's house in Colchester. These were my first steps in disability politics aided by a man who would go on to assist me in taking my first steps into mainstream society.

Of course, at this time there was no indication that my life was about to radically change over the next two years and the possibility of me being at University would never have crossed my mind.

Talking about University, there were some early connections between Oakwood, myself and the University of Essex. Due to the computer programming, Oakwood had a link with the University's computer. Alongside testing programmes, Geoff and others were able to 'use' a programme to play chess against the computer and we would spend hours sending moves and waiting for a response. I don't think I ever got the better of the bloody thing! To be honest I had no idea what a University looked like, so when a student friend of Steve's offered to drive a group of us to and open air rock concert we jumped at the opportunity. Outside of a hospital it was the largest institution I had ever seen, and I was well impressed.

Chess wasn't the only game played at Oakwood. Most of the lads would play wheelchair football and challenge various non-disabled teams to take us on at the local school on a Sunday afternoon. I was allowed to be the sole ambulant player in the team and each Thursday evening we would forego a trip to the pub for a practice in a nearby hall. Geoff had very long legs and either he or Gareth would be the goalkeeper. Alan Haskey, who came with me from Delarue, had restricted mobility but had outstanding heading ability; whilst Neil would simply 'goal hang' until an opportunity came along. The following year would see our greatest triumph, but I'm racing too far ahead. With an increase in daytime activities and various social ones as well, the nightmare of the last years at Delarue were slowly being put to rest. The only real link with the past was my relationship with Carol and with much hindsight I can now see my efforts to 'do the right thing' by her ultimately contributed to the relationship failing.

Getting engaged had been my idea and whilst both of

us understood we had to get to know each other far more than we did before taking even the smallest step forward, the fact we were in such close proximity to Yvonne and John who were edging ever nearer tying the knot, seemed to exert a degree of pressure on us both. Yvonne and Carol became good friends and I guess I looked towards John to be my role model. I remember, without any memory of exactly when it was, a group of us attending their wedding and being entertained by Humphrey Lyttleton, the famous jazz musician who knew the couple. This lack of detail isn't simply caused by the distance of time or fading memory, it is due to a huge trauma that took place in my life; an event which was to change my life forever.

In the months following Christmas my father's health slowly declined and towards the end of March he was taken into hospital and Mum stayed with Mary and David in Dunstable in order to be nearby. Easter was mid-April that year and I planned to go home and visit. I phoned home a number of times, although keeping in touch with my family was never one of my strongest points, the last time being the Tuesday as I was planning to reach home on the evening of Good Friday. From what was said, Dad appeared to be on the mend, as he had left his hospital bed and was sitting in a chair.

When I arrived home, David told me that Dad hadn't looked as well earlier in the day as he had on the Tuesday, but he was probably just tired. The Saturday afternoon saw us all turn up for a visit and I spotted Dad in a corner bed by a large window as we entered the ward. We knew something wasn't quite right when the matron whisked Mum away to see the doctor and told the rest of us to proceed over to Dad's bed. I was extremely shocked to see him so drawn and subdued; this emotion was further compounded when Mum finally came back and the look on her face told us all we needed to know.

No one dared meet another's gaze and hardly a word was spoken as Dad slept for the majority of the long, gruelling two hours we were there.

During this awful silence, I sat trying to hold myself together and as soon as I felt I was going to breakdown, I would look out of the window at the world and life passing us by. Towards the end of the stay two things happened which will probably remain with me for the rest of my life. The first felt symbolic at the time and still does. It had been a bright sunny spring afternoon and as I gazed out of the window, I watched a large orange ball slowly leave the sky bringing the first hint of darkness. Then my Dad woke and sat there saying nothing, but he looked at each of us who were round the bed in turn with a sorrowful expression. When he finally spoke, it was in a whisper; Mum struggled to hear what he was saying but I thought he was telling us to take care of each other. I was the last one to grudgingly leave my seat and make my way to the door. No words can express how I felt when I reached the door, knowing as I turned, that I was seeing my father for the very last time.

Once outside the Hospital my Mum confirmed the worst, the doctor had told her that Dad was dying from a blood disorder and wouldn't see through the following twenty four hours. The trip back to Mary and David's was in silence and the time dragged well into evening. Around ten o'clock the Hospital rang to advise us that it was only a matter of time and if we wanted to be there, we should go sooner rather than later. I wasn't the person I am now back then, I was more passive and less assured, so whilst I indicated a desire to go back, I didn't push the matter when it became clear that no one else was willing or able to go. The tension finally got to me and I was forced to go to bed, but couldn't sleep. Around ten to midnight I suddenly had a wave of emotion sweep over me and just like the time when I knew my dog had been put to sleep, I knew Dad had passed. Shortly afterwards, the phone rang down stairs.

I'll never know if the events that followed were caused by the raw emotions that poured out as a result of the phone call, but Mary reacted badly to me crying and I believe at that moment I internalised my grief. On Easter Sunday I remember phoning Carol at her home and her father sounding not too pleased to hear my voice. Looking back now I realise this was the first of many long and difficult conversations over the phone between Carol and myself during a bleak twelve months. Only a few memories still float around for the period between Dad's death and his funeral.

My brother-in-law David like the rest of us took Dad's death badly and was almost involved in a car accident as a result of a loss of concentration. This simply poured fresh oil on already smouldering embers of raw nerves shared by family members. Dad's death was announced in the local newspaper and as I sat staring at it I had a small panic attack. Perhaps I was an immature twenty-year-old; I don't know, but seeing my father's name (and therefore my own name) in the newspaper column brought the reality of mortality crashing down on me. Of course, I'd known people who had died, my friend at school for example, but this was different. It was as if a part of me was being spoken about in the print, before my eyes.

During the funeral itself I had managed to hold myself together and probably felt I had to be strong for my Mum. Once outside my Mum suddenly left my side to look at some flowers and I was left standing all alone. It was at this moment I crumbled. Fortunately for me Aunty Peggy, Mum's brother Ken's wife, came over to comfort me. Ken and Peggy were the only members of Mum's family we saw and I'd always liked my Aunt and Uncle so I was particularly pleased to see them. Their presence however didn't stop me from having my usual feeling of being ostracised at family occasions and whilst other mourners stood eating and talking in Mary's living room, I sat reading one of the Law books I'd borrowed from Steve.

It wasn't till I'd returned to Oakwood that the full

impact of Dad's death hit me. I started to get sudden mood swings, often calm in the mornings and deeply emotional or irrational in the afternoon. For some reason these mood swings corresponded with Mr and Mrs Eady being on duty and I began to dread seeing them walk through the door. Valium was prescribed for a couple of people at Oakwood and I found myself taking the little yellow pill. Whether or not this had any effect on my fragile mental health is a matter of conjecture, but I do know my health was hit as a result of a terrible vivid nightmare I had. Despite the fact Dad had been cremated I had dreamt of seeing his corpse inside the coffin covered in maggots and worms. I awoke in floods of tears and found it difficult to get back to sleep not just that night, but for the following three months. As time marched on I began to get more and more tired and upset which finally led to deep depression. I was at odds with the world, extremely anxious and distrustful. I knew my erratic behaviour was driving a wedge between me and everyone else at Oakwood, even Carol; but the more I tried to control it, the less I was in control.

I'd stopped writing, but did spend some time painting, thus becoming the Vincent van Gough of Oakwood. One of my paintings was a torso nude of a woman and the broadcaster Chris Davies who was at Oakwood at the time pestered me to sell it to him. It was obvious Chris had a crush on Carol and convinced himself, I'd based the painting on her; which I hadn't. Needing money, I played along with the fantasy and finally sold the painting to him after destroying the magazine cover that I'd been inspired by. I needed the money because I was drinking quite heavily hoping it would help me sleep.

At the same time, I'd convinced myself that being at Oakwood was making me worse and the solution was to escape along with Carol; the solution was dependent on money and gambling seemed to be the quickest route. Needless to say, reality was somewhat different; I was losing more than winning and making matters worse rather than better. The strain on the relationship began to show and Carol ended the engagement, though we stayed together for the time being.

Something had to give and it did; the lack of sleep, depression and a cocktail of drugs left me feeling suicidal. There came a point when it was obvious things couldn't go on the way they were. One day I left my room to go to the toilet and found myself half way up the High Street hovering on the edge of the pavement hoping for a large truck to come to my assistance. After another huge flip out, which saw me hide in my wardrobe because I thought the Nazis were coming to get me, I was taken to a psychiatric hospital in Colchester.

Whatever I was given after admission led me to sleep solid for two days and after that I found myself in a strange environment cut off from the real world outside, but also the world inhabited by my fellow patients. Once I'd left the hospital, I discovered I'd been dosed up to the eyeballs with Largactyl. As soon as my head began to clear, and I was on the verge of escaping my zombie-like trance, I had fresh syrup pushed down my throat. The Largactyl didn't simply suppress my emotions it also affected my ability to speak and I struggled to make myself understood.

To make matters worse the ward I was on was full of men who were of my father's age. A few days into my stay I had another patient grab me from behind, very much as Tony had done in my first school, but I was powerless to cry out for help. Luckily a nurse came in and rescued me. When the weekend came, I had about half a dozen visitors come along at the same time and this was totally overwhelming.

Carol and someone else came from Oakwood, I think Mary and David drove across to see me and Bernard also came with a non-disabled member of DIG. I wanted to see them, but I couldn't relate to them all being there at the same time making me feel as if I wasn't responding to them as I thought I should. The effects of the Largactyl are hard to explain. It felt as if I was under water where I could see things but not really make sense of them. I don't know if they cut the medicine that I was taking in the second week, but I know I was regaining my sense of really because I was paying more attention to my surroundings. It was perhaps the first time in my life apart from being at home, that I wasn't with people who had physical impairments. I felt isolated and lonely in ways I'd never experienced before. The paint on the walls and the paintings hung on them were depressing and you can imagine the reaction I received from a doctor when I said this to him! The décor was there to have a calming influence apparently.

Sitting in a common room all alone one afternoon I suddenly had a huge stabbing pain in the centre of my back and I was struggling to catch my breath. I was unable to move or cry out and while this experience lasted, and I seriously thought I was about to die. The reason I'm recalling this event is because it was the turning point in my life; for months I didn't feel I had anything to live for and certainly didn't want to go on, but as the pain and a sense of panic surged through my body, I realised I really did want to live. Shortly afterwards I spoke with a female doctor who understood the trauma I had gone through and she reached the conclusion that being in the hospital wasn't going to aid my recovery, so I was discharged back into the care of Oakwood.

The only difference between the person I was before going into hospital and the returning one is that I was no longer having sleepless nights or feeling suicidal. My overall situation remained static; therefore, it was felt that I wasn't settling in and therefore my very presence could be considered disruptive. There was a strange incident where Carol and I had a visit out of a blue from one of the Spastics Society's social workers. I wasn't really sure why I had to be questioned by a woman who was clearly uncomfortable talking to a male more than half her age about my relationship with Carol. I saw it more as a bloody cheek when the same person arrived at my Mum's front door and boldly announced that I was 'a sexually frustrated young man' and that she was there to discuss what was to be done about it! Mum told her that as far as she was concerned, I was no different to any other young male of my age and promptly led her back to the door. I think Mum's reaction shows her in a different light compared to many mothers of disabled children. Over the years I knew her she often surprised me with her radical thinking and under different circumstances I could imagine her as a feminist. What's clear is that when it came to her family, she was a 'no nonsense type' and didn't appreciate the authorities poking their noses where she thought they didn't belong.

In hindsight I think Carol and I both knew things couldn't go on the way they were and if I tried to stay at Oakwood, the likelihood would be that I would only make things harder for everyone. Just as I didn't want to go back to Leighton Buzzard at the end of my schooling, I didn't want to go back when the time to leave Oakwood came. Where would I go and what would I do? This is where Bernard came to my rescue; he offered me accommodation in a spare room he had. I stayed there for three months until, he found me somewhere I could move to in a place called Wivenhoe which is just outside Colchester. Leaving Oakwood wasn't like leaving school, I continued to visit in order to play football and in a vain hope my friendship with Carol could turn for the better again.

This has been a difficult chapter to write and I'm aware that the subject matter has been anything but light. There have been issues I could've glossed over or played down, but I wanted to capture how far I fell before making the upward climb. In the next chapter I want to describe what it was likely making yet another transition. Here I've touched upon the journey from school to adulthood, dealing with uncertainty and immaturity one moment and the consequences of life and death in another. After a year of crazy talk and erratic behaviour I found myself outside of my accustomed segregated environment and thrust headlong into a world I barely knew.

Part Two

Mainstreaming my life

Chapter 5

The art of living

Dear past, I survived you. Dear present, I'm ready for you. Dear future, I'm coming for you.

Matshona Dhliwayo

I've called this part of the book 'Mainstreaming My Life'. When I speak of 'mainstreaming' I'm referring to entering wider society and living among mainly non-disabled people as opposed to being within segregated institutions designed for disabled people. Leaving Oakwood was a necessary step but one that was sudden, unplanned and very traumatic. Sleeping on a mattress in the utility room of a large Victorian house might not sound like the ideal place to start a massive adventure for a twenty-one year old, but for me it was just about right. For a short while Bernard Brett, a thirty-six year old Irishman, gave me both refuge and peace of mind.

What can I tell you about this man who touched so many people's lives? Using a communication board and a flashing smile that was accompanied by eyes that sparkled, Bernard spoke volumes. He had spent twenty years of his life being cared for by his parents before being moved into a residential care home for adults with cerebral palsy. The seven years he spent there was to leave a lasting impression on him.

In 1964 Bernard brought a house in Colchester and in many ways established one of the first 'independent living' schemes by having a mixture of paid staff and volunteers catering for his support needs. He also turned both his home and life into a service to assist young homeless people.

As a Quaker he set up a Christian Action Housing Association which included renting out the majority of his house to young people. There was a couple who gave Bernard regular support, but a great deal of the personal support came from volunteers. During my stay there was a young couple there with a baby, two men in their late twenties, one of which went on to be a manager at a Barnardo's Home, and a young woman who kept herself to herself. During the late afternoons I would wander into Bernard's room for a chat and read the local newspaper alongside him. The evenings were spent talking with other members of the household.

Looking back, I recognise that my relationship with Bernard was based upon him taking me under his wing and then having him letting me fly when I was ready. In many ways I feel awkward about my time living in his house because not only did I behave like a fish out of water, I also caused Bernard slight discomfort. I was never quite sure when to leave during the times he was having his support needs met.

Looking back with hindsight, there's a possibility he probably felt my presence was 'institutionalising' him once again. The fact that we both had cerebral palsy and had 'escaped' institutional living might've provided some commonality, but it also threw up a contradiction; the public/private issue that's glossed over in institutions – where the disabled body is public property – couldn't be readily ignored. I was a visitor in Bernard's home, not a fellow inmate therefore I should've given his privacy more respect than I did. This said; I believe Bernard understood I had just entered uncharted waters and was on a steep learning curve.

The early 1970s in Colchester saw the Unemployment and Benefits Offices sat side by side. I often joke that when I went into the Benefits Office, I was told I was 'not disabled enough' to claim a raft of available benefits, yet in the other office I was regularly told I was 'far too disabled' to stand any real hope of employment, although the craggy old Disablement Resettlement Officer (DRO) put me down as being capable of 'light engineering' whatever that meant. For several months whilst I stayed in Colchester and for a short time when I lived in Wivenhoe, I would approach employers looking for work. I was so naïve back then, especially since it was my first experience of mainstream discrimination, and for a while I accepted the pathetic fob offs tossed in my direction. Nevertheless, I was still eager to please, so I agreed to attend a Day Centre for a trial period at the Disablement Resettlement Officer's request. My first, and also last day, consisted of taking toilet fresheners out of one set of boxes and putting them into cellophane pouches before placing them in another set of boxes. I was also outraged that you had to pay for a horrid midday meal. I might've been naïve, but I wasn't prepared to put up with that kind of crap!

Having spent the majority of my life in institutions, moving into Bernard's house was really my first real test of living within the mainstream. I don't count the holiday periods I spent at home from school because for the majority of that time I was still being sheltered and over-protected by my Mum. When I was about fifteen, we had a serious falling out because I wanted to go to town on my own; I did it at school, so what was the big deal? I became so angry with her I scratched, 'I hate you' into a table and stormed off. Even when I'd made this break for freedom, I knew she was following me at a distance. Six years later, was I equipped any better to deal with the mainstream? My social skills were pretty immature, if I'm honest because the number of non-disabled people I'd associated with remained relatively few and tended to be people who knew who I was and where I came from and as a result my experience of public displays of discrimination were limited. Once when watching Leighton Town play when home from school there was this guy getting upset at their poor performance and so he started shouting, 'You're a bunch of useless spastics!' He kept on like this for a while and I was getting fed up with it, so I shouted, 'Oi mate, do me a favour, I wouldn't have that lot in my bloody team!' Not only did this silence him, at half time he came over and apologised.

I wasn't accustomed to walking the streets at night, and though Colchester was an Army town, it was a fairly peaceful place. Nevertheless, I had two incidents I've never forgotten. The first was around eight o'clock and I'd just left the house when a boy aged about twelve approached me and pulled out of his pocket a long chain and made some threatening remarks. I remember thinking that my best strategy would be to remain passive but to hold my ground and stare him out. After a few minutes of this standoff it became clear the boy wasn't expecting that type of response and lost his bottle before legging it. Nevertheless, the experience seriously put the wind up me.

The other experience was at the other end of the scale and involved two policemen who stopped me and asked why I was out on my own. In response I said I was on my way home to which one of them replied, 'And to which institution would that be?' For some people it might be difficult to grasp how unusual my situation was back in 1972. The sight of people with cerebral palsy living openly within mainstream society wasn't a common one and in many ways each day I was breaking new ground. A non-disabled person who hadn't been attached to Delarue had befriended me and begun to teach me how to drive whilst I was still at school, but our friendship was extremely limited and therefore it was during my stay at Bernard's where I started to learn how to relate to non-disabled people as friends.

The woman with the baby in the house was often at a loose end when her partner was assisting Bernard, so we often went for short walks together. She thought it was funny that during one visit to the baby clinic, a midwife who must've seen us out together had asked her if I was the father of her baby. I still had silly hopes of winning Carol back, so I when spotted a beautiful laced nightdress in a shop window, I decided to buy it for her. I couldn't believe the shopkeeper refused to sell it to me and I had to ask my newfound friend to go in and do the deed. They were a lovely young couple and I often wonder what happened to them. There were several other people I made friends with whilst staying with Bernard. As a treat once a week I would eat at a nearby Restaurant run by a Bangladeshi family. Many of my disabled activist friends will no doubt raise an eyebrow or two over the way I was treated by them, but I would argue the complexities involved still leave me bemused rather than offended.

On the face of it, a case could be made that I was being 'discriminated against' because instead of being seated in the main restaurant area I was always ushered through to where the staff sat and eat. Was this merely an attempt to stop the other customers being 'offended' by my presence? To be honest, it never felt that way; I was always made to feel welcome and given any support I needed. Cyclones are a natural hazard in Bangladesh and it is said that the 1970 cyclone may have killed up to five hundred thousand people. When I left Oakwood, I took a couple of my paintings with me and I gave one to the Restaurant to sell in order to raise money for the relief fund. By the time I moved away from living in Colchester I seriously felt I had become part of an extended family.

Another person I befriended was Brian Hall, who made three hundred and sixty-one appearances as a player, scoring thirty-eight goals in eight years with Colchester United. Brian, along with another hero of the famous 1971 FA Cup victory over Leeds United, Ray Crawford ran a local sports shop for a couple of years. I would drop by on a regular basis for a chat in order to pass the time. The Leeds match was the first time I had seen Colchester play and had only gone because Carol was ill in bed with flu and I'd won the final seat in a draw amongst the male residents at Oakwood. When I lived in Colchester and for a while during my early Wivenhoe days, I would attend Friday morning training at Layer Road. The manager at the time was Dick Graham who didn't object to me just turning up. According to Crawford, Graham's training methods were 'ahead of their time' and I would love it when during a Friday night game one of the moves I'd watched them practice in the morning came off. It was due to my friendship with Brian that I was able to arrange a match between Oakwood and Colchester United.

The majority of the players were in wheelchairs, which was a novel experience for the Colchester lads, but there was also one runner in each team. I also played on my feet and had a game of my life. Despite scoring a hat-trick, including a goal with my left foot after a shot with my right had been blocked; I was upstaged by a former pupil from Delarue who powered in the winner with a bullet-like header. Alan Haskey had little mobility, so he sat in his wheelchair and was what one might call a 'goal hanger', however his ability to head a ball was extraordinary. The United team couldn't believe their eyes! The local press came along to the game and took an unusual 'team' photograph which I kept for years till it turned yellow and fell apart. If one looked closely you could spot me trying not to laugh at something Brian was saying to me. Today we hear a great deal about celebrities and footballers doing 'their bit for charity' but this had a different feel to it.

Just before I left Delarue I'd attended a charity cricket match which involved the Spurs team including England Internationals, Jimmy Greaves and Alan Mullery along with the Welshman, Cliff Jones. Jones and Mullery, along with a few others, had a kick-about with me and a couple of others, but the *real stars* were really standoffish. I don't want to over analyse or romanticise things, but I always found the Colchester lads really down to earth and didn't make a big deal about the fact I was disabled. I often wonder if there was a strange paradox at work here. Remember this was still the early 1970s and disabled people were largely 'absent' from all walks of mainstream life, therefore, there were 'no rules' to play by. It was only later when disabled people were becoming more 'present' within society that patronising bastards emerged to support 'good causes' via events such as *Children in Need* and ITV's *Telethon*.

This later era structured what was to become the 'acceptable face of 'the handicapped' (sic) and the famous' relationship. I'm aware that organisations such as the *Stars Organisation for Spastics* and the *Variety Club of Great Britain* had existed before this time, but they had different conventions to the type of relationships I'm talking about. In the January of 1972 I turned 21 and although I invited Brian to my birthday party which took place at Bernard's house, I hadn't really expected him to turn up, but he did.

Another moment, a high spot that year, was when the 'Us' reached the Final of the Watney Mann Invitation Cup (normally referred to as simply the Watney Cup). This was a short-lived football tournament held in the early 1970s. It was held before the start of the season and was contested by the teams that had scored the most goals in each of the four divisions of the Football League the previous season who had not been promoted or admitted to one of the European competitions. Brian offered me one of his 'family's tickets' provided I could get on the 'special cup train' that ran from Colchester to Smethwick in the West Midlands. My destination that day was to the home of West Bromwich Albion, a football team whose ground is the highest above sea level in England; not many people know that! It's funny, but the first two times I attended the

Hawthorns I wanted the Albion to lose. The first was this match against Colchester and the other was a League Cup game against Watford during the Autumn of 1978. How I ended up there and my subsequent switch of support to WBA, we'll reach all in good time. Meanwhile, let me recall the Watney Cup Final as I saw it.

Looking back, I realise this trip broke new ground for me. The only other 'away' match I'd travelled to on my own up to this date had been a first round FA Cup game between Cheshunt and Leighton Town. It was the first time I'd ventured to a game larger than two men and a dog. I had been to some big games with my Dad when Northampton Town had a season in the First Division in 1965-1966, and in particular I can remember the game against Blackburn Rovers. Anyway, I had made my way to the outskirts of Birmingham on my own and had managed to meet Brian outside the players' entrance which I now know is situated in Halfords Lane. Luckily for me, but not Brian, he was injured so couldn't play which is one of the reasons he was able to slip a ticket to me.

The competition was unique that year because there was 'no offside rule' being used and this led to a high scoring game which ended in a four all draw. Much to the delight of Brian and myself, Colchester went on to win the game on penalties. What I do remember vividly was the Albion's first goal scorer, the legendary Jeff Astle; it was the only time I saw 'the King' play other than on TV.

I kept up my friendship with Brian for a couple of years with the odd visit to his shop on my way to see Bernard. Sadly, the working relationship between Brian and Ray off the pitch didn't work and the business folded. It was only through doing research for this book that I discovered the fact Brian died in 2006 at the age of 63. My random contact with Brian was down to the fact that Bernard felt my time had come, and that I should move on. I don't really know the details, but it would seem Bernard had arranged for me to move into a spare room on a couple he knew. Quite what the thinking was behind me going and living with them I've never been sure. The husband had a MS which had developed rapidly; this meant he was severely impaired. His wife was his sole support, so I've always questioned why she and Bernard thought having me stay there would work.

To be perfectly honest I'd felt totally uncomfortable with these arrangements from the start however I wasn't really in a position to argue. Reflecting on this situation I found myself in, I've drawn the conclusion that the couple were having major difficulties adjusting to the sudden change in both of their lives and the nature of their relationship. I'm not in favour of imposing a stereotyped presentation of how people deal with the onslaught of serious impairment as often represented by the 'individual tragedy' approach towards disability, but at the same time I recognise that this experience can result in overwhelming grief for all concerned. In many ways I question whether or not my presence in the house was viewed as a public intrusion into their private grief. During the short time I was with them there wasn't any unpleasantness, but I sensed I didn't really belong there because the proximity of my presence was too close. To make matters worse my bedroom was rather cramped because I had a trolley for my electric typewriter in there. The house itself was situated on the outskirts of a village called Wivenhoe but it was too far to walk to and so I felt rather trapped and cut off.

If I remember correctly, Bernard invited me over to stay one weekend and asked me to accompany him to the local Quakers Meeting House. At the end of proceedings, I was introduced to Bill and Christine who had two young sons called Robert and Daniel from Christine's first marriage. There was a considerable age difference, but as I was to find out later, Bill had been very supportive of Christine when she had had bouts of mental illness and over a period of time, he had talked her into marriage. It turned out that I was about to become their new lodger.

They offered me a room in their house and the majority of the time I spent with the family I enjoyed, especially helping Chris with the boys as this was the nearest thing to a stable family life I'd known. What was obvious from the start was Bill's love for his freshly made family; however, he had had over forty years of bachelor life behind him which meant he was very staid in his ways. This produced some tensions in the household, but I tried to stay out of the 'difficult moments' the best I could. What I really liked about Chris was her down to earth practical attitude which forced me to confront so many issues during my stay with them. Despite the fact Bill was quite traditional in his ways, Chris' laid back nature helped create an atmosphere where I felt able to test my new found freedom.

I loved living in Wivenhoe and would argue it remains my favourite haunt. It's interesting that the village is still a place I often visit in my dreams. So, what was so good about Wivenhoe? I found this useful quotation which helps set the scene:

> The streets are small and quaint, leading into each other and ending at the picturesque waterfront where fishing boats and small sailing craft bob at their moorings. When you fall in love with it you will join the long line of artists, farmers, writers, shopkeepers and sailing folk who have lived here and loved it too.
> (*About Wivenhoe*, unpaged)

Interestingly, there's no mention of footballers, actors or more significantly, students from the nearby University. Important for a young man in his early twenties was the fact that the village had four or five pubs each with its own unique character and client base. On the Quay sat the Rose and Crown which attracted the bulk of the tourists and was always fairly crowded. It was the least accessible from my point of view and I only tended to go there during the summer months or with student friends. Most of my drinking was done in the Black Buoy which was run by a landlady called Ross. The majority of her staff were casuals, mainly students, but she had one regular member, a woman in her late twenties or early thirties, who would chat with me during slack periods. Through our conversations I found out she had been going through a rough period and needed picking up. Among my drinking companions was a quiet man called Derek and over time I realised he had taken a fancy to this woman but was too shy to do anything about it. Despite my own limited social skills, I managed to engineer the pair into going out together.

What was unique about the Black Buoy, and in some ways Wivenhoe as a whole, was the fact that you didn't know from one minute to the next what kind of person would cross your path. I seriously doubt outside of large cities around the world would you have found a more diverse group of people. In the Black Buoy I found myself rubbing shoulders with fishermen and academics, whilst in the bar opposite, Joan Hickson of *Miss Marples* fame was being served. I can even recall the night the painter, Francis Bacon, paid for a round of drinks. In sharp contrast to the Black Buoy and its landlady was the Greyhound. This was a local for students and ordinary folk run by an old East European guy. The first time I entered the Greyhound I was surrounded by members of the local chapter of Hells Angels. I'm not sure what it was about me at the time, but I seemed capable of drawing people towards me and that night I struck up a conversation with a woman who had recently lost her partner in a motorcycle accident.

I've two very strong memories from nights in the Greyhound, both concerning my infamous folder of poetry. Rumours circulated around the village that the Greyhound landlord was entertaining for the week a London 'madam' and her daughter. One evening this stunning young woman breezed into the Black Buoy for a swift drink and all the men quickly circled like wasps round a honey pot. A few days later one of the cocky drinkers announced he was 'on a promise' on the Friday night and his crowd were green with envy. Not wishing to witness the spectacle I had decided to drink in the Greyhound that night and took my folder with me to review recent work. A little while later, the young woman much to my surprise, entered the bar which was still quiet. I managed to pluck up enough courage to say to her that I heard she was supposed to be meeting someone in the *Black Buoy* about then and she smiled before saying how much she enjoyed disappointing macho men. It makes me laugh even now to think about that guy being stood up whilst I spent the evening discussing poetry with a really nice lady! I think it's only fair to say the pubs along with the people who frequented them became the social building blocks upon which I forged my de-institutionalised adulthood.

I did more than drink during my time in Wivenhoe, although Chris might dispute this. We lived in the top house on Clifton Terrace which over looked the public playground and at the other end of the Terrace lived Jon Laurimore the actor and his wife Jill who was a script writer before taking up life as a ceramist. I'm not quite sure how I struck up a friendship with them both, but I would quite often pop round for a chat and a bite to eat on a Sunday afternoon. Jill long after I knew them became a successful novelist.

Living in the mainstream also coincided with me developing a deeper political consciousness. I was still involved with the local Disablement Income Group, but I also started to become interested in another type of campaign which involved non-disabled people. Every time I went to sign on, I would see a gaggle of people handing out leaflets about benefits and people's entitlement. I found out this was the Colchester Claimants Union and getting involved with them introduced me to my first real taste of political activism. DIG meetings would talk about issues and writing letters to MPs, but the

Union meetings were focused on 'taking action' around various issues or representing people at various tribunals. Being part of the Union also taught me how effective direct action can be as a political tool. Quite a number of times when people were being jerked around by the Benefits office staff, we would engage in lightening occupations in order to force them to see people again.

My parents were Labour supporters and Mum was a member of the Co-operative Society, but neither of these things helps explain why I had become an anti-capitalist from an early age. All through my teens I had fairly left-of-centre views, in fact during the final year at school, partly to piss Mayhew off; I had pushed for my class to join the newly formed National Union of School Students. As I've already said, when I was at Oakwood I had debated with Carol over Sociology and one of the subjects we'd discussed had been 'disability'. My ideas were far from worked out, but I was already convinced that disabled people had a raw deal within society due to the nature of our capitalist system. I had read a book called, *A Life Apart* which was an account of research done by sociologists at a Leonard Cheshire Home called *Le Court* and I had concluded the whole thing was oppressive crap! (Miller & Gwynne, 1972) I didn't give the book another thought until towards the end of 1972 when Carol showed me a letter in a copy of The Guardian by a disabled person called Paul Hunt.

I should perhaps explain that during this year, much to the frustration of Chris who had to keep picking up the pieces, I would travel over to Oakwood to play football and try as much as I could to keep the dying flames of the relationship alive. Long and tense conversations over the phone in Wivenhoe's High Street didn't help matters and during my visits I didn't really want to acknowledge that both of us had moved on and after a visit or telephone conversation, I'd emotionally beat myself up. By showing me this letter, I believe was Carol's way of trying to help me find a new direction, and in many ways she was successful. In his letter, Paul Hunt explained that he wanted to establish 'a consumer group to put forward nationally the views of actual and potential residents of these successors to the workhouse' and that he wanted to hear from disabled people who wanted to support this project. I immediately wrote to Paul to say that I wanted to know more about what he had in mind and he subsequently invited me up to London to meet him and his wife Judy. This was the start of a new journey but unknown to me at the time there was going to be a huge detour in the middle.

Let me state quite clearly that I had next to nothing to do with putting in place the foundation stones for the birth of the Union of the Physically Impaired Against Segregation. Paul's letter inspired others, like me, to link up and contribute to discussions, often via newsletter, about the *nature* of disability and the need for a new self-organised group of people with physical impairments. This process went on for between eighteen months to two years before a degree of clarity emerged. Unfortunately, I had grown impatient with the early discussions and by the time UPIAS had be fully formed, I had moved on as an individual. How and why I moved on will become clearer, but for the time being it is enough to acknowledge that the contact I had had with the founders of UPIAS was to have an impact on my future thinking.

The significance of my involvement with the embryonic disabled people's movement wasn't my contribution to the debates but rather the impact the meeting I had with Paul had on my life. During my involvement I had made two contributions to the newsletter and these concerned the proposed name, which I didn't like, and I had put forward an argument for the need to link up with other social movements. Neither of these went down well with the others who were involved. Ken Lumb, who is sadly no longer with us, told me years later during a heated debate about some criticism of the British Council of Disabled People, that I was not too unlike the person I was calling into question. He claimed that my article for the newsletter read as it had been written by 'an angry young man'.

My meeting with Paul Hunt was the first of two meetings I travelled to London for which were to change the nature of my life; the second took place a decade later, but in a political sense they are intrinsically linked. Talking for a couple of hours sat in Paul's kitchen made me feel as if a huge weight had been lifted off my back. There I was talking to someone who understood the issues that had plagued me for much of my life; someone who had a full grasp of the fact that disability was indeed a political question. This was the first step in my own 'liberation' but in some ways I'd to wait until the early 1980s, when I met members of the Liberation Network of People with Disabilities, before continuing my journey.

My involvement in the new movement was limited due to events and needs closer to home. After the football match between Oakwood and Colchester United I'd realised I had come as far as I could not just with the team, but also with any hope of a fresh relationship with Carol and so I broke all my ties with Oakwood. I was at a fresh crossroads in my life but with no obvious signpost to point me in the right direction.

Then one night I once again took my poetry to the Greyhound only this time I ended up entertaining three young English undergraduates with my work and life story. During the conversation one of them suggested that if I was capable of writing poetry of that quality, I would also be capable of doing a degree. The other two agreed and urged me to go and talk to someone at the University. The following day, Bill and Chris were particularly keen to hear about this conversation due to the fact that they had been woken in the middle of the night by the voices of three young women who were dragging a drunken poet up to bed before letting themselves out.

A few days later I took their advice and caught a bus up to the University where I was invited to meet a lecturer called Colin Bell. After hearing my story which included the fact I had no 'A' levels, he invited me to go away and write an essay about myself and why I wanted to attend the University. Following the completion of this essay Colin gave me an option; I could either go to the local Technical College in Colchester and attempt to pass an 'A' level or I could attend a couple of courses at the University and write a couple of essays. The choice was simple for me; I didn't fancy doing another 'A' level course, so I opted to attend the University. The main subject area I elected to study was American Literature which included the work of Walt Whitman and Nathaniel Hawthorne. Although this was relatively interesting, if I'm honest, it didn't float many boats however it gave me an open door to walk through. I spent the winter and spring terms at the University and began to get a feel for campus life.

The first few months I found particularly difficult going and for the most part thought the lecturers were speaking a completely different language. I certainly had no experience of sitting in large airless theatre blocks and during a number of lectures about Enlightenment figures I'd routinely fall asleep. The community in Wivenhoe had helped me to learn how to socialise and express opinions so I didn't find it too hard to join in the discussions and debates in the campus coffee bar. Two of the people I befriended quite early on were Celia Pugh and Eve Hostetler who were members of the International Marxist Group, but it wasn't until the following year that I actually joined the IMG. After my probation period at the University, Colin Bell invited me back to discuss my progress which resulted in him inviting me to apply for a place through the Universities Central Council on Admissions. Obviously, I was delighted by the decision, but I wasn't quite sure if I wanted to do a further three years of American Literature, however Colin said the University had been so impressed by my standard of learning they would be open to a change in direction and so that's how I ended up studying Comparative History and Sociology between 1973 and 1976.

During my first year at University I remained with Bill and Chris, but a number of events took place which resulted in me moving onto the campus and into one of the University's six tower blocks. The house required some work doing to it and two builders were employed. I was studying down stairs on the first day and around eleven o'clock Chris invited them in for a tea break, however only one of them, Dick took up the offer. After Dick had gone back to work, I stayed quiet and, according to Chris, I appeared to be extremely stressed. She eventually asked me if everything was okay, and I said it was, but she knew me well enough by then to know I wasn't being totally honest with her. Using her usual skill of making me talk when I didn't really want to, she finally forced me to tell her what was troubling me. Just like when people throw up, I said in a rush, 'It's you and Dick; you're going to get it together!'

Chris' first reaction was to laugh. Like me she had only just met Dick that morning, she hadn't formed an opinion of him, and I'd agreed neither of them had been flirting or behaving in an inappropriate fashion; so why would I think what I did? Besides, she was married to Bill. I wasn't able to explain my overwhelming feeling of certainty. Events took their course and eventually both Bill and I left the house.

During a visit with my first partner Brenda to Wivenhoe in the mid-1980s we bumped into Chris outside the fish and chip shop and she invited us back to Clifton Terrace for a cup of tea with her partner who, of course, was Dick. As a Marxist I cannot explain what happened that day; it was not the first nor would it be the last time I'd 'know' future events, the identity of strangers or felt personal loss from miles away. I've no control over these events; if I had I'd probably be a lottery winner by now! Whatever took place that morning it nevertheless signalled the start of yet another chapter in my life.

Chapter 6

When two worlds collide

And will love come through as strong as ever to seal the deal, or crash and burn on the dreams of tomorrow? What happens when two worlds collide?

Allie Spoletini

As I've said previously, I'd left Oakwood but still kept one foot in my segregated past by going back to play football as well as mixing with people still living there. Slowly, over the first year at University, I started to take my foot away; throwing myself into campus life. Making major changes in my life not only affected the lifestyle I led, it also began to help change how I viewed myself in terms of who I was. Before looking at life at University as I undertook my degree, I want to consider the transition period from leaving Oakwood to being established at Essex.

In this chapter and the following chapter, I take a break from 'storytelling' to offer a more theoretical and reflective approach to my journey. To do this I've adopted a different style of writing; a style more in line with academic studies, which means I've used quotations to support my thinking. The plan wasn't to get too academic or technical; nevertheless, it has been necessary to employ concepts and language currently found not only within disability politics and disability studies, but also within other fields such as philosophy, psychology, sociology, anthropology, history and legal studies. So, what I'm about to write comes from reflection and putting together bits and pieces I've gathered over the years.

This adds an additional difficulty in that I've introduced language and concepts in relation to a period of history that pre-date some of the associations they have had with disabled people. There are also dangers and difficulties associated with me trying to be reflective and employing up-to-date concepts; I've used 'knowledge' unknown to me at the time and so I'm viewing my life back then as the person I am now.

In one sense there a strong possibility it'll come across as being no different from someone re-writing or at least editing another person's story without intending to do so. The memory isn't a neutral recording of what has occurred either; it's distorted, piecemeal and, therefore, subject to interpretation and censorship. Nevertheless, I hope this chapter will prove to be a useful exercise.

Historically, what the public understands to be 'disability' wasn't discussed in the same manner as it's today. Everything was fuzzy; imprecise, fluid and to a large extent still taboo. How 'disability' was talked about lay completely in the hands of the professionals and over-determined by language employed by them.

Looking back, I shudder at the type of labels I'd willingly accept; even the early writings of disabled people who would go on and form UPIAS seems littered with this stuff. During the early 1970s then, it was extremely difficult for a disabled person to see themselves other than through the gaze of the public or the professionals; however, now and again, something would stir and cause an individual or a group of disabled people to bulk at societal perceptions of them. What about me?

I believe it's fair to say that only during my time in

Wivenhoe and then at University was there periods when I didn't sense I was being made to feel 'disabled' all the time.

Here I'm talking about being 'disabled' in the common sense dominant meaning of being bodily 'different' from those who are considered 'able-bodied' or more oppressively objectified as being 'normal people' (sic). The experience of segregated schools and Oakwood meant that I was surrounded by what appeared to be both 'disabled' and 'normal' at the same time because being impaired was seen as the norm in those settings. My peer group were other disabled people; the only non-disabled people I talked to the majority of the time being teachers and support staff. I wasn't required to question let alone think about what it meant to be 'disabled' because there was no need, the reality as I saw it then, was right there before my eyes.

Contrast this experience to living in a small village where the only disabled person I'd known was the person with MS; a person who as I've already said earlier, resented me being in his home. In the previous chapter I've mentioned how socially inadequate and naïve I'd felt when entering the world of the non-disabled or the 'land of the normal' (sic) as I'd probably viewed the situation at the time.

Critical to my story therefore is the need to recognise how the transition in my life led me to become increasingly aware of two very different worlds where what it was to live as 'normal' stood in opposition to each other. This awareness in turn had ramifications in terms of how I came to see myself and how I began to make sense of how others saw me.

This chapter then explores a variety of interconnected issues relating to how I addressed changing social environments; learning the skills of negotiation and navigation within unfamiliar surroundings. Key within this process is the question of 'identity' and I'll be considering my own 'identities' as they altered during my transitional period from both psychological and sociological perspectives.

The notion of identity has many meanings, for example, it can mean: the condition of being a certain person or thing or the fact or condition of being associated or affiliated with something else. Weinreich and Saunderson (2003; 55–61) put forward the view that:

> ... the formation of one's identity occurs through one's identifications with significant others (primarily with parents and other individuals during one's biographical experiences, and also with 'groups' as they are perceived). These others maybe benign such that one aspires to their characteristics, values and beliefs (a process of idealistic-identification), or malign when one wishes to dissociate from their characteristics (a process of defensive contra-identification)

A crucial factor in identity formation in my opinion has to be how an individual who was born with a significant impairment negotiates between how they see themselves and how significant others view them. This is both a psychological and social issue in my opinion because the nature of one's identity is influenced by the social environment in which a person operates. In the next chapter I explore identity formation in more detail.

As the rest of my story unfolds, I'll explain how I became increasingly aware of the unequal and differential treatment experienced by disabled people. This awareness led to me holding the views I expressed in the introduction. In more recent times the oppressive treatment of disabled people has been called: *disablism*. Carol Thomas (2007; 73) wrote:

> Disablism is a form of social oppression involving the social imposition of restrictions of activity on people with impairments and the socially engendered

undermining of their psycho-emotional well-being.

This chapter therefore will also consider how disablism psychologically as well as socially impacted upon me at this very significant moment in my life. In the early 1970s I was still a long way off from having any rounded socio-political view as to what it meant to be a disabled person and subjected to disablism. Looking back, managing the transition period from segregation to mainstreaming wasn't easy, not just in terms of the realities of day-to-day living, but also in terms of dealing with this on a personal level. I've no intention of using this chapter to analyse what was going on inside my head, but rather to take a look at how the social relationships I experienced influenced how I saw myself and others.

Despite questioning why I'd experienced a segregated upbringing and believing it had something to do with the capitalist system, most of my ideas about being 'disabled' were shaped by dominant societal attitudes and values.

There were however contradictions in how I viewed myself at the time, for example, I'd accept the description of being 'physically handicapped' but nevertheless felt disquiet with UPIAS speaking about 'physical impairment' because to me the word 'impairment' meant 'flawed' and I rejected this way of seeing my body. What I failed to fully register was the fact that society saw the majority of disabled people wholly within negative terms. The overwhelming view of disability held by professionals and academics was that it was a personalised tragedy and this in turn contributed to the cultural and common sense ideas that existed among the public.

Campbell (2008) discusses the harm that can be done by living in cultures where 'disability' is relentlessly and inherently viewed as negative. She argues, it can produce self-loathing, which I experienced in my early teens, and the negativity surrounding how 'disability' – meaning bodily difference – is viewed and this can become internalised by those subjected to societal responses. Micheline Mason (1990; x) explained this perfectly well when she wrote:

> Internalized oppression is not the cause of our mistreatment; it's the result of our mistreatment. It would not exist without the real external oppression that forms the social climate in which we exist.
>
> Once oppression has been internalized, little force is needed to keep us submissive. We harbour inside ourselves the pain and the memories, the fears and the confusions, the negative self-images and the low expectations, turning them into weapons with which to re-injure ourselves, every day of our lives.

Looking back, I'm not exactly sure how I saw myself as a person. I fully accepted that my body was affected by cerebral palsy which in turn impacted upon my functional ability, and as a consequence, readily went along with the notion of being 'physically handicapped' (sic). This however doesn't really reveal very much about my own self-perception in terms of how I *actually* saw myself.

Clearly, I made a distinction between having a body which was restricted in function and viewing myself as being flawed or abnormal; this suggests to me that there was an embryonic understanding that 'disability as personal tragedy' was an unacceptable way of seeing disabled people.

I'd argue that for a person like myself, the identities I've both now and especially in the early 1970s were in part shaped by societal attitudes towards both my body and, consequently, my impairment. This shaping in turn influenced my own self-perception and the identities I acknowledged. This process has huge implications for how I and other disabled people make sense of 'the self' and how it also impinges upon our individuality. Celia Cameron-Smith (2004; unpaged) writes:

> The self rests on inter-related physical, cognitive,

emotional-affective pillars, and responds to environmental currents. Thus the self is essentially a process and is given the feeling of form through the narrative capacity inherent in the individual. The self is situated in a self-space created by the interrelationship of the physical, cognitive and affective components in relation to the environment.

I accept the general view that humans are always located somewhere and at some time; therefore, our awareness is profoundly influenced by the fact that we have a body. In many fields of academic study there has been a shift away from talking about 'the body' towards exploring what is referred to as: 'embodiment'. Thomas Csordas (1999; 143), in *Perspectives on Embodiment*, puts forward the opinion that:

> If embodiment is an existential condition in which the body is the subjective source or intersubjective ground of experience, then studies under the rubric of embodiment are not 'about' the body per se. Instead they are about culture and experience insofar as these can be understood from the standpoint of bodily being-in-the-world.

From this particular stance it's then possible to discuss *how* the 'impaired' body is both seen and treated in relation to the 'unimpaired' body. Clapton and Fitzgerald (2011; unpaged) for example write:

> Historically, our bodies have framed our futures and explained our past; our bodies write our stories. But it's not our bodies per se which write the story; rather it's the way in which we, as a society, construct our bodies which shapes our history and our future.

My body, therefore, has been subjected to how different agencies within society have constructed what it means to be 'disabled'. Crucial to these social constructions are ideas around what is considered to be the bodily norm and how those bodies which deviate from this norm should be both seen and treated. Clapton and Fitzgerald (2011; unpaged) explain that:

> Bodily difference has for centuries determined social structures by defining certain bodies as the norm, and defining those which fall outside the norm as 'Other'; with the degree of 'Otherness' being defined by the degree of variation from the norm. In doing this, we have created an artificial 'paradigm of humanity' into which some of us fit neatly, and others fit very badly. Life outside the paradigm of humanity is likely to be characterized by isolation and abuse.

When introducing this type of discussion, it's necessary to address both the external and internal forms of oppression that's experienced by disabled people. It's for this reason I spoke in the introduction about agreeing with Paul Abberley (1997a) that the impaired body becomes a site of struggle because it's at the same time the site of oppression.

The social construct of the 'disabled identity' occurs through stereotypes and definitions of who is and who is not disabled; not only does this give rise to oppressive identities, but at the same time it also implies the ageing process is 'natural', which in turn constructs impairment as exceptional, thus distorting the amount of 'perceived disability' (sic) that exists within society. In later chapters I'll discuss in more detail the political significance of having a 'disabled identity' externally imposed and how I, along with other disabled people, sought to forge new 'disabled identities'; but here I'm focusing upon the oppressive identity many of us have learnt to internalise.

Donna Reeve (2014; 93) speaks of what she calls 'acts of invalidation' which can be found in looks, words or behaviour of others in relation to a person with an impairment. She presents an example I can all too readily identify with:

> So a common experience for disabled people with visible impairments is that of being *stared at* by others when away from home because they look or behave differently to 'normal' people. It may be understandable to attract a glance because of this difference, but it's at the point at which the casual glance turns into a hardened stare that this gaze becomes pathologising and an act of invalidation.

Until I left Oakwood I was only periodically exposed to the public gaze and looks of disapproval. Nevertheless, it made me feel self-conscious of my difference when subjected to these looks, the finger pointing and strangers laughing at me in the street. Once I was involved in mainstream activity, I soon realised that I'd entered an unknown world inhabited by non-disabled people; a world I was in truth ill-equipped to deal with at the time. Here I want to introduce the notion of paradox.

A paradox is said to be a statement that apparently contradicts itself and yet might be true. Having been in a segregated environment, my world had been quite 'normal', until I'd to consider what lay beyond it; the world of 'normal persons'. Once on the outside of the 'disabled' world, which had appeared 'normal', I was confronted by the world of 'normal persons' and, subsequently, found myself to be 'disabled'.

This strange twist brings to mind a number of texts I've read over the years relating to the experiences of non-disabled people becoming 'disabled' and how various types of rehabilitation programmes assist people to 'adjust' to their new identity and the unfamiliar territory of the 'disabled' world.

There was of course no rehabilitation scheme to assist me to make the transition into the alien world of 'normal persons' or offer me advice on living within a disabling society. On reflection then, it's necessary to ask: how did I internalise the fact that at any given moment I could be subjected to an accepting or rejecting public gaze? It's a commonly held view among disabled people that one of the consequences of being subjected to the public gaze is that we somehow become public property at the same time; to be prodded, poked or interrogated. If I did internalise how public attention made me feel, how did this influence my coping strategies when dealing with changing social relationships; did it assist in altering my identities, sense of self and individuality?

Perhaps key to attempting to answer these and other questions is to assert that my transitional period led to what I'll describe as 'paradoxical positioning. Phillippa Yaa de Villiers (2006, unpaged) in my opinion offers a good example of paradoxical positioning when she writes:

> As a mixed-race African and adoptee I feel, paradoxically, oppressed and completely free .... My adult life has been largely devoted to healing this rift. The freedom of my paradoxical position, is in fact that I don't have the constraints of a traditional role and I've access to the world.

The paradoxical position of being oppressed and completely free is something I can relate to as I've already indicated. The immediate period after leaving Oakwood I felt free of segregated living; one of the core institutional forms of social exclusion found within society. The paradox exists because I was entering mainstream society where disabling barriers existed at every possible turn; nevertheless, my own personal experience of mainstream living wasn't one of total rejection or exclusion. Wivenhoe life hadn't segregated me, it wasn't an institution; it was the mainstream and at this micro level of society I'd encountered very few disabling barriers. I don't want to paint a totally idealised picture, there were difficult moments and of course within the bigger picture until I went to University, I was unemployed with no employer willing to take a second look at me. It may sound strange but the full social significance of this experience of institutionalised discrimination didn't register with me at the time. Of course, it was painful and disappointing, but the young man with CP simply accepted that this was the way it was. Hence, I'd internalised my treatment as being 'what to expect' and therefore going to University was an escape from this social predicament.

Whilst I may have faced few social restrictions in Wivenhoe, the reality was that I remained a recent escapee from institutional living, dependent on Chris and Bill within an unfamiliar environment. How did this affect me? I recall desperately wanted to be accepted and probably, unconsciously, developed various forms of denial in order to 'fit in'. The University of Essex offered a completely different contrast compared to Wivenhoe because it was just like Delarue or Oakwood, an Educational institution. It had rules and regulations; it was part of the mainstream, yet it had its own campus which produced distinctive cultures, sets of identities and environment, thus making it both similar and very different to what I'd experienced before.

There were only a couple of other disabled people on campus and our relationships rarely touched upon issues of impairment or being outwardly facing disablement. In truth, once I stopped going to Oakwood or being involved with UPIAS, I didn't go out of my way to be with other disabled people for a while. Was this a deliberate choice on my part or not? I believe the answer to this question is a complex one. In my opinion there was never a rejection of other disabled people or a conscious desire not to be viewed as one of 'them'; it was more a case of feeling I'd done my time and I wanted to fully explore this new world I'd managed to stumble into. Nevertheless, I do believe I sub-consciously feared that too close an association with the world I'd left behind might hinder my survival chances in the new one. I can't be certain if this is true or not or how long it lasted because by my third year, I was friends with two other disabled students.

This uncertainty I speak of relates back to the issue of internal oppression because as Campbell (2008) suggests, internalised oppression is the driver behind the distancing of disabled people from one another – a close association with other disabled people could lead to rejection by non-disabled people because you're still viewed as part of an 'out' group and therefore you don't really belong in the new environment. Swain and Campbell (1999, p.69) explain that the 'pressures to pass as normal or aspire to some approximation of normality, on non-disabled terms, are manifest for all disabled people.'

There are many reasons why disabled people internalise their oppression; in my own situation, I believe the attitude fostered at Delarue, that we were 'the cream', had an adverse psychological effect on me. It always felt as if this was the language of compensation, it also sat comfortably beside the view that in order to be fully accepted one has to become what is known as a 'supercrip' – that is some who, according to Reeve (2014; 95), 'overachieves in order to prove that they are better than normal, thus widening the gap between that which is loathed (disability) and that which is desired (non-disability).' Most conscious members of oppressed sections of society will be able to identify with the notion that it isn't enough to be 'as good as' members of the dominant group; there's always a need to go that extra mile in order to be acknowledged.

Spending two terms on campus had helped me repair what was a fragile confidence – damaged by my experiences at school and Oakwood – so I began my degree course with an amount of optimism, though I still retained my inner sense of inferiority. Many non-disabled people or those who have never lived in segregated environments might struggle to comprehend how difficult it is to adjust to being in the mainstream. Although two years had passed since I left Oakwood, I often felt like an escapee, a fraud or as someone who didn't really belong and without warning could be 'exposed'.

Dealing with this inner turmoil meant I felt vulnerable and therefore believe part of my coping strategy was to deny my identity as a disabled person as much as I could. If we recall what Micheline said about internalised oppression, how it can result in self-harm, I can recognise this as a contributing factor in the ways in which I can beat myself up or turn inward. Much of this stems from negative self-appraisal brought on by various signs of rejection and forms of disapproval experienced over the years. Institutional living, for example, is very cold and dispassionate, therefore, one is expected to bury or at least control one's emotions.

I see another paradox here; part of my coping strategy was to deny my imposed disabled identity, but at the same time I was self-conscious of being 'different' to the majority of people around me. It was like trying to hide in plain sight. Knowing I was 'different' took on various forms; not least of which was being aware of the differing reactions to my participation in lectures, classes and social activities. Among the reactions was the inability 'to see me' or to chat over my contribution.

At times I witnessed unequal power distribution and now, years later, I can relate some of this to being viewed as 'Other'. Sara Rismyhr Engelund (2012; unpaged) informs us that:

> According to Michel Foucault, othering is strongly connected with power and knowledge. When we 'other' another group, we point out their perceived weaknesses to make ourselves look stronger or better. It implies a hierarchy, and it serves to keep power where it already lies.

There is an actual duality at work here because needing to highlight others' 'perceived weakness', also contains an uneasy recognition – like a mirror being held up – that the person is engaged in staring at their own perceived vulnerability. I've heard non-disabled people say to each other many times: 'There but for the grace of God, go I.' Tom Shakespeare (1997) has described disabled people as being treated as 'dustbins for disavowal'; this treatment projects anxieties of non-disabled people, perpetually anxious to deny their own mortality and physicality. This process can often give rise to awkwardness when disabled and non-disabled people encounter one another. Both can have a sense of embarrassment at not knowing how to 'behave' within the company of each other. I'd to learn how to deal with this 'awkwardness'; the lack of eye contact, non-recognition of my presence, and the physical demonstration of non-disabled people being 'uncomfortable' with having to relate to me. This type of social interaction is wounding because it displays different degrees of rejection; making the disabled person probably feel more self-conscious than they probably would've if the 'othering' hadn't been recognised as taking place.

The psychological or emotional experience of trying to negotiate the mainstream varies greatly from individual to individual and is itself very fluid. I've read a book chapter by Heikki Ikäheimo (2009) called *Personhood and the Social Inclusion of People with Disabilities – A Recognition-theoretical Approach*, which sought to address many of the issues I've touched upon already within this chapter. The concept of 'personhood' is subjected to much heated debate across numerous disciplines and, much as I'd like to, I can't unpack it and explore its properties in this chapter to any great extent. Personhood is often defined as 'the state or condition of being a person, especially having those qualities that confer distinct individuality'. Within anthropology, for example, personhood is used as an analytical term to indicate who, within any given culture, is regarded to be a fully functioning and accepted member of adult society. This way of viewing personhood immediately 'disqualifies' many people with significant impairments and, as a result, calls into question their status. I believe it's important to consider how dominant values and perceptions within our society can damage disabled individuals' own sense of self.

I spoke earlier about how disability is usually discussed in terms of being viewed as a personal tragedy; a key element of forming this perception has been ideologies associated with individualism and normality. In many instances being viewed as 'disabled' equates with negative appraisals ranging from viewed as abnormal through to being classed as non-human. Knowing that in certain social contexts you aren't even considered 'human' can hit a person extremely hard. Thus, when a person has internalised their social oppression, it's likely they will have low self-esteem. How does this occur? Voigt (2009; unpaged) suggests:

> Our society places emphasis on looks, speed, and being the same as everyone else. Thus, people with disabilities might place additional pressure on themselves to try to meet society's impossible standards.

Ryan Howes is quoted by Margarita Tartakovsky in (2013, unpaged) as saying:

> Deep down we've all constructed an idea of who we 'should' be: how we should look, act, think, feel and be regarded by others.

Understanding these common and dominant responses is important because if we're constantly reminded that we're lacking in social worth, then it becomes increasingly likely individuals will internalise these 'woundings' and, therefore, develop low self-esteem. Being 'acted upon' as lacking in social worth of course can take many forms, therefore I want to focus briefly on how Ikäheimo (2009) looks at personhood in relation to disabled people's experience of social exclusion because I believe it helps throw fresh light on my own experiences during the first eighteen months at Essex. Ikäheimo (2009; 87) writes:

> When you try to speak to them, you seldom see the light of understanding illuminating their faces, but more often a humiliating mixture of pity and confusion. Indeed, how would they count, if someone asked them to count the number of persons in a room where you are?

Treating someone as invisible or as a non-person means that psychologically their very existence as a social being is denied. Every aspect of the individual's personhood – their psychological capacities, ability to exercise responsibility and authority; to make value judgements as well as having an opportunity to contribute something positive to the lives of others – vanishes as a result. Ikäheimo (2009; 87) concludes:

> What is lacking here really is one of the components of what it's to be a person in a full-fledged sense: interpersonal personhood. In other words, what is lacking is that relevant others should see you (at least to an adequate degree) in the light of person-making significances and that you should thereby count in the concrete contexts of interaction with them as a person who has authority, a seriously taken claim to happiness, and/or something gratitude-worthy to contribute.

In a psychological sense this type of denial according to Ikäheimo is another form of social exclusion; in other words, being prevented from full engagement in *social life*. Earlier I referred to Weinrich and Saunderson's view that 'significant others' play a crucial role in identity formation and Ikäheimo believes they also feature in how disabled people experience psychological social exclusion. What if significant others lack the ability to view your personhood because your life experiences and lifestyle are completely alien to them? They may want to accept your 'humanity' but only through making you a token 'normal person'; not really understanding or wanting to be bothered to deal with you as a disabled people. Often this can result in inappropriate responses which compound one's 'Otherness' and social exclusion.

In specific or established social environments for example, Wivenhoe and the University, this form of social exclusion was less likely to occur compared to visits to Colchester or Leighton Buzzard because I'd already challenged to a degree people's first impressions of me. I often view myself as an explorer in a strange land and as a result I'm required to 'make peace' with the natives; allow them to sniff and stroke me, tell them stories to put them at ease whilst at the same time attempting to make myself acceptable to them. It's still the case that I've a sense of ill-ease when I enter new environments or need to establish fresh social relationships. I'm self-conscious of being a disabled person and therefore never quite sure what kind of reaction to expect, and in part, this explains why my transitional period was such a big deal for me. I was required to both learn and unlearn, address being a disabled person now in a primarily non-disabled culture which was alien to me – a double bind one could say.

There is nevertheless a further consideration to be made regarding the University which may have made the transition slightly easier than just wandering into the big, wide, open mainstream society. While my presence on campus may have shocked or amused certain people; the fact it was a University and I was participating in campus life by fulfilling expected social roles meant a tacit acknowledgement that I'd a right to be there. In one sense then this forced them to accept me as a 'person' psychologically, but at the same time as I've already indicated, it meant that my 'difference' was nevertheless a potential flash point as I was unlike most people they had known. What I'll never know, of course, is how many staff and students viewed me as a 'super-Crip' simply because I was *there*.

University gave me the social space to find myself, to discover that I could relate to non-disabled people and become a significant figure in the life of the community. My transformation was rapid, though uneven, and it's difficult to explain how it was possible that within a short space of time I went from being virtually 'invisible' to a situation where I was recognised by many as a leading figure within campus politics. Not everyone shared this view of me or my actions; here then is the final paradox, the moment I'd 'arrived' and announced my presence in the world, 'significant others' sought to socially exclude me and in the process tried to deny me my personhood. How and why? You'll just have to wait and see!

Chapter 7

A sense of self

Far from the still small point of truth inside us, identities actually come from outside, they are the way in which we are recognised and then come to step into the place of the recognitions which others give us. Without the others there is no self. There is no self-recognition.

Hall, 1995;8

In chapter six I looked at the transition in my life where I journeyed from segregated existence into the disabling mainstream of social interactions. Within the chapter I touched upon identity formation to explore the sense of self and internalised oppression. It's not my intention to cover the exact same ground again however I do want to consider the complexities around both identity and politics. During the writing of this book, I delivered a talk to students at the University of Birmingham entitled, *'More Than A Left Foot* – Nothing special, but quite unique!'* The talk was about connecting my personal journey through life with a specific emphasis on my engagement with education as well as the Disabled People's Movement. I chose the title because I felt it captured the duality of my identity as a 'disabled person'. I've spoken about how disabled people have come to be viewed within society and why many of us have had to deal with the oppressive consequences of the ways in which we've been both seen and treated.

My desire throughout the writing of this book has been to show that I'm a person who acknowledged that I had an impairment, however that I rejected seeing disability as a personal characteristic. It follows then, when I came to accept myself as a disabled person, I was taking the conscious decision to embrace what I considered to be a collective political identity. This said, I believe that those of us who embrace the political identity of being a 'disabled person' also create issues for ourselves in terms of all other identities we may have.

As a disabled person I also have had the identities of being a husband, father, writer, activist, and now pensioner; all of which are subjected to denial and distortion due to how dominant ideologies socially construct disabled people as 'special' – meaning that people like myself have been 'set apart' from the rest of society and viewed more often than not as incapable of fulfilling ordinary social roles. By speaking about myself as a disabled person I'm signifying that I'm an individual who considers himself subjected to the impact of disablement rather than using disability as a personalised identity. In my opinion this is where much of the confusion around how the duality of identity as a 'disabled person' is constructed exists, and I will explore this as part of the discussion.

I spoke about my uniqueness in my talk because I outlined, as I've done in this book, how I've fought against the possible life expected of someone 'like me'. Within the imposed identity of being part of 'the disabled' (sic) other 'disabled identities' are at work e.g. spastic, person with CP, physically disabled, etc. The management of the dual 'disabled identity,' which consists of the imposed identity and the self-defined political identity that many disabled people struggled for, will be a main theme in this chapter. Issues around identity and politics will be explored with reference to key points from Margaret Wangui Murugami's paper on disability and identity.

There's much in her paper which coincides with my own approach towards disability and identity, however, there are also considered differences. Discussing this paper is complicated by language and cultural issues which are open to interpretation and therefore create certain ambiguities. At times, for example, it's difficult to know the ways in which she employs the word disability. Murugami's starting point is that:

> The gist of this paper is the premise that a person with disability has the capability of constructing a self-identity not constituted in impairment but rather independent of it, and of accepting impairment as a reality that he or she lives with without losing a sense of self. (Murugami, 2009; unpaged)

The central focus in her paper is on the psychology around identity formation. Earlier in the book I stated the view that a substantial part of disabled people's oppression stems from how society views us and the impact it has in terms of how this becomes internalised. The idea of 'constructing a self-identity not constituted in impairment but rather independent of it' is the crucial debating point for me and one that needs carefully taking apart.

Murugami's paper looks at several assumptions that have been made in relation to identity and disabled people and these include the idea that identity can be structured upon shared social experience; that there are fixed identities of disabled people; and that the self plays a significant role in the formation of identity. What's key for her is the need to:

> .... understand the rhetoric versus practical realities in order to assess what can free persons with

disabilities from fixed identities that have been enforced overtime by regulatory regimes embodied in cultural and societal prejudices.

This is very much in line with my own thinking as I'll seek to demonstrate. The definition of disability employed in this paper is open to interpretation because it could sit within either a straight social approach or accept the multi-dimensional framework found within the World Health Organisation's ICF. Murugami outlines three basic methodologies that employed in considering the relations between impairment and society – the traditional view which focuses upon the individual's personal incapacities resulting from a defect or impairment. The second approach is the reformist one which seeks accommodation and individual rights. Finally, there's the social oppression approach that's been advocated throughout my book. Having outlined the differing approaches towards viewing disability, Murugami introduces the question of the essence of self in the process of identity formation. She uses the following definition to work from:

> Identity is 'the condition of being a person and the process by which we become a person, that is, how we are constituted as subjects' (Kidd, 2001).

Her starting point is to suggest that the universal construct of 'the self' results from the fact that every human becomes aware of their individuality. Based upon this premise, it's argued that human beings are consciously aware of their own lives and by reflexing upon this, we become aware of a consciously constructed self. Thus 'self' is seen as something we own and therefore,'… something that we must all possess and a characteristic that we must all develop. Self in this context enables us to reflect on who we are, whom we choose to identify with, and what we choose to do as matters of choice, not compulsion.'

There has been much debate down the years on the relations between 'the self' and disabled individuals. I've indicated I believe it's complicated by influences which are both conscious and unconscious. (Goffman, 1963; Linton, 2007; Dunn and Burcaw, 2013) Murugami asserts:

> Self in this context enables us to reflect on who we are, whom we choose to identify with, and what we choose to do as matters of choice, not compulsion. Group membership in this kind of reflection is no longer synonymous with identity formation. We are able to choose our identity and ignore and even reject identities fostered on us as a result of ascribed characteristics. We do all these by creation of narratives about the self which, provided we can sustain these narratives, work to maintain our sense of self.

This approach is explored by Dunn and Burcaw, however Murugami believes it's a way of trying to address the problems that are associated with 'conflating identities into essential, fixed, pre-ordained, singular categories', as well as viewing disabled people as 'the disabled' with a single identity. It should be noted that our sense of self evolves and therefore we 'reconfigure' ourselves throughout our lives. This was my argument in the previous chapter.

It's at this point in her paper that Murugami introduces the self-concept and states:

> Self-concept may be defined as 'knowing oneself, accepting oneself with one's limitations, not being ashamed of the limitations but simply seeing them as part of the reality one is in, and perhaps as a boundary one is challenged to expand' (Murugami, 2002:2; Berne & Savary, 1981).

This contains two elements which aren't necessarily mutually exclusive. It's possible to recognize one's limitations without having a negative appraisal of them. Similarly, whether one seeks to challenge any specific boundary can be dependent upon many factors, internal and external. Self-management of impairment has been subject to debate within the arena of disability politics over many years. (Finkelstein, 1990; Zarb and Oliver, 1992; Crow, 1996) I want to look at self-concept in more detail. Cherry (2018) informs us that:

> According to a theory known as social identity theory, self-concept is composed of two key parts: personal identity and social identity. Our personal identity includes such things as personality traits and other characteristics that make each person unique. Social identity includes the groups we belong to including our community, religion, college, and other groups.

As I've argued elsewhere the interactions between the two identities – personal and social – are often very problematic for many disabled people. Cherry refers to Psychologist Bruce A. Bracken who suggested in 1992 that there are six specific domains related to self-concept:

- Social: the ability to interact with others.
- Competence: the ability to meet basic needs.
- Affect: the awareness of emotional states.
- Physical: feelings about looks, health, physical condition, and overall appearance.
- Academic: success or failure in school.
- Family: how well one functions within the family unit.

Murugami considers these domains in relation to personal development and the lack of self-actualisation. Self-actualisation within psychology is concerned with reaching one's personal potential, whether that means 'becoming a painter, a politician, a philosopher, a teacher, or anything else.' (Positive Psychology Program, 2017) Disabled people's sense of self is often distorted by an array of factors. Dominant ideologies and practice can result in psychological and material disadvantages leading to experiences of underachievement and, for many, a sense of inadequate fulfilment. It's possible therefore to talk about self-actualisation in terms of having low esteem, poor self-image and negative self-concept which in turn has implications for people's individual identities. To a certain extent this can legitimate well established stereotypes of disabled people.

From this psychological approach to self and identity, Murugami acknowledges that there may be additional issues in relation to how disabled people cope with the realities of impairment, be that in terms of practical or emotional issues, if they haven't acquired 'knowledge and gaining experience in confronting obstacles, meeting challenges, and engaging in activities that develop problem-solving strategies.' (Ibid.) I'd argue that the lack of knowledge and experience in these areas quite commonly stems from the failure to gain access to peer group support and positive role models.

Being isolated from other disabled people and subjected to normative values instilled by professionals, family and society can hinder a disabled person's ability to develop impairment-based strategies for addressing disabling barriers. I found it interesting that Murugami refers to Yanchak (2005:135) who argues that disabled people 'often encounter difficulty forming a secure vocational identity because of self-identity issues rather than decision-making problems.' (Ibid.) I would argue this is because most vocational identities are highly structured around conformity to normative values and work practices (Russell and Malhotra; 2002).

Having considered what self-actualisation can mean to disabled people, attention within the paper shifts towards what Murugami refers to as 'normalcy' in terms of addressing self-identity. She draws upon various academic texts including Nick Watson (2002) who argued that it wasn't necessary to side-line 'impairment' but instead to challenge what's considered to be 'normal'. Drawing upon Watson, Murugami states:

> In this context, a person with disability challenges the social construction of what is regarded as normal and a normal body and embraces the difference of a body with impairment as what is normal to him or her. Self-identity hence becomes a product of a conscious action that questions identity dominated by social ascription.

Murugami equates this type of challenge to the social approach I've taken in this book. She argues that by challenging social systems, in which disabled people 'are subordinated through relations that are contradictory to their own views of self, helps.... [disabled people] ....to create self-identities that are far removed from biomedical models that present disability as tragedy.' What's interestingly from my perspective is that Watson (2002:521) is quoted as saying that 'the self-identity created does not necessarily show off difference; is it not about celebrating difference or diversity, or taking pride in identity through labelling, but about defining disability in its own terms, under its own terms of reference.' By contrast, Hughes et al. (2005) are presented as arguing that identity formation among disabled people is regularly immobilized by the way society constitutes them 'as strangers in the contemporary world.'

Murugami proceeds by considering a variety of other approaches then by disabled people which include those who despite daily encounters with disabling practices don't incorporate impairment/disability in their identity. Instead they regard themselves as 'normal' person while viewing their 'biological' self as not important provided they are able of engaging in life roles alongside their non-disabled peers. Watson (2002:509) suggests that many ascribed to a social approach where 'daily life with impairments as what is normal, as long as restrictive measures are removed.'

Other disabled people were viewed as taking a person first approach which saw disability as just one of the characteristics in his or her personality, Murugami however raises the issue of who decides who is a disabled person and I've discussed this elsewhere nevertheless there's a need to acknowledge the existence of problematical areas around how societies seek to legitimise what's considered to be disability and who is and who isn't a disabled person.

Where I find Murugami's argument difficult to address is her comment about 'accepting a disability enables one to reflect on capabilities and limitations so as to balance oneself between the two.' I assume she is referring to impairment and impairment reality here. She goes on to suggest that the 'facilitation of such acceptance can be enhanced through observance of the obligations of the UN Convention on the Rights of Persons with Disabilities', but this doesn't adequately address how specific societies and their governments respond to the Convention. What she does acknowledge is that:

> Despite the noble function that rights are expected to perform in human life, violation of the same rights is experienced from all directions. Most often the violation becomes so legitimate that the rights of persons with disabilities are privileges and are thus not given adequate recognition. Disability is both a human rights and social issue.

This is how the violation of disabled people's rights are currently viewed in Britain post-2010. What needs noting is that a large proportion of the violations have been fostered through stereotyping. Murugami proceeds to discuss the role of stereotyping in relation to identity formation and most of what she writes has been well documented in my book. The central point she makes, and it's crucial to remember:

> Stereotypes tend to homogenize persons without consideration of the uniqueness and diverseness that the persons may present.

Murugami points out that stereotypes are in fact an abuse of human dignity because they tend to assign to disabled people a group identity – for example being viewed as part of 'the disabled', 'rather than allowing individuals to formulate a healthy self-concept based on their individuality and uniqueness.' Murugami extends her argument by pointing out that misconceptions about people with impairments act in a similar fashion to stereotypes, thus tending to give them attributes they don't possess. Her illustrations relate to how some of the misconceptions rob disabled people of their aesthetic and identity values because they employ normative ways of seeing people and therefore are value laden. Finally, she introduces the negative impact language can have on identity formation.

The messages contained in Murugami's paper are that the self-concept is of vital importance in terms of identity formulation, but not only that, it's seen as the first step towards fighting for individual rights and opening the potential for engaging in both forging the collective identities disabled people have and participating in the emancipation struggle.

By taking control over the stories that are told about us in terms of 'the self', individuals can choose their own identities and thereby create the space to ignore and, under the right conditions, reject identities forced on them by the ascribed characteristics society imposes. A core element of Murugami's argument is that through developing a strong self-identity and a positive self-concept, a disabled person becomes empowered because it signals 'a clear understanding of the self, first as a person and secondly as a member of a group of persons in similar circumstances.' She also believes that:

.... the actualization of the self-concept would also enable one to fight for individual rights apart from group rights. Moreover, group membership in this kind of understanding does not affect one's self-identity formation.

The duality contained within the identity of 'disabled' can be challenged and in many cases overthrown by speaking about who we believe we are and validating our own self and lifestyles. I would go beyond the argument Murugami makes and say that our ability to sustain our stories, which take us beyond being 'acceptable Crips' or 'token nondisabled people', is often influenced by our ability to connect with the knowledge and experiences of other disabled people and this in turn supports us to maintain our sense of self. I've argued that in many instances 'disabled lives' are invisible and therefore without transforming this situation so that our lives are both visible and meaningful, it's extremely difficult to challenge, yet alone overthrow, the oppressive experiences associated with conflating identities into what Murugami describes as 'essential, fixed, pre-ordained, singular categories.'

This view of 'disabled lives' leads me to visit the quotation that is at the beginning of this chapter from Stuart Hall. One reading of Hall's assertion is that identities come from the outside and then we step into the place of recognition that others give us, which might suggest that this goes against all that's been said here, but I've an alternative reading. In my opinion it's precisely at 'the place of recognition' that self-actualisation takes place. The individual either accepts and embrace external identities or they seek out alternatives which coincide with their own self-concept. It's quite common to hear disabled people talk about the 'lightbulb' moment when they discover the collective disabled identity of being among others who are 'disabled by society'. This also relates to the Affirmative model of disability developed by Colin Cameron (2013; unpaged) who argued:

> Disability is a role imposed on people with impairments which leaves us unable to relate positively to impairment. So, we are always expected to be too busy trying to prove how well we've overcome impairment. Or too busy with feeling sorry about our own tragedy.' He added, 'And this has a role in reinforcing and validating the idea of normality being a good thing.'

While this is a different approach to disability than the one that I advocate, I nevertheless believe Cameron's use of 'role' here corresponds to the notion of imposed identity that we've been discussing. He links his model to the development of disability arts and culture and I would argue this is part of 'alternative place of recognition' I've just referred to. Of course, there's a fly in the ointment; a major barrier to developing both individual and collective identities has been and continues to be, is the actual *nature* of both our oppression and world disabled people inhabit. There's a paradox here; what unites us, also keeps us apart. I believe Paul Abberley (1997b: 41) captured this when he wrote:

> .... we need to develop theoretical perspectives which express the standpoint of disabled people, whose interests are not necessarily served by the standpoints of other social groups, dominant or themselves oppressed, of which disabled people are also members. .... Disabled people have inhabited a cultural, political and intellectual world from whose making they have been excluded and in which they have been relevant only as problems.

Disabled people's oppression comes from being either excluded or marginalised and denied identities which don't ascribe them as being 'individuals with problems' (sic). The oppression as experienced makes it difficult for disabled people to come together not simply as a social group but also as a socio-political community with a collective identity.

It's necessary therefore to question to what extent it's possible to talk about a disabled community or disabled communities. Murugami's paper explored the issue of identity formation and the implications for disabled people however it was primarily focused upon the issue of self-actualisation with very little time spent on the question of embracing the collective identity of being 'disabled people'.

Chapters six and seven stepped out of my personal journey in order to explore issues around identity and self. I saw this as a way of situating my 'disabled life' within the context of coming to terms with the implications of the psychological, social and cultural baggage that comes from living with significant impairments in a capitalist society. Within the rest of this book I'll be demonstrating how my personal journey developed my own understanding of both disability, identities and politics. This journey involves both fighting to be part of mainstream society and being within disabled communities. The immediate task however is to explore my time at the University of Essex because it had a profound impact upon the rest of my life.

Chapter 8

Glory days

The bravest are surely those who have the clearest vision of what is before them, glory and danger alike, and yet notwithstanding go out to meet it.

Thucydides

Without a doubt 1973 was an important year of the transitional period in my life; it marked the end of the disabled person who had felt 'like a fish out of water' no matter where he was and the beginning of the journey of a disabled person who was ready to break the chains that had been holding him back. The next four years, more than any before or since, were to shape the person I became.

When looking at my four years at Essex I want offer an insight into my overall experience; however, the academic year 1973-1974, will be presented as being a significant part of my life. One of the shocking things I've discovered during my preparation for this book is the amount of knowledge and history I've 'lost' over the years. I graduated in 1976 with a second-class Honours degree in Comparative History and Sociology. I went to University to study and to achieve, however I left with so much more than a degree. My studying and political exploits, set me up for life with a grounding that I've drawn upon again and again ever since; however, I was surprised to discover that I've a clearer memory of the history side of my degree compared to the sociological side. Yet, the lecturers who had influenced my thinking the most were sociologists rather than the historians! Sure, I did the basic sociological theories and influences – Marx, Durkheim, Weber, Parsons, etc. Had the pleasure of exploring social history with Paul Thompson, but beyond this, I've a complete blank. History, on the other hand, I recall studying European History from the French Revolution of the 18th Century right up to the Second World War. In addition, I took two courses on Comparative Fascism and Comparative Imperialism. In my final year my dissertation was on 'The History of British Trotskyism' from a socio-historical perspective.

Studying at University was a challenge; I was unable to take notes and I wasn't keen to rely on my fellow students, so my memory and written texts were my main source when it came to essay writing. I know I'll sound like an old fart, but the environment and culture I was learning in during the 1970s was a million miles from the experience of many disabled students around today. As I've said previously there were only a handful of disabled people on campus and no support systems; everything was down to the individual to negotiate the disabling barriers they encountered. In many ways as I inferred in the previous chapter I was treated like a 'token normal' (sic) and assistance was offered by staff and students alike under the: 'it's no big deal' philosophy. Jean, the Coffee shop manager, would carry my drinks and food over to the table and in the two restaurants I'd a variety of strategies which saw me by.

Getting use to campus life was easier than I'd imagined it would be and I suppose my introduction was not much different to those who had left home for the first time. I stayed in three different tower blocks during my time at Essex, starting off on the North side for a short while in William Morris Tower before transferring to Rayleigh Tower and ending up in Bertrand Russell on the South side of campus. The North side had four Tower blocks which made it very windy and extremely difficult to walk down to the main campus at times. And if the wind wasn't a problem then avoiding missiles from bored and/or anti-social students on top floors was! Essex was a modern campus designed into squares at different levels which were serviced by stairs, lifts and a ramp. As a person with limited mobility it did require careful planning to get around and I'd only attempt the stairs between square 3 and 4 during the quiet periods.

As I've explained, dealing with complete strangers has never been a strong point with me, so I tended to socialise with people I already knew or tagged onto existing groups. It wouldn't be true to say I only socialised with like-minded people either, among my friends was a son of a well-known millionaire. As students the type of socialising we tended to do was focused upon where the best parties were or what the Film Society had to offer late on Friday nights.

The Students' Union was divided between the political fringe, of which I became a part, and the non-political entertainment fringe that ran the bar, the discos and booked bands. Essex had an incredible record of bringing top bands and artists to the campus; for example, during my time there I saw *Lindisfarne, Dr John, Tom Petty and the Heartbreakers,* along with a folk group often associated with the University, *Fairport Convention.* Now, I've just said I was poor at talking with strangers, but I didn't seem to have too much trouble chatting with their lead singer Sandy Denny. Back in 1974 there was little evidence to suggest that her life was about to crash and burn. I'll never know why she came over prior to the gig for a chat; it's only during research for this book that I discovered the fact she started training as a nurse early in her adulthood, perhaps this influenced her decision, I don't know.

The relationship between disabled people and celebrities is a complex one which I'll avoid discussing beyond what's been said already; however, as a disabled individual, I've met my fair share and had a mixture of responses. When I was a teenager the *Baron Knights*, a local group in my local town of Leighton Buzzard, befriended me and I attended a party to celebrate their first silver disc as well as being invited back stage at the Palladium Theatre. Forty-five years or so later, as an ageing adult, I was shunned by an original member of the group who had spoken with me back then. At University there was no smiling for the cameras and as far as I could tell the artists I spoke with, who included the two sisters from the all-female American rock group *Fanny*, were genuine. The only truly negative experience I had was with a singer called Vin Garbutt. I'd written lyrics to a song called *Empty Shore* and two fellow students, one a wheelchair user with a wonderful voice, wrote the music which was recorded onto a tape. I asked Vin Garbutt if he was willing to have a listen to it, however he did the gig and then went off with the tape!

There was one midweek gig during April 1973 I'll never forget. Even now I laugh when I recall listening to the unusual sound coming from the stage and thinking, 'this band might have a few 'hits''. Their new album's first single, which they had brought out that week, was on the coffee bar's jukebox. I wasn't wrong; the album was called, 'Catch A Fire', and I was at a Bob Marley and the Wailers gig during their first UK tour!

I'm not sure when it was, but by 1974 I'd one of those blue invalid cars (sic) so I wasn't trapped on the campus. The 'Noddy car', as they were known, had three wheels and a single seat in the middle. There was enough space to carry a wheelchair or illegally transport a small person who had to sit illegally crouched on the floor. Most of the time I lived on campus I spent as little of my existence as possible in the box sided room with its single bed, wardrobe, table and chair. The communal kitchen was there to service the two wings of the floor with eight people in each wing. It was possible to sit around the edge and socialise, however, some students objected to having an audience whilst they cooked and eat. I rarely cooked for myself; didn't know how to for starters. During my second year I'd forgotten it was Easter, not sure why I hadn't my car, and therefore I was shocked to discover everywhere closed. For three days I'd a diet of spaghetti and salad cream as they were the only things I could find in the cupboards.

During the 1970s the University of Essex was associated with Left-wing militancy and student unrest. There's no denying that I was deeply involved in many of the internal and external campaigns. Alongside reading material for my courses, I supplemented it with literature on Marxism, Trotskyism and a whole range of political issues ranging from racism through to the crisis in the Middle East and revolutionary struggles in South America. One book was about a peasant leader called, Hugo Blanco, and not in my wildest dreams would I've believed that forty years later I'd have an opportunity to talk with him.

My first political activity was to go on an anti-National Front march through Leicester. It was rare for me to participate in anti-racist or anti-fascist activities because the IMG were frightened for my safety and how my presence could put others at risk. I remember having a heated debate with Eve about this, but with hindsight, I realised they were right. Two incidents brought this sharply into focus. A year after the Leicester demo there was a clash between NF supporters and anti-fascists in Red Lion Square, London where a student from the University of Warwick was killed by a police baton. His name was Kevin Gately and he had been part of the IMG contingent. I remember vividly how Celia returned completely drained and shocked by the unfolding events. The other incident involved me directly, but I've no idea when or even what the protest was about. During a protest in London I was singled out for abuse by a large contingent of NF supporters who started to follow my section of the march. They were calling me names, pointing, laughing and, of course, trying to provoke a reaction from my comrades. It took all my effort to persuade Patrick, a French student from Essex, not to take a break-away group over to 'sort them out'. The way I was targeted brought home what Eve had said.

I remember going on other protests such as supporting the Portuguese Revolution and the National Abortion Campaign. There was also the campaign around the unjust prosecution of the 'Shrewsbury 24'; building workers who were charged following the first ever national building workers strike in 1972. The decision to prosecute them was a political one; the Tory government had strong links with the building industry which opposed the unionization of building sites. The first of the trials of building workers from North Wales was held at Mold Crown Court, beginning on 27 June 1973. Des Warren (2007; 33) recalled them:

> These were of great importance and a dress rehearsal for Shrewsbury. What they meant was described to me by one solicitor: 'Like a West End impresario, the Director of Public Prosecutions used the Mold trials to cross out the faults in the production, prior to the Shrewsbury run'.

The Mold trials resulted in only minor charges being upheld by the jury, resulting in small fines ranging from £5 to £50. A second trial at Mold commenced on 18 July 1973 and all three defendants were found not guilty. Colchester IMG organized for a minibus to travel overnight to support the workers and I remember waking up stiff at five o'clock in the morning in a car park. Des Warren was sentenced to three years in prison and Ricky Tomlinson was jailed for two. In 2014 the campaign for justice was still going on.

Other early starts and minibus rides from Essex took place in 1976 when the Students' Union supported the striking workers in the Grunwick Dispute which was also about union recognition and working conditions among film processing workers, mainly Asian women, who were working in North London. Mass pickets and Days of Actions took place during June and July with loads of arrests being made, including the National Union of Mineworkers President, Arthur Scargill and Labour MP, Audrey Wise. I was almost arrested twice at Grunwick however on both occasions fellow pickets pulled me to safety; in one incident a large IMG member called Carl, from London, jumped onto the back of my potential arresting officer and pulled him off me as others snatched me away.

Another campaign I was heavily involved with through the Colchester IMG was the Troops Out Movement. This was always tricky because Colchester was a garrison town. TOM was started by Irish solidarity activists in West London in late 1973 and campaigned for the withdrawing of British troops. As well as being involved in national events we would annually target the Colchester Tattoo for leafleting. Quite often we were aided by bandsmen who secretly smuggled leaflets inside because they objected to being sent to the North to serve. One year I caused utter uproar in the local press because of a TOM poster I designed.

The period from October 1973 until August 1977 there were two critical political periods. The first of these ran for most of the academic year of 1973-1974 and were referred to as 'The Troubles'. What had begun as a Day of Action in support the National Union of Students' Grants Campaign developed into a protracted struggle between the students and the University authorities. It was a struggle that had repercussions well beyond the confines of the Essex campus and involved demonstrations, mass meetings, occupations, picket lines and clashes with the police. A constant theme that ran throughout these events was the various positions taken in relation to the demands that emerged from an unofficial occupation by the students and then were embraced by a large section of the student body.

Alongside using material produced by the students, staff and the mass media, I've re-read three specific accounts of the events: these include the official report into the 'disruption at the University of Essex' by Lord Noel Annan, an unpublished book by Susan Wolf and Michael Mann (1975), plus a pamphlet written by Colin Beardon, who became the President of the Students' Union. I'd argue all three publications are flawed in various ways but nevertheless helped to jog my memory. The other critical period I'll be covering is the 1976-77 academic year; unfortunately, these events are less well documented.

Rather than offer a blow by blow account of 'The Troubles' and a critique of the unpublished book by Susan Wolf, a PhD student at the time, and Michael Mann, a Sociology lecturer, within *More Than A Left Foot*, I aim to publish a pamphlet on the subject at a future date. In this book I'm focusing upon my role and how 'The Troubles' affected me. It will be necessary to acknowledge the Wolf and Mann text from time to time because I appear within it and in my opinion the style of commentary, worked to construct negative presentations of all the political groupings on campus. Whether intentionally or not, their caricature of the IMG in particular served to collude with how the mass media and the University authorities constructed their 'reds under the beds' narratives within the 1970s at Essex and beyond.

Before looking at 'The Troubles' and my role within them, I believe it would be helpful to offer some background to the historical and social context in which the events unfolded. David Jobbins (2013) from University World News was a major source in providing me with the following background information. In 1960 there were just twenty-six universities in the United Kingdom, a decade later this had increased to thirty- nine with Essex being among the newer ones. Forty- four years on it's now possible to add another hundred and nineteen to this list. Overall participation in higher education increased from 3.4 per cent in 1950, to 8.4 in 1970, 19 per cent in 1990 and 33 in 2000. What about student numbers? In 1973 I was one of 217,000 full-time students however by 2011 the number had reached 1.92 million. It's also crucial to remember, because it plays a vital role in my story, that under the 1962 Education Act, tuition fees for most students who secured a university place were paid by the State while relatively generous maintenance grants meant that student loans, bank overdrafts and credit card debts were largely unknown. Wolf and Mann not only situate the University of Essex as a product of this era they go on to argue that central to the narrative of 'The Troubles' was Dr Albert Sloman, Vice Chancellor, and his approach to both 'governance' and how he viewed student participation in the life of the University. They stated the view:

> There are those who argue that the ghosts of 1968 still haunted the establishment as 'The Troubles' unfolded, therefore the stance Sloman and the University took was bound to lead to various forms of conflict within the University as the personal and political were merged on both sides. The majority of commentators agree that the events of 1973 were not a re-run of 1968 where three students were initially expelled following the throwing of paint at a visiting lecturer from the chemical research centre at Porton Down.

The authors believed the events of 1968 had created a strong mythology with a well-established set of stereotypes, various forms of collective nostalgia, and distinct ideas on 'community'. One example being that basic solidarity can bring about collective action and therefore taking direct action can produce results. Mass meetings were also idealised by sections of academic staff as 'common ground' where all could come together to discuss differences. This idealised view was shattered by 'the Troubles'. For the conservative elements, the events of 1968 had been humiliating, a bitter blow to the idea of an academic environment above and beyond grubby politics. The power of authority, therefore, lay in being consistent which meant never 'giving in' to extremism.

What is not disputed is that the mass media, staff and students often characterised Essex as a 'red base' and this notion continued well into the 1980s. Where did this notion come from? At the second conference of the Revolutionary Socialist Students' Federation held in November 1968, the organisation launched its own manifesto which contained the following Action Programme:

- All power to the general assembly of students, staff and workers – one man one vote on the campus.
- Abolition of all exams and grading.
- Full democracy in access to higher education.
- All power to the general assembly of students, staff and workers – one man one vote on the campus.
- Abolition of all exams and grading.
- Full democracy in access to higher education.
- An end to bourgeois ideology – masquerading as education – in courses and lectures.
- Abolition of all inequality between institutions of higher education – against hierarchy and privilege.
- Abolition of all inequality between institutions of higher education – against hierarchy and privilege.
- Break the authority of student union bureaucracies and institute mass democracy.

The manifesto appeared in New Left Review I/53, January-February 1969. The significance of these issues will become clearer when I comment on Lord Annan's analysis of the events that unfolded. Interestingly, in an article called, The Student Movement Today, from *International Socialism* (February 1975), Alex Callinicos and Simon Turner trace the links between the activities of the RSSF of the late 1960s and the events that had occurred over the previous year and a half. The article reported that:

> British students are on the move again. The last 18 months have seen a series of revolts unknown since the late sixties. At Oxford, Essex and Kent in 1973/74 thousands of students found themselves engaged in bitter battle with the authorities. This involved a determined effort by the authorities to break the student movement. Each Vice-Chancellor was keenly aware that he was being watched by others as to how he dealt with the militants. In the event, large scale victimisations took place but not before the intervention of the police and the courts invited by the authorities. At Essex no less than 105 students were arrested for picketing the university. The first months of 1974/75 have exceeded anything that took place in 1968. Thousands of students have occupied their colleges or the local education offices, boycotted lectures, refused to pay excessive prices, and other protests. In London 40,000 marched in support of the NUS grants campaign. The cuts taking place in education have ensured that students are going to take direct action on an unprecedented scale.

I could be accused of jumping the gun by using this quotation here, but in offering a backdrop to 'The Troubles', I want to show that they should not be seen in isolation and that they form part of a wider picture. So, while some of the legacy of 1968 acted as residue for the events of 1973 – 1974, the focus initially at least, was very different. Despite this fact, the 'red base' notion had an influence on how the events of the 1970s at Essex were interpreted both internally and externally. What caused the upsurge in student politics in the early 1970s needs locating in the shifts within society as a whole. A decade after the events a book was published called *Policing the Crisis* (which charted the emerging disorder and tension that took place in Britain and other western societies from the late 1960s. Key factors in these developments were class conflicts which grew in intensity in relation to the demands of trade unions, on the factory floor and in the pits, not to mention the pressure for increased welfare expenditures. In addition, other social movements began to emerge, for example, generational conflict witnessed by the already mentioned student revolts of 1968 which fostered a teenage culture subversive of adult authority. Feminism and the Civil Rights movement in the United States added to the clamour for social change.

The authors of *Policing the Crisis* argue that opposition to the Vietnam War had brought many of these social movements together. The 1970s therefore are often characterised as a decade underpinned by uncertainty and crisis. In relation how this period impacts upon Higher Education, Steven Fielding (2008; unpaged) argues that:

> The expansion of higher education also saw previously dispossessed groups enter universities as students and teachers who then criticised established views of the state. Socialists and feminists, enjoying a uniquely loud voice during the 1960s and 1970s, outlined alternative ways of practising politics, hoping to develop more popular forms of participation in decision-making.

Even within 'A Brief History' of the NUS which appears on their website under, *Our History*, there is an acknowledgement of this shift in how the organisation saw itself:

NUS became an integral part of the labour

movement, extending its connections with trade unions and playing a key role in the liberation and anti-apartheid movements.

What significance, if any, lies in the fact that the class composition of the University of Essex according to Wolf and Mann was across the middle stratum with very few from elite backgrounds? I believe the ideals of Dr Sloman were alien to the bulk of students and his sense of 'community' was an abstract one for those who were living in the bleak towers and limited spaces for self-expression. It's precisely the young from the middle stratum of society who embraced the principles of the emerging new social movements. It's within this context that I intend to discuss my role in student politics at Essex.

My role in 'The Troubles' however can't be told or understood in isolation as it's part of a series of narratives that involve other students, members of the academic staff and University administrators among others. I hope I can reveal aspects of these narratives as I attempt to broadly paint a picture of what took place and how I influenced, and was in turn, influenced by them.

Leaving aside the early weeks of my life as a now registered student and the issues I'd to deal with, I want to turn my attention to the National Union of Students' Grants Campaign and the Day of Action which was planned for 15 November 1973. Essex's students' union was in support of the campaign and on campus there was discontent due to high rents and prices. Talk of militant action was in the air. The Day of Action rapidly became the focal point of attention for the seven IMG members who made up the campus group under the leadership of the well-established member, Celia Pugh. [IMG had non-student members in Colchester as well.] The group had recruited a number of 'sympathisers' during the Freshers' Fayre and they were involved in our strategy meetings. Celia played a major role in shaping our strategy for the term, however, what isn't widely known is that as the future events unfolded, Celia became less and less involved due to the fact she had obtained a day job and this, plus the events themselves, thrust new responsibilities onto untested activists like myself.

In relation to the specific Day of Action we discussed the various tactics that could be brought into play to build the day and support the ongoing campaign because we wanted to influence our Union's Executive who had in late October started talking about plans for the day and whether it should simply involve a lecture boycott. Internal resentments existed and talk of occupation was in the air.

Publicly, the IMG argued that a demonstration would have a more public profile, but we were aware that many activists wanted to include the possibility of an occupation. It was agreed that an academic 'strike' would take place followed by a demonstration in the town which would be supported by the local Technical College.

The lecture boycott had been well organised with a mass picket outside Lecture Theatre Block. A few lecturers and students sought entry and a certain degree of pushing and the odd scuffle took place, but the only violence stemmed from individual right-wing students who used force to enter LTB. One of these right-wing students as a result he had his jacket ripped. I'd personally been pushed around by this conservative student who had flung himself at the picket with two arms flaying everywhere. With hindsight I believe the lecture boycott would have been quickly forgotten if an additional dynamic hadn't intervened.

What took place inside the LTB and the reaction towards it in my opinion influenced the overall direction 'The Troubles' took and why the students, academics and administration failed to contain or resolve the conflict. Like ships passing in the night, there was no common understanding of the issues involved. On the picket line itself Ronnie Munck, a postgraduate student who was also a member of the trade union ASTMS and the IMG, grew frustrated with the fact that lecturers were escorting students through the picket lines without any attempt by either side to discuss the issues involved. He proposed that representatives from the picket entered the lecture rooms to ask the lecturers' permission to address the classes and put the Student Union's case for an academic strike. Half a dozen pickets, including Ronnie and another IMG member Will Rich, undertook this task. Once inside the response differed greatly and it was only after hostile responses from some of the lecturers did the IMG members respond in kind.

Rightly or wrongly, those involved believed they were supporting a collective decision to boycott lectures. I don't believe the notion of '... the absolute value of the idea of academic freedom', as raised by Wolf and Mann in their book, played any part in the thinking of these particular students; therefore, is it possible to reject something that isn't part of your terms of reference in the first place? There appeared to be an underlying assumption that all students should've been aware of and accept without question '... the idea of academic freedom as traditionally understood within universities.'

At no time did the University view what took place as anything beyond the actions of intolerant individuals or politically motivated groups. For me this begs the question: how did the academics view the lives of their students beyond the walls of the lecture rooms? The academic outrage at this attack upon 'academic freedom' and the students' determination to defend their right to collective action in the face of the attack upon their living standards kept both sides firmly apart with only a handful on each side seeking to bridge the gap as the year wore on.

Unknown to the SU Executive, secret negotiations had taken place between the University Left and the college union to turn the demo into an impromptu 'occupation' of the Town Hall. Not only had this been badly thought through, for example, how long would it last? To make matters worse, I'd committed an irresponsible act by phoning Celia the previous night to tell her our plans, so when we arrived at the Town Hall, we were met by a strong line of police who claimed to have 'anticipated' our course of action. Unfortunately, the demonstration itself was small, the speakers had failed to show up and the police presence all culminated in increasing tensions.

Thwarted and frustrated, the activists trundled back onto campus to hold a post-demo workshop led by the revolutionary Left. The outcome of this workshop was a proposal put by the IMG to instigate an occupation and use this to forward localised demands. I was elected as part of the organising committee.

On Monday 19 November at 7.30pm, a fire alarm went off as a signal that the plan for the occupation was about to be put into action. I was already stationed in the University Bar with equipment needed to secure the Administrative area we planned to occupy and I'd already enlisted support from students who had gathered there. The start of the occupation saw a constant flow of traffic with fifty to a hundred students maintaining a presence while others went to collect provisions. There was a sense of excitement, a deep conviction to transform words into action; however, with hindsight, I recognise the committee hadn't paid much attention to the practical side of running an occupation.

All of us involved were entering unchartered waters, many including myself, were new to taking leadership responsibilities and were found wanting. After the initial high of instigating the occupation I felt politically isolated because no other IMG member could be present.

Maybe I should've taken the initiative and been more proactive in establishing 'house rules and self-discipline', but it's so much easier to be wise after the event. After an initial confrontation with the security staff and Dean of Students the occupiers were left to their own devices.

I can't refute the claim that some ran amok during the early period of the occupation; a number were ill-disciplined and engaged in irresponsible activities such as vandalism and searching private files.

Those involved entered the occupation for a mixture of reasons and among them were a small group of 'independent activists' led by a charismatic white middle-class male who was driven not by well thought-through socio-political positions but rather by an anti-establishment spontaneity which saw him behave like a whirlwind.

Having inspected the havoc caused, I was of the opinion then and nothing has changed my view since that time, that the University exaggerated the scale and cost involved. Late morning the follow day the University informed us that they were going to take legal action against the occupiers. Before the University's legal threat had arrived, the Occupation had produced its first broadsheet with three clear demands:

- An immediate 15 per cent reduction in ALL catering prices, with no staff redundancies.
- Firm guarantees that catering and accommodation facilitates will be expanded to cope with the expected increase in student numbers (over the next quinquennium).
- An immediate 55 per cent reduction in rents, back dated to 1 October 1, at the University's off campus properties.

These demands had originated from the workshop held on 15 March and were put forward by the IMG and the International Socialists. It's interesting that Mann and Wolf refer to the demands as being 'almost too moderate' because other commentators later sought to spread the foolish notion begun by Sloman that the IMG had deliberately targeted Essex as a launch pad to smash capitalism from. I'm not going to explore the demands as that would add little to the central story; all I'll say is that the demands were viewed as reflecting real 'bread and butter' issues concerning Essex students and therefore it was argued that the demands would be supported by a large cross section of the student population.

These were hardly demands designed to bring about the fall of capitalism! I fully appreciate that the economic and social considerations faced by grant supported students of the 1970s were completely different from those being experienced by fee paying students during the second decade of the 21st Century; nevertheless, it's important to place the demands in their historical context. A fourth demand, 'No Victimisation' was added when it was realised the Proctor had been collecting names and nine students were specifically named in the Writ issued against the occupiers.

I'd spent much of that morning briefing both staff and students on what was going on in the Coffee Bar directly below the occupation. Others on the committee were ensuring that the Student Union called an Emergency General Meeting for eight o'clock that evening. The Union President, Rusty Davis, was off campus due to illness and therefore other officers and the Executive had to decide whether to call for support for the occupation or not. There were executive members on the original occupation committee and they had helped plan the event, but the occupation hadn't been officially sanctioned by the Students Union.

The Left were keen to obtain SU support and looked to the Executive to put forward a motion that would ratify the decision to occupy and back the demands retrospectively. There was no problem securing a quorum by the time the clock struck eight o'clock with between 700 and 900 students filling the two lecture theatres that were opened up. This was an unusual situation because nothing like this had occurred for several years and to make matters even stranger the Assistant Proctor had asked to address the throng.

Perhaps in another place at a different time the speech

by Keith Ovenden, a Lecturer in Government, may have gained more than polite acknowledgement. Talking about being sympathetic to the students' demands but suggesting they should be targeted at the Government rather than the University cut no ice in an atmosphere which was strongly polarised as being 'them' versus 'us'. After many passionate speeches, included one from me, the Executive motion was put with only eight voting against supporting the occupation and its demands. With victory secured, the students emerged from the meeting only to discover a pinned notification of a writ on the barricaded entrance which meant further discussions had to be held well into the night. The meeting had agreed decision-making powers were in the hands of daily general meetings inside the occupation and fresh 'committee' was elected from those meetings to share the responsibilities and to dispel the notion that there was an 'established leadership' pulling the strings. Students began to furnish the occupied area turning the 'Essex Free State' into a home from home.

Chapter 9

On the barricade

Enjolras: 'Now we pledge ourselves to hold this barricade.'

Marius: 'Let them come in their legions, and they will be met.'

Enjolras: 'Have faith in yourselves, and do not be afraid.'

Rebel: 'Let's give 'em a screwing they'll never forget!'

Victor Hugo , *Les Miserables*, 'The Barricade'.

Having presented the background to 'The Troubles' what follows is the briefest of account of the events I witnessed and was involved in, but it by no means covers all the twists and turns that took place between 15 November and 11 December. Over this length of time seven formal meetings of the Students Union of various kinds were held with attendance ranging from approximately 900 to 250. I attended and spoke regularly at them. It was the University's swift response to the occupation that set the tone for a cat and mouse confrontation. The occupation was notified by 11.45am that unless an immediate evacuation was forthcoming, legal action in the form of an injunction would be issued. We took the decision to stay put until at least the Union meeting that night and support pressing ahead with the tabled demands. By 9.40 that same evening a writ had been issued citing nine students. Some feared immediate police action and proceeded to strengthen the barricades. With the decision to give the occupation meeting the power to make day-to-day decisions, a meeting took place well into the night and it was agreed to send two named students down to the Court of Appeal in London to oppose the injunction. Vicky Price, a member of the International Socialists and I were elected. Years later Vicky and I still discuss our adventure and not so long ago we incorporated it into a joint lecture we delivered at the University of Wolverhampton.

I knew Vicky vaguely before our journey down by train to London, but the trip began an association that has lasted over forty years. The central part of the story is that we were met off the train by a reporter from the Daily Express, according to Vicky who still has the documented evidence, and a photographer. The following day the report featuring our unsuccessful bid to have the injunction overturned, carried a photograph only of 'the attractive young student, Vicky Price' (sic); I was nowhere to be seen. Here we have not only an example of sexism, but also disablism as well. Vicky corresponded to the stereotype of a 'female revolutionary' – Patty Hurst and Angela Davis spring to mind as I write this – but, my image, that of a disabled person, would have been totally incongruous in terms of the message the newspaper sought to convey. Here then was my first experience of a deliberately constructed invisibility and denial.

The failure to secure a victory in London led to the occupation being extended to include the whole administrative floor as an attempt to increase its security. What is unclear is at what stage the University, with the VC returning from a conference, decided to delay the implementation of the court order. My impression is that the VC sought to portray the students' actions as being those of an 'irrational minority' and therefore hoped to bring the weight of the majority of the campus 'community' down on them. The President had sought a concession from the V.C. to justify continued negotiations, however, with nothing forthcoming from this meeting many students hardened their position on talking to the University. All of this, plus an incident involving myself, led to a feisty students' union meeting on the 3rd of November.

In reporting on this meeting, Wolf and Mann make specific criticisms of my behaviour and I believe these are worthy of comment because they throw some light on the different interpretations that can exist regarding political motivation. The meeting's atmosphere was very intense, and this wasn't helped by the fact that two small children belonging to Colin Beardon, the Secretary of the Union, were running around making a noise. A few people complained about this disruptive behaviour and asked for them to be escorted out. Both parents were students and entitled to be there, nevertheless a fierce argument broke out and as a result, Colin resigned as Secretary on the spot and marched all the family out. Wolf and Mann characterise the immediate aftermath of Colin's resignation as being where '... the IMG were seen by some to overplay its hand and sectarianism was brought out into the open.' (1975; 53) What was it that I and the IMG did that was deemed so sectarian? Wolf and Mann state:

> Bob Findlay who was already establishing a reputation as one of the most effective spokesmen for IMG policy suggested that in light of Beardon's resignation a new delegate should be selected for the NUS Conference in Margate that weekend. This was seen by some students as a power-play. (1975; 54)

In their book the authors generalise how the IMG, CP and Union Executive were perceived by the main body of students. As a result, my comrades and I are characterised as being 'adventurists', although this doesn't fully square with us being also described as a tight-knit humourless sect. I believe I can justify the rationale behind my call: the Essex delegation was going to Margate not only to vote on conference motions but also to seek support for our campaign, therefore, if Colin wasn't going this would leave us with a vote short. Make no mistake, I would've welcomed seeing an IMG supporter go instead of a Broad Left one, but that was never the primary motivation behind my proposal. I don't see where either the charge of sectarianism or power-play comes into this. IMG believed a large meeting provided the most democratic way to select a replacement as there was no time to organise a campus wide ballot. Calling a snap election of this kind favoured no specific political faction therefore Colin was just as likely to be replaced by a Broad Left candidate as an IMG supporter. I'd argue that those who questioned my actions were failing to consider the nature of the politics I and the IMG were engaged in and therefore were guilty of imposing their own assumptions upon us. As it happens, Colin's resignation wasn't accepted, and he did eventually attend the Conference.

I've included this incident because it represents the first of a series of occasions in my life where my political actions have been called into question by people who hold very different views to my own. In nearly every case I've felt the ways in which my actions were misconstrued implied some underhand or dishonest intent on my part. Now, I'm not going to say that I've always been squeaky clean or without a hidden agenda, but at no time within my involvement in politics have I sought to trick or hoodwink anyone. Perhaps I'll go as far as to say that often my weakness and downfall has been because I've sought to be open and transparent in my views as possible.

I believe the Left were the most likely to speak at meetings, but not exclusively; non-aligned students made their opinions known. It's also a mistake to assume all the Left-wing students were political hacks well versed in making speeches; very few had that kind of experience. In my own case, I was learning as I went along, and I remember one specific meeting where the audience anticipated my opening line and decided to shout out with a collective voice: 'Well, basically ....' I was stunned into silence as the air was ruptured with laughter.

The meeting on 23 November proved to be a watershed because it marked a shift in how the students' demands were viewed by both sides, with both sides coming under pressure from academics and trade unions frustrated with the lack of progress and continued disruption. Measures designed to break the deadlock split both camps with a hard core seeking 'no compromise therefore no negotiations' however talks did take place unofficially and this cause further splits and distrust. The weekend following this meeting saw the occupation well attended with over 200 students being entertained by a film and workshops. Wolf and Mann sarcastically write: 'Even the IMG workshop on the grants campaign drew 20 students.' (1975; 57) It has been argued that the IMG sought 'maximum disruption' as being the only course of action, but this once again misrepresents the facts. Students have no actual power therefore within negotiations they have nothing to bargain with unless they have something the University wants. Without the occupation having a material impact upon campus life, the students had nothing to force the University to the table.

On 30 November, an impromptu meeting of the occupation run by non-aligned students voted to seek negotiations. I've no idea why I or any of the Left weren't in the occupation on the Saturday night in question, but unknown to anyone at that time, the Executive had begun talks to end the dispute. The writing was on the wall for the occupation with the Christmas vacation only three weeks away and dwindling numbers supporting it. Given the climate it wasn't surprising that only 200 students attended the next meeting called by the Executive. The

Broad Left (CP and Labour Party students) supported the Executive's motion to negotiate on three of the four demands and to end the occupation on the 7th. The IMG and others attempted to strengthen the motion without success. It was argued that the fourth demand, the call for 'no victimisation', could be suspended until there was a need for it.

So, the term petered out, but not without fresh verbal attacks upon the occupiers from both the VC and the CP who were re-positioning themselves as the 'party of reason' and in sharp contrast to the hot-headed revolutionary Left. Three weeks in student politics seemed a very long time, however, unknown to anyone at the time this was nothing compared to what was to follow during the Spring Term. What can't be disputed is the fact I returned home for Christmas completely drained.

The Spring Term was all about the repercussions following the occupation. Essex was one of a dozen educational institutions that saw disruptions during the first term of the academic year, but only Oxford and Kent reached serious proportions on a par with Essex. Although the issues involved were different, there was soon to be a basis for solidarity; all three were about to witness disciplinary processes unfold which would side-line the original issues and the demand for 'no victimisation' would take centre stage. Not only would the fourth demand be back on the agenda, it once again divided the University community as the students held to the position that the occupation was a 'collective action' not the activity of individual 'trouble-makers', thus disciplinary charges were by their very nature unjust. A further argument along these lines was the considered arbitrary nature of the way the University selected which students would face disciplinary charges; why were some charged and other participants ignored? A third of those charged had political affiliations.

By the end of the Christmas vacation twenty-eight of the thirty-six who were to face charges had already been informed. I learnt my fate on returning from Leighton Buzzard. I'd just the three standard charges facing me:

1. Conduct which unreasonably obstructs the satisfactory conduct of the administrative work of the University;
2. Conduct which obstructs the holding of a class given by the University;
3. Conduct which obstructs the holding of research in the University;

Will and Ronnie along with a few others faced additional and more serious charges. From the outset there were deep divisions within the students' community as to whether we should participate or not. Very few people expected the proceedings to be fair or impartial given the make-up of the panel, however in the final analysis, there seemed little political mileage in boycotting them. Whatever the University's motives, the hearings were delayed until well into February. Prior to this the University Grants Committee paid the campus a visit and whilst the Student Union Executive and the fringe group, the Essex Independent Activists, organised a series of protests, most of the student body, including most of the Left, seeing little or no point in taking part.

The disciplinary hearings first verdicts were mixed with one student being acquitted and another found guilty of disrupting a lecture; the sentence was reserved. It had been agreed by the Union that on hearing the first 'guilty verdict', a peaceful 24-hour occupation of the V.C.'s suit would go ahead, and this was duly carried out. I hadn't been involved in planning this but was one of the hundred and fifty students who had taken part. When the first sentence was passed down, a suspended expulsion, the atmosphere on campus suddenly changed. In the eyes of the students the disciplinary process had confirmed the University's rejection of 'collective responsibility' and as a result was about to engage in wholesale victimisation. The rejection of the idea that students had a collective identity was viewed as a direct challenge to the very existence of a Student Union. The Student Union recalled its representative from the panel, which in the University's eyes was viewed as confirmation that the students were rejecting the legitimacy of the academic community.

This reading of the situation was compounded by the students' next move which was to adopt a strategy more akin the trade union movement's 'industrial action' than 'protest politics' which is associated more with the students' movement. I see two reasons for this shift in strategy; firstly, the IMG had a member on the local Trades Council and he had briefed them on the ongoing situation on campus. Whilst the previous term's occupation had caused 'significant' disruption, it hadn't led to the University coming to the negotiating table and offering a reasonable way forward; the Secretary of the Trades Council suggested that instituting a picket line would impact directly on all aspects of running the University and therefore would be more effective than another occupation. Secondly, the picket was regarded to be an 'appropriate' response in what the students increasingly saw as a 'dispute' with the University.

The picket line was set up on 27 February and during the day received a mixed reception from traders. The contempt for the picket, in some cases driving straight at them at speed, resulted in the students erecting a chicane barricade. Unknown to me, the Head of the Computing Department had spoken to both the S.U. President and an early shift of the picket, about an important delivery of a new computer from Wales. If this wasn't delivered by the end of the month, the University could lose up to £70,000. The message hadn't been passed on, so at roughly 7.30pm that evening, a half a dozen pickets including myself spotted a large lorry coming towards us. The initial conversation with the driver had been amicable; however, as soon as he grasped our intent was stopping him delivering his load, the very thought of having a two-way fruitless journey caused him to become rather vocal.

On fearing the worse as well as understanding what a coup this would be if we could turn the shipment around, I sent a runner up to the University Bar to enlist the assistance of a group of striking Miners who were being housed by the students during their strike. Within minutes our ranks were swollen by some pretty beefy men and after a conversation between two Miners, the driver and a student, the driver agreed to respect the picket line and head back to Wales. A sense of victory filled the crisp night air.

Alongside the picket, there was a call for the suspension of the hearings and a call for an independent enquiry which was supported by a section of the academic staff; however, it became increasingly clear that the nature of the picket line would shortly become a flashpoint. Having a barricade made the picket effective, but illegal. One of the University's own publications, *Nexus*, reported the negative impact the picketing was having on fuel supplies and catering. The University were desperate to get the computer in that I helped turn away, so they consulted the police. It's not clear who instigated the next move, but reports say the police didn't want to be involved but were happy to warn the students about their conduct; others maintain that the police insisted on being involved when the Administration punctured the picket line in case there was a breach of the peace. Whatever the truth, early on the morning of 7 March, a collection of University staff and the police escorted the computer equipment through after casting aside the barricade. As a direct consequence of their action, the battle lines were firmly drawn. Anger spread across the campus stoked by a leaflet that argued that the role of the picket should now be to close down the University entirely.

Meanwhile, the President of the Union was invited to meet a senior member of Essex Police. The aim of the meeting was to put the frighteners on the Executive and other students by warning them that they risked arrest and charged with obstruction, theft of property and conspiracy. Another occupation also risked police intervention. The students' meeting that night was tense and bloody, with the Executive urging caution and a return to orderly, legal picketing; the militants, on the other hand, spoke passionately for the need to turn up the heat rather than back down. A hastily worded amendment called for an academic strike, stepping up efforts to gain trade union support and a rally with the aim of hitting recruitment to the University. It carried other innocuous proposals that cut little ice with the largely despondent audience. Once the 'climb down' motion had been passed the meeting disintegrated like a smashed pane of glass – I've chosen this as a very apt metaphor. Stunned by the day's events, IMG members and a few others stayed behind to discuss their next move; whereas a group of International Socialists opted to drown their sorrows in the Bar. It wasn't long however before reports began to filter back into the meeting room that all Hell had broken out across campus – there was a riot going on!

In all the narratives I've read on the incident, including the national press, it was never articulated as being a spontaneous riot. I'd also challenge the official view that the entire Left were involved. I can't be certain of my facts because outbursts took place all over the campus, but I saw very few members of the revolutionary Left out that night, those that were, faced disciplinary action inside their own ranks. The truth is that the bulk of the disturbance was carried out by members of the Communist Party and Broad Left who felt betrayed by their own leadership; this was totally out of character and probably explains why it was 'played down' in most accounts. The E.I.A. and a handful of independent activists also took part. Will, a Lebanese student and me, were dispatched to investigate a break in at the University bookshop. When we arrived it was all quiet, so we assumed it was a false alarm and decided to go our separate ways. I'd only gone a few yards before I heard a tremendous crash coming from behind me; as I turned, I think I saw some people running off, but it was too dark to see.

I thought no more about this incident until weeks later because I'd more pressing issues to deal with. The riot had reached the national press and marked an extremely low point in the campaign. Newspaper headlines screamed: 'Essex students in £6,000 Wrecking Orgy' and in Parliament the militants were soon labelled, 'The Wreckers'. I was further angered by the main culprits trying to deny any involvement in such 'ultra-left activities' as they called them. Despite this huge set-back which changed the landscape of the University in more ways than one, there was a picket line to maintain and I found this extremely grim. Maintaining a legal picket was soul destroying because it was totally ineffective and in a matter of days the University had replenished its stocks. The backbone of the picket was no longer the 'Left activists', but rather more social democratic and mature students who believed the actions of the University were morally wrong. The weakening of the picket, the riot and overall climate however gave rise to a conservative led backlash among both students and staff.

The events of 13 March finally brought everything to the boil. The Disciplinary Committee recommended that both Will and Ronnie should be expelled for disrupting lecturers. Both were immediately excluded from campus until their appeal hearing. The new occupation was strategic because earlier that evening an emergency meeting students' union had agreed to go back to mass picketing and put the barriers back up. The Ballroom became the command centre and I took up residents there. Three days later the Union was host to a national NUS 'victimisation' conference which had over 200 delegates from various institutions were disciplinary action was taken place. A popular slogan initiated by the IMG was: 'Oxford, Essex, Kent, unite – One struggle, one fight!'

The police also visited the occupation and warned students that they risked police action against them if they didn't leave; everyone stayed put. At Christmas I'd promised my mother that I wouldn't do anything stupid, like getting myself arrested. Famous last words and all that, as they say! On the Sunday evening of the 17 March rumours circulated that a police presence would occur within 24 hours. The occupation was jammed packed that night and it was so hot, I'd to take my vest off and stored it in my coat pocket. Because I didn't sleep well, I volunteered to do the first picket shift. It was still early when the twelve pickets, mainly activists, saw van after van arrive full of police. Their first action was to tear down the barricades which was met with token resistance and led to a couple of arrests. It was not until deliveries began to arrive did things begin to heat up and more arrests followed. People began pouring out the Ballroom and from the Towers to see what was going on.

Looking around I could see a mixed sea of angry and frightened faces; the possibility of panic and humiliating retreat was on the cards. It was this realisation, a watershed moment, that drove me to make a political intervention: I felt the need to become a cause celebre and ignite the flame of resistance. When the next vehicle approached, I walked out into the road in front of it and as its bonnet brushed the front of my legs, I placed my hands on it. No sooner had I done so, I felt both of my arms being grabbed and I found myself being dragged backwards down the road towards the awaiting vans. I was briskly pushed into a van and handcuffed along with three others; shortly after I was joined by IMG rookie, Liz. Twelve men and three women from the CP, IMG and IS, were arrested that morning. Were the activists deliberately picked off; I don't believe so. The next few hours were an education; the women were treated reasonably well, whereas the men had a mixed reception. I was subjected to a particular set of 'special measures' which singled me out. My experience began with the processing; I offered as little co-operation as possible and as a result, when the command to 'empty your pockets' was issued, I stood still and crossed my arms. I was wearing a long army coat and the lining in each pocket was ripped. A middle aged policeman began to remove my belongings which were lying deep inside my coat. Painstakingly, he withdrew countless coins, pieces of paper, and eventually, the vest I'd removed the night before and had forgotten about. He looked me in the eye and said: 'Don't tell me, the next thing I'm going to pull out will be a fucking rabbit!'

We spent hours in the cells before being individually called. I was the last one interviewed. I could've at one time written a whole chapter going over the interview because it contained so much material, now with a dulling memory, I can only recall the salient points that remain. Two detectives entered and looked at each other before beginning this short dialogue:

'What the fuck is that?'
'Jesus; is it even human, I wonder....'

For a split second, it had worked, the anger inside me rose like a tidal wave, but then something else took over; a political consciousness kicked in and I realised that I'd been subjected to a psychological punch which was meant to anger and catch me off guard. Okay, I thought, if you want to play silly buggers, then that's fine by me. Using my impairment as an instrument against me is how I viewed it at the time, now a degree of uncertainty has crept in; was their reaction less about winding me up and more to do with the macho culture of the police force? I guess I'll never know. The following hour was dominated by a verbal game of chess, a war of manoeuvre involving bluff and counter-bluff. Each time they tried to entice me into admitting an illegal activity, I'd turn the tables and offer a justifiable explanation:

'So, you admit to being on the picket line and

convincing drivers to turn around? In other words, you prevented drivers entering the University.'

'No, I didn't prevent drivers from entering the University.'

'How could you convince them to turn around, if you didn't stop them, eh?'

'I stood on the picket line, they drove up and stopped. We spoke to each other and they elected to turn around. Call it Free Will, Detective.'

After a short period of time the lead detective grew so frustrated that he started asking questions and then rewording my answers. So, I stopped talking and his colleague recorded a made-up dialogue. Bored, and concerned by this turn of events, I seized back the initiative and said I wanted to make a statement. The colleague enquired as to where to record this fresh statement and the lead officer almost beside himself with eagerness was saying, 'In the book, in the book ...' It took all my strength to stop myself laughing.

My statement was fairly short and said: 'I've nothing more to say without legal representation, especially since all that lies about this sentence is made up bollocks.' I did ask if he wanted me to sign it, but I'll refrain from telling you his response. Very shortly afterwards I was back in the cell. What followed was a harrowing coach journey from Colchester to Chelmsford, handcuffed to the seats. I'd to spend the night in a cell, ironically, with Colin Beardon.

The next morning, we were driven back and remanded on bail charged with obstruction. As soon as I got back on campus, I made two important phone calls. The first was to my mother and told her I'd disobeyed her instructions. The second was an audacious call to the headquarters of the National Union of Miners; I wanted to speak directly with Arthur Scargill its leader, but he was unavailable. I'd met and talked with him a number of times and I was seeking solidarity support as we had given them. I did outline what was going on and a few days later the President of our SU, Rusty Davis, received an open cheque *to cover legal costs* alongside a short note: 'Just don't go mad – Arthur'. Very few people knew about my actions.

The Tuesday was relatively quiet apart from a de-briefing meeting for those arrested. It wasn't until later that night, when rumours of another assault on the picket was likely to occur in the morning began to filter through, did I really consider the reality of the situation: my role in the struggle had changed. I had to withdraw from the front-line and that was going to be extremely difficult for me.

I woke up on the Wednesday in completely different circumstances to the previous two mornings; I was neither sleeping rough in the Dance Hall or in a police cell, but back in my own bed once an occupation meeting was over. I felt strange, somewhat isolated, I was instructed to stay clear in case I was arrested again and, not surprisingly, this left me feeling of powerless. What was about to go down, no one could've predicted and there are numerous accounts of the events as they unfolded.

The SU were once again tipped off that the police would be arriving in force once again. This time they were met with a mass of resistance which began to build up from 8.30am. At 10.a.m an oil tanker arrived accompanied by roughly 200 police who stood by as University staff removed the barricades. Within minutes the picket numbers swelled to an estimated 500 students with a similar total standing watching from balconies and hills. Given my bail conditions all I could do is observe as one of the bystanders.

Peter Townsend, Professor of Sociology, gave a collapsed account of the two arrest days together, but there's an interesting section I'll recall here:

The blockade had lasted many days but was at the time occupied by only a dozen students, including a severely disabled sociology student who was one of the leaders. But when they were marched off by the police a hundred took their place. The police moved in again and marched off this hundred to the cells. A thousand students then moved forward in support. At this stage some of us on the deck of what we affectionately called our aircraft carrier realised there was likely to be bloodshed.

The student President, Rusty Davis – fittingly a red-haired woman – and myself went up to the Deputy Chief Constable who was leading scores of police towards hundreds of milling students and begged him to withdraw. Soon there was a thin red line of staff and students separating the prospective combatants. We felt lonely and tense.

The Deputy Chief Constable was plainly taken aback by this evidence of staff disagreement with the Vice-Chancellor's action. He agreed to take us to meet the Vice-Chancellor, who had resisted earlier pleas to negotiate. He tried to remain aloof, and seemed determined to let matters take their course. This was an uncomfortable meeting. No compromise was offered. However, the police read the situation for the first time and, back on the access road, decided to withdraw quickly. (2004; unpaged)

The day's confrontation was over; 90 students had been arrested and the entire campus was in shock. These events were two days prior to the Easter vacation and I agree with the view that this defused what could've been a very explosive situation. There was however enough time for the students to organise a 1,400 strong protest demonstration via the police station and for Senate to announce an 'independent enquiry into the troubles' which went down like a lead balloon amongst the students. The Easter vacation was a lull in proceedings, but in truth, I was totally unprepared for was what lay ahead of me in the aftermath of my arrest.

The verdict of my own disciplinary hearing was made public on 27 March. I was found guilty of charges i) and iii), but not guilty of (ii) and fined £55 of which £40 was suspended unless a further breech of discipline occurred. In addition, there was a yearlong suspended exclusion order issued with the same conditions attached. At the time I paid little attention to the penalty because there were signs that further legal action might be coming my way, firstly, with the announcement that the cases of those arrested had been sent to the Director of Public Prosecution, and secondly, I'd an interview under caution with the police regarding the night the windows were smashed around campus. Things were certainly heating up with talk of possible conspiracy charges in relation to the picket line. If this wasn't enough to unnerve me one lunch time, and I can't recall when exactly, I was told I was wanted by security and so I visited their reception. I was merely told I'd visitors waiting for me in an office and I, unsuspecting of anything untoward, followed a security officer to that room. Without warning or an opportunity to obtain representation, I was confronted by a fresh pair of police Detectives who wanted to interrogate me. Clearly, I was far from impressed.

Three things emerged from this meeting worth noting. During the questioning I must've made some comment that struck home because the lead Detective looked up from his paperwork and said, 'Yes, we were warned you're a clever bastard'. That made me smile at least. Unknown to me at the time I was about to construct a terrible case of mistaken identity in relation to the Lebanese student who was with Will and I when we visited the bookshop that fateful night. I didn't know, until a few weeks later, that there were two Lebanese students involved in the occupation and so I told the police in all innocence that the third person couldn't be interviewed by them because he had been tragically killed back home over Easter in a car accident. Will and I were eventually charged with criminal damage – the only students arrested and charged over the entire incident – and faced a High Court trial. When this news broke the other Lebanese student approached us and said that I'd made a mistake and it was him, not his friend who was with us; should he go and tell someone? Will and I looked at each other in disbelief, however we were clear headed enough to suggest that there was no need to complicate matters further by giving the police another person to pin something on. After a chat he saw that coming forward might not be such a good idea and that his friend would've understood. The trial itself didn't take place until well into the summer vacation long after all the dust had settled.

Meanwhile the new term had begun with all sides wanting to take a step back from the brink but struggled to do so. It was a make or break month with the University following the disciplinary route and the SU Executive counter attacking with the demand for their suspension until an independent enquiry had been held. The campus trade unions, led by ASTMS, put forward a peace plan which sought to bring all the parties together around the table. The rawness of the previous term's events meant little progress was possible. Years later one of the ASTMS negotiators then a colleague of mine in the MSF told me how they had grown frustrated with the inflexible stance of the Student leaders like me. During the following academic year, the proposals made by the Unions were the basis for talks and in truth made the Students' grievances much clearer than we ever did. Crucial was recognition of SU autonomy and the right to have and control our own building.

The picket line wasn't the only action the SU had been engaged in. Will and I successfully moved a motion for a rent strike and this had been moderately successful, however with the arrival of the summer term, it was rapidly approaching crunch time. Once again this highlights the powerlessness of student politics; students were over a barrel because anyone considered in debt to the University wouldn't be allowed to sit their exams. Time was running out. BOB 2

Speaking of the exams, I made an interesting discovery during the research for this book. Within the notes on 'The Troubles' I found a piece of paper which recorded key events in March 1974 and among them was the rumour that: '... one [of] those to be charged with being part of the troubles is a spastic and normally requires considerably more time to complete his exams than other people. This time has been considerably curtailed this time, it's to be seen if other spastics are also given the same treatment. This time is apparently condensed into one day.' I've no idea who wrote this or where the rumour started, but it does reveal how some saw me and it illustrates the atmosphere that existed at the time. It's true that the methods used for my exams kept changing over my degree period, but at no time did I feel unfairly treated. In the first year, I'd the same format as other students, although I dictated my answers to lecturers who wrote them down. Subsequently, this was method was changed and I was expected to produce six extended essays over two weeks. It was hard work but suited me rather than having traditional exam questions to be completed in a short space of time.

Sometime during February, the Vice Chancellor had supported a proposal from a member of the Language Centre to have a 'teach-in' in order to restore the academic credibility of the University. The idea was to have staff and students debate topics such as 'academic freedom' as a means of addressing issues arising from 'the Troubles' however in typical Sloman style, within days of the mass arrests, he had requested that Department Heads should select students to take part in the event. This went down like a lead balloon and resulted in around a hundred students confronting him in his office. Unfortunately, there were successive invasions of his office during this academic year and they have all blurred into one in my mind. I do have a vivid memory of one where there were outside students present. A Birmingham student at the time, who became a friend of mine years later, happily recalls meeting me for the first time and watching me harangue the VC and three members of the press. I don't believe this was the same incident however, but Wolf and Mann report that on this occasion Sloman looked at his watch around five to seven and announced that he had another pressing engagement and promptly walked out his office leaving the students staring after him.

The following few weeks saw various rituals played out; well attended SU meetings passing motions of solidarity, the sudden arrival of police determined to demoralise the picket and the University assisting Lord Annan to prepare his 'independent enquiry'. Perhaps if it had been a game of chess, stalemate would've been agreed by then. As it happens, when least expected, a further twist took place out of the blue. No one expected much from the Appeals Committee, but its Chair was Doctor Spicer who was President of the Essex Branch of the Association of the Union of Teachers, and it's likely he took a more sympathetic position on why Will and Ronnie behaved as they did. Whilst they were still found guilty of three of the four charges they faced, the penalties were vastly reduced, and the expulsions were overturned. Everyone was left in a state of shock with the right-wing academics beside themselves with anger and the students divided on how to read the situation. Many students simply put it down to Spicer being the right man in the right place at the right time; the Left were less philosophical, believing the original decision had backed the University into a corner.

Was it all in vain? I'd like to think not; the University did begin to take the SU seriously and eventually they were given their own Union building. Rents and cost of living continued to be issues over the next year or so, but apart from another rent strike taking place, very little internal politics took place on campus until the autumn term of 1976.

Other political activity did occur during that summer term. The IMG agreed that we should stand me in the SU elections for president of the union. At no time did I believe I could win against the smooth-talking Colin Beardon, the Broad Left candidate, but we were hoping to make a good showing. As it happens Beardon ran out the easy winner with 410 votes, a right-wing candidate called Dennis Slattery came second with 271, and I was third with 98. The fourth candidate was an International Socialist member, Phil Benson, secured 54. With hindsight I don't believe the result was too surprising because the Broad Left had a strong base within the CP and Labour Club and they were always viewed as the 'moderates' within the Left.

The fact Slattery, an independent candidate, did so well was that he echoed the views of the Moderate Alliance who claimed to speak for 'the silent majority' who was sick to death with all the disruption and hardship caused by the militants. This was a constant theme during this term from both the right-wing students and staff, however, there were many who believed this wasn't just a natural backlash to the events. A week prior to the closing down of the picket-line, the conservatives had invited John Biggs-Davison, a leading member of the Conservative Monday Club. The mass media was all over this like a rash because it was part of a campaign Biggs-Davison had begun in the Commons where he raised the issue of left-wing students and the National Union of Students and their efforts to suppress free speech; saying that some '... university *authorities behaved with the utmost cowardice in banning Monday Club speakers'*.

I'd been involved in national discussions within NUS concerning the rise of fascist and considered racist activities on campuses during early 1974 when the National Front were making headlines and Jewish Societies were promoting what was viewed as Zionist propaganda. There were those on the Left who wanted a clear position of 'No Platform for Fascists' meaning organisations like the NF and Column 88, however, some SUs sought to extend this to include those who supported Apartheid in South Africa or sided with the views of Enoch Powell. The position I held was that no matter how much we disliked Biggs-Davison's views, all tendencies on the Left at Essex agreed he wasn't a fascist and to deny him a platform would be a huge error.

A protest was held outside his meeting and some entered the lecture room and begun singing *Jerusalem* and heckling; however, just as it began to get disruptive, a SU officer addressed the meeting and said that the behaviour was against union policy and people should leave. Only a handful of Tory students and the media remained. The police had nothing to do as it was a relatively peaceful protest, nevertheless on the World Wide Web it states: '[Biggs-Davidson] subsequently spoke at Essex University, but had to have police protection, while a mob outside demonstrated singing *The Red Flag*.' The constructed media narrative during the early 1970s was very much within the framework of 'the empty within' which both Sloman and Lord Annan employed.

Chapter 10

The aftermath

Anytime anybody pulls you down
Anytime anybody says you're not allowed
Just remember you are not alone
In the aftermath
You feel the weight
Of lies and contradictions that you live with everyday
It's not too late
Think of what could be if you rewrite the role you play

Adam Lambert

It had been decided to maintain a picket and invite other University students to join us over the Easter vacation. I had to stay on the edges of the picket, but acted as a host when I was around however, there was one incident when I wished I'd stayed away. One beautiful afternoon in the spring sunshine, I joined a small group of 'outsiders' and began chatting to them. A woman, sympathiser of the IMG, said I'd just missed out on seeing her 'teddy bears' and would I like to see them? I wanted to be a good host, but I had no idea what she was talking about, so I naively nodded. Feminism clearly wasn't on this sympathiser's training programme as I discovered to my acute embarrassment; but I had learnt a new euphemism.

The verdict of my own disciplinary hearing was made public on 27 March. I was found guilty of charges i) and iii), but not guilty of (ii) and fined £55 of which £40 was suspended unless a further breech of discipline occurred. In addition, there was a yearlong suspended exclusion order issued with the same conditions attached. At the time I paid little attention to the penalty because there were signs that further legal action might be coming my way, firstly, with the announcement that the cases of those arrested had been sent to the Director of Public Prosecution, and secondly, I had to have an interview under caution with the police regarding the night the windows were smashed around campus. The heat was certainly turned up with talk of possible conspiracy charges in relation to the picket line. If this wasn't enough to unnerve me one lunchtime, and I can't recall when exactly, I was told I was wanted by security and so I visited their reception. I was merely told I had visitors waiting for me in an office and I, unsuspecting of anything untoward, followed a security officer to that room. Without warning or an opportunity to obtain representation, I was confronted by a fresh pair of police Detectives who wanted to interrogate me. Clearly, I was far from impressed.

On 24 June, the long anticipated court case of those arrested on the two picket lines begun. Most of the students decided to put up a collective defence and the brief was given to a barrister called Anthony Hooper. Years later Mr. Justice Hooper was to preside over the Damilola Taylor trial; Damilola was a young black boy who was found with fatal stab wounds in a stairwell, but those charged with his death were acquitted. For some reason which escapes me now, I'd decided to represent myself in court, and the Barrister was happy to see me conduct my own defence. It made no difference because ninety-nine of the defendants were found guilty and given a two-year conditional discharge and a fine. Six were acquitted, including the new President and his partner, who saw their cases dismissed on a technically. Beardon argued they weren't actually on the road, therefore not obstructing the Highway. I still smile to myself when I recall this. One Labour student faced an additional trial for criminal damage because he had tried to resist arrest by grabbing hold of a van's wing mirror as he was being hauled away. I attended his trial, but I've forgotten the outcome.

There was a short break before I was back in the thick of things with the publication of the Annan Report. While sections of the University had called for an independent enquiry, the Vice Chancellor was determined to have someone appointed who 'knew' the University well and understood its background. Lord Noel Annan certainly knew the University because in September 1961, when the Provost of King's College Cambridge, he became the Chairman of Essex's Academic Planning Board and was therefore instrumental in the selection of Albert Sloman as the new University's Vice Chancellor. Essex University also awarded him an honorary doctorate in 1967. There's little doubt that Annan had a distinguished career in Education, and was well respected, which meant any voices of dissent about his appointment were quickly muted. I want to suggest it's not just his association with Essex that's worth noting, there are two other factors which may have helped influenced the nature of his Report. During the Second World War he was a British military intelligence officer who ended up working in Winston Churchill's bunker. It's also said that while at King's he was recruited into a secret debating society called the Cambridge Apostles whose members included the Soviet Union spies Guy Burgess and Michael Straight. Did these factors colour how he saw student politics and the role of the Left?

It's not my intention to offer a critique of the Annan Report as that would serve no useful purpose, besides I've already outlined my own perspective on 'The Troubles'. My focus will mainly be on how Annan viewed student politics at the time and how this subsequently impacted directly on me. I believe Wolf and Mann have a valid point when they state that:

> [The Report] was certainly not a 'whitewash' of the Administration, as the students claimed, for it frequently criticised the Administration and the V-C. But its criticisms were mostly from a 'hard-line' position. (1975; 157)

It certainly wasn't 'independent' or without an agenda. I would argue the Report wasn't written primarily for an internal audience, but rather was a clarion call to other institutions and agencies of the State who were being too soft in dealing with what Annan and others saw as a threat from 'the enemy within'. All through the year, as I've already indicated, Sloman made reference to 'outside influences' within the protests. In my introduction to 'The Troubles' I spoke about how Essex was viewed as a 'red base', however I see this as being only a 'symptom' in the ideas of the Establishment. In 1971 Angus Maude had written a *Sunday Express* article entitled, 'The Enemy Within' in which he wrote:

> As we try to grapple with our major imports from America - violence, drug-taking, student unrest, the hippy cult and pornography - our own permissive leftists have been hailing them as signs of progress.

Throughout the 1970s there were a series of *moral panics* concerning the well-being of British society within the mass media and they certainly jumped all over the language used by Annan. He gave a brief summary of 'The Militants' thus:

> Their aims are clear. On any issue, and if there is none they will want to invent one, they wish to raise the temperature and create a situation in which the

University authorities will be cornered and, so they hope, capitulate. For them the University authorities are not only the tools of the Capitalist State but the weakest link in that Stake, and to strike at them is to promote the destruction of that State and achieve the political objectives nearest to their heart. No one would doubt their sincerity; but equally the University authorities must regard them for what they are – wreckers. (1974; 7)

He goes on to link the Left to their counterpart in 1968-9. I don't know how many times I've read this since 1974, but each time I'm left bemused by the simplicity of the argument and its embarrassing reductionism. It is true, of course, that people like Alexander Cockburn offered a strategy in which 'the emergent student revolutionaries aim to turn the tables on the system, by using its universities and colleges as base areas from which to undermine other key institutions of the social order' (Cockburn, 1969) but this wasn't the principle motivation for the Essex Left to join the NUS Grants Campaign. Nevertheless, in his Report's conclusion Annan wrote:

The immediate cause of the disturbances at the University in 1973-74 was the action of a small number of militant students, well-organised, unscrupulous in their methods, and determined to cause a confrontation with the University authorities. They disrupted lectures, ran the occupation and directed the illegal picketing of the delivery area. (1974; 38)

This presentation of the 'militants' underpinned the entire Report and became the focus on attention within the mass media and Parliament – Essex Wreckers! The lead story in *The Times Higher Education Supplement*, published 2 August and written by Laura Kaufman, runs with this narrative. By constructing the 'wreckers' narrative, Annan could neatly explain away how the SU were manipulated by the wreckers who were in turn backed by gullible members of staff referred to as *Staff Sympathisers*. When it came to the SU demands, for example, Annan could conclude, 'After studying the evidence on all these demands I must record my belief that the militants never intended to negotiate, nor to allow the Union Executive to do so.'

How were the militants able to manipulated proceedings? In a sense Annan simply offered a more extreme version of students' meetings than the one we saw Wolf and Mann paint. The whole section seven, 'THE METHODS OF THE MILITANTS', is quite mind-boggling however I will limit my remarks to only a few paragraphs. One of the striking features of the report is how Annan, using 'the evidence' he had gathered, speaks through other people's voices. Here, for example, he writes:

> It was done [militants getting their own way], so it has been put to me, by employing the well-tried methods of the extreme left. Motions hostile to their purposes would be swamped with amendments, the chairman would be switched and a new one appointed by the outgoing chairman. Procedural points would multiply and ideological rhetoric would flow until many uncommitted students got bored and left the meeting. (1974; 22)

Other examples of so called unscrupulous behaviour were detailed from unnamed sources that, just like Annan, appeared to be totally ignorant of SU procedures which even the Left had to follow. Anyone involved in student politics in the 1970s will recognise the chaos that existed in meetings, but there is a deliberate undercurrent here that I would argue completely distorts the dynamics in the majority of Essex SU meetings. Annan's time in intelligence clearly weren't wasted. When I saw this particular section, I was livid but far worse was still to come. Annan went on to say, 'It was put to me that when support waned in a meeting it was a tactic to ask a cruelly crippled student who was a militant to speak and gather sympathy.' Nothing could be further from the truth, but I'll let Wolf and Mann address this slur:

> Bob had in fact played a major role in determining the strategy of the IMG throughout the year. His physical handicap did give him one advantage – it was impossible to listen to him casually. If one was to understand his speech one had to give him total attention. Then one realised that he was indeed a fluent and witty speaker, and he played an important role in articulating IMG policies at Students General Meetings. (1975; 147-8)

I had over the years experienced various negative reactions to my impairment that were hurtful and discriminatory, but never before had I been singled out for a personal attack on me within an official narrative. I was both shocked and belittled by the experience. A few weeks after the report was published, I was approached by Professor Townsend, a Pro Vice Chancellor, who said he personally wanted to apologise profusely for the scandalous lies that were told about me by Annan. I don't wish to appear churlish but at no time since this Report was written has the University of Essex acknowledged the discriminatory manner in which my impairment was 'unscrupulously' used to discredit the Left's behaviour. Wolf and Mann, who as I've suggested were far from supportive of the Left, nevertheless stated in terms of the Report that in their opinion:

> There are a fair number of inaccuracies, and the interpretation of student politics was silly. Those like Annan who blamed a few student militants could only explain the extraordinary fact their line was popular among students, at all moments of crisis, by

imputing to them amazing powers of cunning and deception. (1975; 159)

I had little time to brood over how I had been treated; academically, I had come through the year which was pleasing, but towards the end of summer, Will and I were facing a week-long trial in the Crown Court. A little like our trips to Grunwick, the SU minibus would carry us and the observer supporters to Chelmsford. The morning of the first day was largely taken up with swearing in the jury and I had a slight twinge of guilt when I knocked back a man with hearing loss but I needed people to understand me as my head was on the block. We were before Judge Greenwood and Will and I felt his wrath because we were late back from lunch due to not being served in time. This was deemed disrespectful to the court and therefore we were refused bail during court proceedings. The rest of the week we ate HMP food locked in a cell which presented barriers for me.

The following day, Tuesday, was a farce. We were forced to travel down to Chelmsford and then travel back to campus handcuffed inside a prison van in order to accompany the jury to 'the crime scene', yet within minutes, we were back on the road again!

Most of the prosecution's evidence against us was based on eyewitness accounts from Security men and a storeman who was working late. I was less freaked than Will by the proceedings and worked alongside the Barrister to identify inconsistencies or plain lies. We cross referenced the evidence with a detailed drawing of the surrounding area and the library building. Fortunately, my eye for detail paid off as I discovered we could discredit two of the three Security men's testimonies by demonstrating that their claim to have seen me hurling a brick was either a complete fabrication or the two men were from the planet Krypton because to witness what they said they saw from their stated hiding place, they would've needed to have seen through a brick wall! This put doubt in the jury's minds.

Will nor I could fathom out why the storeman had been called because his evidence as presented in court was complete gibberish and no use to the prosecution whatsoever. He was a small elderly man who came across as utterly confused. On the Friday, half way through the Judge's summing up, we had to break for lunch and I'll never forget sitting in the cell listening to Will giving me a pep talk on what to do and not do, if we were sent down – 'Don't turn your back on anyone, right?'

As it happened the jury failed to reach a verdict and were split seven to five in our favour, (I'm relying on the students K3 newspaper for the details), and this meant we had to go through the entire process again in early December. A few weeks later I was selling the IMG weekly newspaper in Colchester when an older woman stopped to buy one. She'd done so before therefore I wasn't expecting what she went on to tell me. 'My husband was forced to give evidence against you; they threatened to lay him off if he didn't do as they said.' He'd been injured apparently by a can of paint which fell on him when he was in the back of a University van that had sped through the picket-line.

Unimpressed by the University's treatment of the students and himself, he had decided to have a lapse of memory in Chelmsford; hence, the mystery was solved. The second trial was fairly uneventful; Judge Petre was willing to grant us bail, provided we kept to time, which we did. I can only recall one significant incident which took place during the Judge's summing up.

Bored stiff having heard the details so many times before, I absent-mindedly looked across at the jury and almost leaped out of my skin when I spotted a female juror wink at me! Was this a positive sign I wondered; unfortunately, a sense of déjà vu took over when the second jury failed to reach a majority decision. Locked at eight for and four against acquitting, Judge Petre had no option after three gruelling hours of deliberating to do anything other than to dismiss the jury. What followed was the strange procedure where the Judge begins a third trial and asks the Prosecution if they wish to present evidence before the court.

When they declined the opportunity, the Judge then stated there was no case to answer and that we were free to go. In a sense it was not a satisfactory way to end proceedings; we weren't found 'not guilty' as we should've been, but I take small comfort in the fact that a couple of the jury members stayed behind and wished us well. My lasting memory remains: the bemused look on the faces of the waiters at a nearby Indian Restaurant who witnessed a dozen happy students eating, drinking and singing raucously, the *Internationale*.

Living in Colchester during my final year or so meant I was relatively inactive on campus. In truth, once the dust had settled from 'The Troubles', SU politics were reduced to the odd campaign around rent increases, attending marches on national or international issues, or passing motions on a wide range of subjects for the rest of my undergraduate time at Essex. During my final year I wrote a dissertation on the History of British Trotskyism which combined a historical exploration alongside a sociological analysis. A disabled friend of mine who had been a secretary kindly typed up the final draft for me. A PhD student called John Charlton was working on a similar subject and not for the last time in my life, I believe I became a stepping-stone in someone else's career. In the summer of 1976 I obtained a Bachelor of Arts degree in Comparative History and Sociology, but then came the big question; where would I go from here?

I lived at 5 Gladstone Road, Colchester. I was one of a number of students who lived there, although the brother of an IMG comrade called Marian also moved in, but in truth it was fairly untypical of student accommodation. There were no late parties with loud music or anything like that therefore it came as a bit of a shock when one morning we were raided by the police and Customs and

Excise looking for a large quantity of drugs. I was far from impressed when a young copper burst into my room and starting asking me what I used the collection of plastic tubing for.

Sarcastically, I said he had a choice of believing I used them to drink with, or alternatively, we could report that I pleasured myself by sticking them where the sun didn't shine. He quickly left. Another bright spark rushed into the kitchen from the garden holding a plant pot and demanding to know what was growing in it. Julian, a fellow History student informed him that it was a tomato plant, but not satisfied with the answer he decided to waive it under his Sergeant's nose. Those of us gathered round the kitchen table struggled not to laugh at the interchange between them:

'What do you think this, Serge?'
'Like he said, it's a *tomato plant*; now put the thing back where you found it.'

Very much to our surprise, one student was caught with half an ounce of cannabis for recreational use, but apart that the house was clean. I mention the house because Marian and I would sit for hours talking around the kitchen table. Marian's area of postgraduate research was in the field of 'the sociology of literature' where she was researching the German Marxist literary critic Walter Benjamin. Our discussions prompted me to take an interest in the life and work of Franz Kafka and to follow her footsteps onto the M.A. course run by David Musselwhite, who had initiated the Sociology of Literature Project which attracted a worldwide reputation. I was happy to spend another year at Essex.

The academic year 1976-1977 begun with me meeting up with the new postgraduates I'd be studying alongside. It was a small group which included the cousin of Clare Short who became a Labour Member of Parliament for Birmingham Ladywood and someone I came to know quite well. As a member of the Workers Socialist League, he and I were the only really political people on the course.

The weather was quite balmy for early September, so I recall a fateful lunchtime sitting out in the sunshine talking to a friend about the year ahead. When he asked me how I was, I said jokingly that I was bored and thought it was time we had another occupation. This was supposed to be a little quip between two friends, but I'd forgotten he wrote for the SU newspaper *K3*; so, imagine my horror, when I discovered this had been blown up into 'a story' of possible things to come? What I wasn't anticipating was that three months later Shirley Williams, Labour's Education Minister, would announce not only an increase in student fees, but additional costs for overseas students. This announcement led to the launching of a massive NUS campaign across the country. Initially, students were joined in their protests by their University authorities and trade unions, but while continuing to voice concern, they in affect climbed down.

At Essex during the last weeks of the first term there was a 48 hour token occupation. This was a busy time for me personally because I was not only involved in the tuition campaign, but I was also a candidate in the election for the officer post of External Affairs. This resulted in bitter rivalry between the Broad Left candidate and me; however, I came out the victor after a truly acrimonious campaign.

One of the difficulties of trying to write a book concerning historical events which took place almost forty years ago, where little documented evidence exists, is that it's almost impossible to offer an accurate picture. My memory of the tuition fee campaign is extremely vague and my source material limited to two articles in the SU's newspaper. It's for this reason I'm unable to provide details of the occupations that took place. I do have a memory of a particular occupation, but I'm not sure if it relates to this campaign or was part of 'The Troubles'.

I can recall one 24 hour occupation being secretly extended to 48, (which baffled all but a select few), because a group of students had tried to break into the V-Cs office via the roof and had managed to put a foot through the ceiling. A couple of mature students were former decorators and we managed to smuggle material in and out of the occupation under the noses of security. The occupation was extended on the false claim of intimidation, but in reality, it was done to let the plasterboard dry! The University never found out.

What I can tell you about the tuition fees campaign is that it's fair to say that there wasn't an appetite for engaging in a longer occupation among the majority of students. However, as time went on overseas students grew increasingly more anxious and frustrated with the lack of support, and sections of the Left recognised the need to keep making a case for extended direct action. In February 1977 the Essex SU finally voted in favour of a further occupation but for several days it was unclear as to whether it would go ahead or not. In the meantime, talking about Education Ministers, by another quirk of fate student politics at Essex were once again thrust back into the national headlines. At the same SU meeting that voted for an occupation, a motion was passed instructing the Executive to inform Sir Keith Joseph that 'his presence would not be welcomed' the following Friday.

Here was a prominent Conservative MP who sought to 'defend free speech' as Biggs-Davison had done previously. Again, the question of no platform' was raised and, despite Joseph's controversial 1974 speech, where is argued 'human stock' was being threatened by unmarried mothers from the lower classes; very few students viewed him to be a fascist.

A picket was arranged, and an alternative meeting organised, however some in the Left, including myself, decided we would make political interventions against him in the meeting. After he spoke on 'Conservatism and Free Speech', I was one of a number of people who asked him questions. I stated that, as we both supported 'free speech', why couldn't we jointly organise a debate on 'the Irish Problem' in Trafalgar Square? This was pure theatre on my part, I was fully aware that in November 1976, the British state and mass media were quite happy to promote the Peace People's rally in Trafalgar Square but would take the exact opposite view to hosting an event which allowed a Republican perspective to be heard. Sir Keith knew where I was going with my question and tried to blank me, but the audience also understood the narrative and began to bait him. Finally, he relented, and simply stated, 'It couldn't be done'. He refused to elaborate even when pressured to do so and everyone knew at that precise moment, I had caused a political embarrassment.

I don't believe it was the fact Sir Keith was met by a hostile jostling crowd armed with some flour bombs and eggs that drove the Sunday Times' Editorial on the 13th of February 1977 to demand: 'Shut down Essex'; I honestly believe the trigger point was the fact that a disabled, left-wing student had humiliated him. Years later, Conor Gearty captured the political point I was making that day when he wrote:

> Thatcher was protecting Keith Joseph's free speech while simultaneously making CND, Irish Republican and trade union protest next to impossible, through a mixture of specific laws, repressive courts and police action. (2015; 20)

When I turned on the BBC's Six O'clock News later that day, imagine my surprise to see myself standing there with my hand raised as the opening credits rolled. The question remains; did my antics come back to haunt me from that day forward?

The visit of Sir Keith Joseph was just an interlude. Previously, the 48 hour occupation held in December had saw the Proctor and the rest of the University administration take a relax view of proceedings and no repercussions developed. When 800 students at an emergency general meeting on 7 March voted for an immediate sit-in, the climate changed. The occupation came two days before a huge national demonstration in London against the tuition fees increases. Essex was represented by well over seven hundred and fifty students, staff and trade union representatives. The motion to occupy supported six demands:

- Non-implementation of fee increases.
- No discrimination between home and overseas students.
- No quotas on numbers of overseas students.
- View Education as a right not a privilege.
- That there are no redundancies among staff.

Faced with a second occupation the stinging criticism from Annan suddenly came looming back into focus for the Administration and so Essex became the only one of forty universities and colleges to instigate disciplinary proceedings. Given the fact that the academic staff had petitioned the SU not to go ahead with the occupation because it might damage the broad support for the national march and Conservative students opposing the sit-in may have been influencing factors in how the University reacted.

This time round it wasn't the V-C who became the figure of both fun and hate but the Proctor, John Oliver, who featured in cartoons and pieces of street theatre. In one piece of street theatre I'm left asking myself if I was behind one of the masks captured in a photograph. I remember little about the occupations of that year which is ironical because the core argument within my disciplinary hearing – yes, I was disciplined again – was that I was 'the most recognisable student in the occupation'. As the only male student with an obvious physical impairment which stood out a mile, I would imagine that it would be very hard to miss me!

Eventually, around the end of May and into June seventy two students were fined a total of £3,300 and there were five expulsions and ten suspensions. I, along with a guy called Pete Moore, were not only expelled but also served with a High Court injunction which banning us from campus. It was argued that we might disrupt the degree ceremony and summer school; again, a total fabrication as no such plans existed! The SU supported us contesting the injunction, but the High Court upheld the right of the University to exclude whomever they liked, but we were allowed three hours a day to attend the SU in order to prepare our appeals.

The other expelled students and I were very isolated, however, in my case the situation became more complex because within days of my expulsion news broke that I had received a further grant 'to carry on revolting' as the *Daily Mail* reported it. David Musselwhite, the Sociology of Literature leader, decided to write a strongly worded letter to the *Daily Mail* in defence of me and my academic standards. Nevertheless, the media was intent on stoking up outrage at the folly of public money being wasted on a revolting Left-wing student and, as a result, the leadership of the National Union of Students advised me to keep a low profile until the appeal had been heard.

The role played by NUS in supporting Essex students in both 1974 and 1977 was mixed. I had dealings with many of the sabbaticals during this period; Charles Clarke was extremely ineffectual, Sue Slipman showed real distain for 'the Trots' and in one particular meeting Alistair Stewart tried to bait me by waiving a copy of the Communist Party of Britain's 'British Road to Socialism' in my direction without letting the platform or audience see what he was doing. I really didn't like the leadership of the NUS/Broad Left and the feelings were reciprocated. I find it interesting however, given Annan's early background, that in a talk Robin Ramsay gave to Labour Party branches in late 1996, called 'The influence of intelligence services on the British left', he refers to Charles Clarke in the following manner:

> The point I'm trying to make here is this; from their early twenties Clarke and Mandelson were already in the Whitehall system, young men on the make; players, albeit minor ones, in the Cold War, Foreign Office game. We might call them premature careerists.

I've no regrets about being involved in the campaigns I took part in, although I wish things had turned out differently and I'd been able to finish my MA studies. The fact I had to find a new place to study gave me a fresh challenge.

Chapter 11

New beginning

Every new beginning comes from some other beginning's end.

Seneca

The period between being expelled from the University by the Disciplinary Committee and the decision by the Appeals Committee to change the punishment to a two year exclusion order was full of incidents. Fortunately for me, a good comrade of mine called Joan Twelves, was heading back to London for the vacation to be with her partner Greg Tucker and she let me stay in her flat in Colchester. Joan a number of years later became Leader of Lambeth Council and Greg, who was also a councillor, became a leading member of the RMT along with another comrade of mine, Pat Sikorski. Sadly, Greg died in 2008. I have one specific memory of being in Joan's flat and I'll never forget it. It was 16 August 1977 and I remember sitting alone on the floor listening to the radio when the news broke that Elvis Presley had died. It certainly felt like an end of an era that night.

Staying alone in Joan's flat was difficult so I had an invite to stay with some people in Sheffield until the dust settled. It was my first visit to a city other than London and I took in everything I saw. My main recollection was being taken to a large meeting of trade unionists and left-wing groups; an experience unlike any I had had before. On my return from Sheffield I had to face the future and it quickly became clear that my days of living in Colchester were coming to an end. In many ways the appeal process was a non-event; the Student Union argued that the expulsions were too harsh, and the panel listened to mitigating evidence before deciding to impose a two year ban. One of my supporters at the appeal told me afterwards that she had overhead the panel discussing what to do with me. The argument centred upon them making comparisons between a leading figure from 1968 and myself in terms of following a political career. I laughed then, and still do, at the very thought that three senior academics thought there was a strong possibility I could follow in the footsteps of Lord David Triesman and end up in the Houses of Parliament!

Apart from the stigma of being expelled being removed, the material impact added up to roughly the thing: I had to find another University to go to on the back of negative national publicity. Following a string of rejections, including the University of Sussex, I was offered a telephone interview with Richard Johnston from the Centre for Contemporary Cultural Studies at the University of Birmingham. Richard and I had two conversations, one of which was from a telephone kiosk on a road in Wivenhoe, and it had begun with me over hearing Richard's wife saying, 'It's that spastic chappie on the phone ...' Nevertheless, the upshot was that I was accepted by CCCS and given a starting date of matter of weeks. As it happens, things didn't begin smoothly at all because someone at the University of Birmingham must have twigged who I was, and I was subsequently 'suspended' for two weeks while I was investigated with both Stuart Hall and Richard having to give assurances that I would not be an undue disruptive influence. In a short while I'll give a hint as to who I believe that person to be.

Despite having spent five or six years in or around Colchester, I'd find it hard to argue that I had firm roots in the area. Apart from the crowd in Wivenhoe most of my friends were just passing through on their way to other destinies. Suddenly packing up and leaving wasn't an uncommon experience for me and someone in my position had to accept beggars can't be choosers. Birmingham was somewhere I'd heard of because of the pub bombings in 1974, but the nearest I'd been to the city before had been my trip to the Hawthorns. I had to arrange for my three-wheeler Noddy car to be transported to Birmingham at some later date as I was venturing to Birmingham with nowhere to live; so, the first few hours I spent in Birmingham were both hectic and comical as a result. My first port of call was the University's Student Accommodation Services who were as helpful as they could be. Within a short space of time they had organised a trip to a nearby Professor's house where there was a room to let.

The Professor and his wife appeared to be very nice people and the house was well situated, but there was a snag, one huge snag I couldn't handle, despite the predicament I was in. As soon as I heard his name, a small alarm bell started to go off and this bell gradually grew louder as the good Professor explained that they had taken an interest in me because their son was a Professor at the University of Essex; perhaps I knew him? It can be a very small world at times; their beloved son was one of the leading right-wing lecturers who had been most vocal in their opposition to the students' protests. The desire to laugh almost overwhelmed me, but I managed to avoid blotting my copy book on the first day and after making up some excuse, I made a swift exit

Rather than having to justify my excuse to the University, I set about finding a short-term solution to my problem. Despite the differences that existed among the

Left student groups, it was still common in the late 1970s to see them support each other in times of need. My reputation had preceded me and after a drink in the Guild of Students coffee bar I was approached by a couple who were members of the International Socialists and they offered to put me up for a few nights until I sorted myself somewhere to stay. I took up their offer but was keen not to impinge on them too much and so later that evening I managed to find my way to the Hawthorns to watch a League Cup match between West Bromwich Albion and Watford. I can't remember how I got there and back again however I do know the game ended with a goal-a-piece!

Before I was suspended by the University, I had managed to meet several members of the local IMG and one in particular, who was called Glen, took me under his wing. I remember this as being slightly awkward at the time because I left the IMG and had ended up in an even smaller organisation called Big Flame. It would be useful to explain briefly why I'd made this political transition. The transition from IMG to Big Flame hadn't been a straightforward one.

As I've already said, Marian and I had spent many hours sat round the kitchen table discussing the internal politics of the IMG which, not for the last time, was being dogged by factionalism. Two leading figures within the IMG at the time, Brian Grogan and Jonathan Silberman, had held heavy discussions with us about our disquiet which in fact only served to push us even further away. Ironically, both men almost a decade later were expelled from the Socialist League which was the name IMG adopted in 1982 and with others went on to form the Communist League.

Part of the dissatisfaction Marian and I had centred upon the IMG's brand of Leninism and how it sought to build 'the' Party. Writing this now brings a wry smile to my face as I'm now part of a political party called Left Unity which has a number of former IMG comrades in it; but I digress slightly. We had obtained a pamphlet written by the Revolutionary Marxist Current which critiqued the IMG and subsequently decided to make further contact with them. To cut to the chase; within weeks of being involved with the RMC, we found ourselves in discussions around their interest in Big Flame's Project for a New Revolutionary organisation.

I'm using a quotation I've taken from a website run by ex-Big Flame members because it captures where both the organisation and I were at the time:

> One of the key sentences in the platform published in each issue of [Big Flame's] newspaper was the statement that a revolutionary party was necessary but that 'Big Flame is not that party, nor is it the embryo of that party'. This had the advantage of distinguishing them from some small groups who saw themselves as much more important than they were, but posed the problem of the 'party's' real reason for existence. (Farrar, 2009; unpaged)

So, as Max Farrar records it, '.... Around a dozen RMC members joined Big Flame. There were groupings in Liverpool and London with individual members in such places as Birmingham, Brighton and Nottingham.' The awkwardness I experienced was short lived due to the fact that Glen decided that I was going to spend my first Saturday night in Birmingham at a Moseley party hosted by a prominent member of the IMG! The party has stuck in my mind for several reasons, some of which I'd rather forget, but I'll recall here as light relief. The house owner Brian, and Glen weren't the only IMG members I knew at the party, so I wasn't a complete fish out of water. The person who latched onto me that night however was a complete stranger and a woman probably four or five years older than I was. I remember dancing quite a bit with her and having my drinks held for me however as the night wore on, she increasingly paid me more and more attention. I hadn't been involved with anyone for a number of years, so I found the situation both exciting and frightening at the same time. The crunch came when I said I needed to go to the toilet and she offered to come and assist me. Well, as a newbie in town, I felt that was a step too far and quite unnecessary; so, I politely declined the offer.

A few weeks later I saw her again at another party and she approached me for a dance, which I accepted, but when there was a break in the music a new friend, now a very old friend of mine, pulled me to one side and told me to be careful because her husband could get quite jealous. In the darkened room we were in I doubt Steve would've noticed the blood drain from my face. Taking a break from dancing at Brian's party led to me sitting next to Pat, softly spoken woman from Manchester, studying German at the University. In the weeks and months ahead Pat and her circle of friends soon became mine; a couple of whom I still see now and again. My first weekend in Birmingham was certainly eventful.

Getting to grips with a new and vastly different University presented me with a real challenge however joining the Centre for Contemporary Cultural Studies was something else. David Morely, Professor of Communications at Goldsmiths College, was quoted by Annette Naudin as saying in 2014:

> The Centre taught me many things, including the pleasures (and of course, the inevitable difficulties) of collective intellectual work, in dialogue with others – rather than as an isolated pursuit.

To have any understanding of the pleasures and difficulties David speaks of here, it's necessary to offer an insight into the unique cultural practices of the Centre. Stuart Hall, the Centre's Director whilst I was there, noted:

> Cultural studies have multiple discourses; it has a number of different histories. It is a whole set of

formations; it has its own different conjunctures and comments in the past. It included many different kinds of work. I want to insist on that! It always was a set of unstable formations. It was 'centered' only in quotation marks, in a particular way.... It had many trajectories; many people had and have different trajectories through it; it was constructed by a number of different methodologies and theoretical positions, all of them in contention. Theoretical work in the Centre for Contemporary Cultural Studies was more appropriately called theoretical noise. It was accompanied by a great deal of bad feeling, argument, unstable anxieties, and angry silences. (1992; 278)

This was the social environment I found myself in. During the early days it was both personally and intellectually extremely challenging. As part of a project to mark the 50th anniversary of the Centre, Kieran Connell conducted a number of interviews with former staff and students in 2014. I believe this snippet from an interchange between Hazel Chowcat (nee Downing) and Kieran reveals a particular aspect of the Centre's culture and, in passing, how I tried to deal with it.

Kieran:
I guess the centre was different from most academic institutions in the sense that it was political, we talked about before the kind of melting pot of politics from across the left, the spectrum of the left, you know from SWP to Big Flame to the Labour Party I guess. So even with all that, that political engagement you still felt it was like naval gazing?

Hazel:
Absolutely because it was, it was in the tower, you know. I remember, I mean you've spoken to Bob Findlay, I remember, I told you this because it's

worth just reminding you of this because it was just hilarious. We did spend a lot of time deciding where we going to form ourselves into a mass party. What was that about? That, out of the On Contradictions paper, there was loads of debates about this stuff and Bob sat in the Centre and he said, 'Well I give you warning, if you go and form yourselves into a party then I'm going to go off and start a tendency'. It was, I mean looking back I just wonder really, whether people are still engaged in those sort so debates or was it because we were all so political? If we had not been avowedly political, an avowedly political Centre, would we have been engaged in all that stuff? (Connell, 2014)

Of course, I was using humour to make a political point; I do believe some Centre people took themselves too seriously. Ironically, this was a year or so prior to *Monty Python's Life of Brian*, but I've always saw connections there! Nevertheless, on reflection I owe a real debt to the Centre; my time at Essex had introduced me to an analytical way of thinking, but the enrichment I gained from my time at the Centre has proved priceless. Initially, I held out a hope that I could put together a dissertation on Kafka and submit it to Essex once my suspension had been lifted. Michael Green, who had a literary background, agreed to supervise my work but after a year of fairly isolating research, I found myself being drawn in a completely different direction and, as a result, poor Kafka remains an enigma. The pull I was experiencing was both internal and external. Part of the draw away from Kafka came from my engagement with the Centre's own culture; the weekly meetings and collective working. At the time of my arrival, for example, the Women's Studies Group was deeply involved with producing the seminal *Women Take Issue* (1978). Michael O'Shaughnessy, who like Hazel also interviewed by Kieran, spoke briefly about the start of the week at the Centre:

And then I guess the Mondays there was a big meeting every Monday which was for everybody in the Centre and I can't say that I participated much in that in terms of contributing to it; I was just kind of listening and watching, because there was a lot of stuff going on. (Connell, 2014)

Thankfully, my association with members of both Big Flame and the International Marxist Group, kept my politics fairly grounded during these heady days. It was also these external politics which influenced my interests at the Centre. Within a week or two of arriving in Birmingham I had met with Brian Parsons who was the Big Flame contact in the City and I subsequently moved into his spare room in the flat he rented in Moseley for a couple of months. Brian and a teenager called Mark France were all that existed of Big Flame in the City and so my main political activity was once again within student politics and supporting local campaigns.

If I recall correctly, I was the only Centre person involved in the Birmingham Guild of Students and in little or no time I was on their Council and an ex-officio officer in the role of External Affairs, the same position I held at Essex. BUGS was fairly right-wing, and the Conservatives were led by Anna Sourbry, a person I clashed with frequently inside the Council Chamber, but surprisingly was quite amicable with outside it. Anna was Minister of State for Small Business and Enterprise in David Cameron's government from 2015. BUGS did have a few Left-wing speakers appear in the debating chamber and Dennis Skinner was perhaps the most entertaining followed by Tariq Ali. To be fair to Tariq, he was restrained by the fact that he was seconding me at the University of Birmingham Debating Society, debating: 'This House believes capital punishment is wrong.' What was really bizarre about this whole event was the fact we had to have a meal with the opposition; their side included a senior member of West Midlands Police. I still smile at the memory of Tariq being so engaging and inclusive; I love listening to him speak as he has similar qualities to Stuart Hall.

Chapter 12

Going down the Brummie road

Oh, me lads,
Should've seen their faces
Going down the Brummie road
To see the Albion Aces.

WBA Supporters

It wasn't too long ago that I was reminded of my time at the University of Birmingham while attending a meeting. A former student approached me and said she could still recall me making one of my first speeches in BUGS during a debate on a woman's right to choose and how powerful it had been. BUGS was also where I did most of my socialising on campus. Pat Bridgwood, the student from the German Department I mentioned earlier, met me in the coffee bar one lunch time and introduced me to two other women from the Department, Debbie Orpin and Helen Singer, who shared a house with an IMG comrade I was familiar with, called Andy Pritchard. Over the next few months, I regularly met up with this group, went for drinks with them and had visited their house in Harborne. Two other students, Trevor and Pauline, lived in the house as well.

Returning from home after Christmas in early 1978, I found out that my room at Brian's had been used as a cat tray and I suspected one of Brian's associates had stolen a velvet jacket of mine, but there was little chance of proving it. This was the last straw. Tensions were mounting because I'd become increasingly disillusioned with Big Flame. Unhappy with my situation, and knowing the house in Lonsdale Road in Harborne had an empty antic room, I virtually begged my friends to let me move in with them. Obviously, I can't speak for them, but I know my time in Lonsdale Road was really an enjoyable one.

Living in Harborne meant that it was an easy drive to the Hawthorns, so despite watching West Bromwich Albion lose by a single goal to Liverpool mid-January 1978 I was hooked and still make my way to the Hawthorns for Home games. Periodically I also relive this time by meeting up with Debbie who is currently a lecturer at the University of Wolverhampton. Debbie and I became close friends and spent a lot of time together in the house. Many people came and went during my time in Lonsdale Road and I was disappointed when Debbie decided to go to Berlin a short while after Pat Bridgwood had done so, but I paid her a visit in the Christmas of 1978 in minus twenty Celsius temperatures.

Britain during the late 1970s saw a lot of racist and anti-racist activity and because Birmingham was a very diverse place, it was very much involved in things. Quite a number of Centre members were in the Anti-Nazi League and Rock-Against-Racism. I'd already taken a keen interest in anti-fascist and anti-racist work at Essex however this interest grew after the Centre itself published the book Policing the Crisis: Mugging, the State and Law and Order in May 1978, which created a great deal of discussion and debate. After reading the book I decided I'd like to research how race and racism were reported upon in the mass media with an emphasis on how 'Otherness' was being constructed. As an aside, it could well be that I was making internal connections with how disabled people were portrayed, a subject I was to study twenty years later. I spoke of being 'Other' in a previous chapter, but Dr Zuleyka Zevallos (2011) provides a useful explanation when she writes that:

> The idea of *'otherness'* is central to sociological analyses of how majority and minority identities are constructed. This is because the representation of different groups within any given society is controlled by groups that have greater political power. In order to understand the notion of The Other, sociologists first seek to put a critical spotlight on the ways in which social identities are constructed. Identities are often thought as being natural or innate – something that we're born with – but sociologists highlight that this taken-for-granted view is not true.

After talking to a newly arrived student called Paul Gilroy, we both concluded that our own individual work might be enhanced by the formation of a new sub-group – The Race and Politics sub-group. This sub-group was made up of people from an array of backgrounds and not just CCCS students either, for example, Anne was a single mother from Handsworth and Raghib Ahsan worked at Land Rover before becoming a local Labour councillor. Recent folklore suggests that the sub-group was made up of an entirely Black membership however this is untrue. There is no doubt that the driving force came from the Black members of the sub-group such as Paul Gilroy, Hazel Carby, Errol Lawrence, Pratibha Parmar and Valerie Amos [who became Baroness Amos], but others also made both an impact and contribution. Errol when talking to Kieran Connell (2014) explained that:

> Paul and Hazel, in particular, were I'd say quite well read in terms of they had already done quite a lot of associated reading around the way race works, racism works. They had talked about it quite a lot. They had thought about how it intersects with

gender and class. And I think that the two of them were quite pivotal.

However, Errol then went on to say who he considered had played a directional role:

> Obviously, Paul and John [Solomos] ... he joined later. Bob was also very influential in the group. Pratibha and Valerie, as well, Paul and Valerie were quite close friends and I was just there.

It's true that in group discussions Errol was the quiet one, especially when compared to Robin and me, but he did make a huge contribution. The Race and Politics sub-group wanted to do more than debate, and it was Val Amos who came up with the idea of writing the book, but she moved on before we really got down to writing *The Empire Strikes Back: Race and Racism in 70s' Britain* (1982); however, Errol made a significant contribution to the book. I was able to play a major role in the sub-group until I left the Centre in 1979, making fleeting appearances when I could, and I shaped the first chapter along with Simon, before Paul polished it up. My main contribution, I say this tongue in cheek, was that I came up with the title for the book and as a result of attending a march in Blackpool, I was given a leaflet with a stunning photograph on it, which in my opinion, captured what our book was all about. Luckily, both the group and publishers agreed.

Errol in his interview mentions some of the influences but I believe it's difficult to pinpoint the key influences. Carnie (undated), writing about the Centre, says:

> Indeed, the work done in *The Empire Strikes Back* was built upon the groundwork laid by Hall in *Policing the Crisis*. Both works emphasize the need to re-examine racism in reference to its specific historical and social context instead of viewing it as a universal constant

across the range of human experience. This work on racism and sexism was in concordance with Williams and Hoggart's early attempts to use personal experiential accounts as ingress to the investigation of more extensive cultural phenomenon. In this way, the Centre's investigation into racism and sexism was a further exploration in the ways in which 'the personal was the political.' (Unpaged)

All the people involved with the production of *The Empire Strikes Back* I believe understood the interconnections between the personal and the political; it was this 'understanding' that had brought the Race and Politics sub-group together in the first place. I know Paul and I've differing views on the importance of the group's dynamics; however, I've expressed my take here because I believe the folklore acts to undermine the way in which we worked and how this captured and resonated with all the 'noise' surrounding debates both inside and outside the Centre.

Working on *The Empire Strikes Back* enhanced my analytical and writing skills, as well as deepening my commitment to challenging all forms of social injustice. Before moving on, it's necessary for me to acknowledge the legacy of *The Empire Strikes Back*. In 2014 Michael Keith (2014; 1815) within an article entitled: *How did the empire strike back? Lessons for today from The Empire Strikes Back: Race and Racism in 70s' Britain,* wrote:

> *The Empire Strikes Back* made a landmark and sometimes controversial intervention in the scholarship of ethnicity and race when it was first published. This article considers both the continuities and breaks that linked and separated the volume from the Centre for Contemporary Cultural Studies' work and tradition that preceded it. It also suggests that the balance between ethnographic engagement and critical scholarship sets up a necessarily iterative

process that values both but also recognizes the differences between the two.

An off shoot of the sub-group's work had been the involvement of Paul, Errol, John and I, either together or separately, in delivering sessions to undergraduates on an interdisciplinary course. One session saw me act as a facilitator of a group discussion, however having arrived early, I'd to sit patiently as the students filtered in. At two minutes to nine, a couple of students grew anxious, they wondered if the tutor had forgotten, resulting in wasted journeys. I decided to put them out of their misery, so clearing my throat I said authoritatively, 'Shall we get started?' I just wish I'd been able to capture the dismayed looks on their faces! Can I confess that this wasn't the last time I pulled that stunt? A joint session we presented was based upon textual readings of newspaper articles in relation to race. One of the examples we used was that at the time the West Bromwich Albion striker, Laurie Cunningham, was often referred to as 'the Black Pearl'. Paul, John and I would regularly attend matches together at the Hawthorns; in fact, *The Empire Strikes Back* carries a Preface which includes this sentence:

> Cyrille, Remi, Brendon and Laurie restored on Saturday afternoons the momentum we lost in midweek.

Going down the Brummie Road became a major aspect of my life and even now, thirty years later, John Solomos and I occasionally meet up before a Home match. Football and politics, of course, weren't my only recreational interests. My love of music is indicated throughout this book and I suppose there's a bitter-sweet irony involved. If my childhood hadn't been so isolating, my opportunities for play so limited, would I have spent so much time buying and playing music? I'd heard live music with my parents and the odd outing with Carol however it was going to gigs at Essex that truly sparked my interest in live music. Moving to Birmingham actually increased my opportunity to see groups live. The Moseley and Kings Heath scene not only consisted of pub crawls and crashing parties, but also included going to live music gigs. Also, my involvement with Rock Against Racism and knowing Martin Culverwell at the Centre brought me into contact with local bands. Jane Munro, the bassist with the *Au Pairs*, said in a 2008 interview with Tommy Gunnarsson:

> I joined the band by a kind of happy accident, really. I was on the periphery of the Moseley music scene and the other band members and I'd a mutual friend, Martin Culverwell, who later became our manager. .... Martin said he knew a band who were looking for a female bass player. Lesley rang me. The four of us had a jam together at a room over a pub, and the rest is history.

Lesley Wood was the lead singer and lyricist and we shared the same Birthday, so more than once we celebrated together at parties. The *Au Pairs* weren't the only local band I went to see; *Steel Pulse, UB40,* and a little later, *The Beat,* all entertained me. I'll tell you a story about Ranking Roger from *The Beat* in the next chapter. During the late 1970s and early 1980s I regularly attended gigs where top artists performed, and in all honesty, I can't recall any real hassle. The Birmingham Odeon held some amazing gigs, for example, *Culture Club, Adam and the Ants,* not to mention Patti Smith. Digbeth Civil Hall played host to top groups as well with American groups such as *The Ramones and The Motels* interrupting IMG meetings fairly frequently. Another popular venue Barbarella's where I saw *The Clash* more than once and *X-Ray Spex* with Poly Styrene. These were truly heady days.

As I've already indicated my University grant ended before the book was published and given the commitment to the sub-group, I'd made little progress on my own research. In a final bid to stay at Birmingham I stood in the election for President of BUGS, despite knowing I didn't have a cat in hell's chance of winning! Liz Wakefield, a final year student, was also standing for one of the posts and during two weeks of extensive campaigning and hustings we found ourselves spending a great deal of time in each other company. What was so different about our sudden relationship was that we were like chalk and cheese.

Liz came from a Christian traditional rural background and was stunningly beautiful as a person; then there was me, the brash revolutionary socialist who, and for the life of me can't remember the context, stated boldly that I didn't believe in marriage. Who knows why we hit it off, but we did; and I found myself courageous enough to ask her out for a meal. In typical Liz style she said she'd rather entertain me herself than go to a flash impersonal restaurant. I recall the quiet night together and the peck on the cheek when I left; such events had been few and far between in my life. In all honesty, I wasn't sure if Liz had a boyfriend or not, it didn't seem to matter for some reason. After the Elections we went our separate ways, but I did receive a postcard from her tell me that she missed me; months later our paths crossed once in Birmingham and after a fleeting hug, she fluttered away again. I did hear much later that she had become ill after University; unfortunately, I was unable to follow up on these rumours. Perhaps the fact I wanted to include her here shows how much of an impression the lady with a flower in her hair had made on me.

My time at Birmingham was over, not only did this bring down the curtain on my second phrase of studying; it also forced me once again to confront the tough environment of looking for employment. In one sense I felt my University days had done very little to enhance my prospects of getting a decent job and therefore I was no better off than when I left the Oakwood Further Education Centre. What I needed above all was some employment experience. At first it felt like a repeat of the early years after Oakwood, shunned by the labour market and the State, however, this time around I'd a social network to draw upon and this led to an opportunity. The following four years were to shape my future and commitment to disability politics.

The first year of the 1980s was untypical of the rest of the decade which saw my life completely transformed. Leaving CCCS and Lonsdale Road was a huge displacement for me however I was fortunate that a student attached to CCCS through the English Department started going out with a Spanish student called Vincente, who was also a member who of the IMG. My friendship with them and another overseas student from Honduras called Carlos paved the way for me having temporary accommodation with Vincente. I remember one extraordinary event involving Carlos, Vincente and myself.

There was a rumour that an international fencing tournament was taking place at the University and a Cuban team was in town. We decided to go and have a look and sure enough a female team was involved, and my Spanish speaking comrades began talking to them. Their Russian coach wasn't too impressed and when we accepted an 'invite' to meet up at their hotel later; he was at the front door to 'see us off'. This was not before one of the women had taken an interest in me and had asked Vincente to tell her about 'my story'. I'd little idea as to what was going on until he asked me for some details about my past. When I quizzed him on his conversation, he told me that she was wondering what kind of life I had in England and would it be improved if I went back to Cuba with her! The Russian made sure that idea didn't progress. It would be another twenty years before I put foot on Cuban soil.

At times my experience of living with Vincente was very similar to living with Brian, minus the cat shite, because I was never quite sure what to expect. Time and watches were alien concepts to Vincente therefore relying on him to turn up for shared meals, meetings or anything else for that matter, was completely out the question. His flat was a place to crash and for the most part, I was left to my own devices. Talking about time, I'm struggling to piece together a series of events which led to my first ever paid job. Fortunately for me IMG comrades, especially Vincente, rallied round and gave me their support. Vincente knew a couple of IMG comrades called Dave and Pia who lived in Wolverhampton and he mentioned to them my difficulties finding suitable employment. Dave worked with another IMG comrade called Anne on the biggest Youth Opportunities Programme running in the West Midlands in Brierley Hill which is on the outskirts of Dudley. Brierley Hill had a large British Steel plant called *Round Oak* which bit the dust along with many others in the 1980s. Chronic unemployment was a feature of the local economy however one Conservative councillor, Bruce Meredith, viewed this as an 'opportunity'. Meredith as Co-ordinator of Dudley Council for Voluntary Service (DVSC) introduced the YOP scheme in 1979 with 80 trainees however by 1982/3:

> .... according to the DVSC Annual Report, acting as a management agency, the organisation employed no less than 1,099 people under various MSC headings. (Johnson et al, 1984: 35)

With Dave's assistance I became part of this rapidly expanding evil empire. At the time of my recruitment I don't believe either of my comrades fully appreciated the full extent of the nature of the beast we were dealing with because both of them were fully committed to the young people they trained. I do remember my interview with Bruce and thinking what a smooth operator he was. From the outset I knew my recruitment wasn't some kind of charitable act, but rather an opportunistic adventure based upon the belief that employing a disabled man looked good for business and added further brownie points with the Manpower Services Commission (MSC). I was employed as a full-time tutor initially covering both Social Life Skills and Literacy and Numeracy.

My first couple of months weren't easy because it was one thing having Meredith appointing a tutor with a speech impairment but it's another having that decision accepted by the rest of the staff. The majority of the staff were straight from industrial backgrounds and had had no or little previous experience of relating to disabled people let alone accepting one of them as a colleague. My main supervisor, Sheila, called into question my ability to do the job from the beginning, so I was under pressure from the off to prove myself capable. Obviously, Dave gave me support and Anne soon won Ruth around who was the other literacy and numeracy tutor. Generally speaking, I'd very few problems with the trainees as far as my impairment went; there were a couple of macho lads who wanted to throw their weight around but co-training with Dave put a stop to that. Dave had good awareness as a nondisabled ally and I can recall a funny incident which took place in a local cafe one lunch time. We were at the counter ordering and the owner asked Dave if I wanted sugar in my tea. Rather than answer him, Dave turned to me and said: 'Would you like to inform him how much sugar you want; then let him know I don't take any.' The incident was never repeated.

Once I proved I could train, the focus shifted onto what I was training. There was an Australian called Colin who was in his early sixties and ultra conservative. The trainees one afternoon asked about the 'Troubles in Ireland' and so I, as a historian, explained the partition of Ireland, the Easter Uprising and the development of Republicanism and Ulster Loyalism. At break time in the staff room, [a small changing room in a Lodge on the edge of a park in Quarry Bank], Colin hit the roof excusing me of teaching IRA propaganda! For my part I simply asked, which one of us has a degree in History?

Travelling between Birmingham and Brierley Hill each day proved arduous with the expectation of reaching Headquarters by nine o'clock. Not only had I to deal with rush hour traffic, there was the little matter of having my three wheeler trike break down more than once on a very steep incline called Mucklow Hill. One time I arrived at work in the back of a police car with both staff and trainees wondering what the Hell was going on! Anne Walters was still living with her parents after returning from going to University in Hull. Now and again when the weather turned bad, I'd stay there for the night. Anne's Dad was Scottish, and her Mum was Welsh; a lovely couple I grew very fond of. My plight, plus her own desire for independence, spurred Anne into action. A friend of a friend wanted to rent out a house which was within walking distance of DVSC, so Anne and I moved into Adelaide Street.

It was a beautiful terraced house with three bedrooms, two downstairs rooms and a spacious kitchen. The back downstairs room was converted into a temporary office for a while as I struggled to complete my contribution to the *Empire Strikes Back*. In the short space of time we had known each other, Anne and I moved from being work colleagues and IMG comrades, to being really good friends. We had our own friends and activities, including watching rival football teams, which resulted in outbreaks of friendly banter regarding her support for Wolves and my allegiance to the Baggies. We also spent a considerable length of time together going clubbing, watching films and going to concerts; we also covered for each other going into work still hung over from too much vodka and late night dancing to the Clash and New Romantics in our living room. At this time Anne, Ruth and I were working in a church hall in Brierley Hill away from the main activities happening in Quarry Bank therefore staggering into work wasn't a big issue.

Over time as Meredith's empire grew, the project was moved lock, stock and barrel to an old steel plant in

Brockmoor. Dave and Ruth had left by then and I believe both Meredith and Sheila wanted to reduce my influence over the trainees therefore I was switched to literacy and numeracy full-time. A new guy, a Wolves supporter called Rob, was brought in to oversee us. He had no background whatsoever in training therefore spent much of his time doing timetables and observing. Our team was boosted further by the arrival of Debbie and Sarah, plus a little later the son of one of Meredith's friends and a past boyfriend of Anne's. This didn't go down too well, but she was very professional about it. Sarah and I became good friends and often escaped off site Fridays for lunch.

Although Ruth had left, Anne and I still socialised with her and her partner, Tim. Apart from my initial issues over my speech, and a crazy incident where some of the staff thought I was fighting a trainee when in fact I was assisting him during a seizure, disability was only a minor factor in my working and private life until one night the four of us decided to go clubbing together. I had to park and became separated from the others, so I arrived first at the nightclub only to be confronted by a doorman who refused to admit me because, according to him, I was improperly dressed. I knew this was bullshit, but waited for the others and eventually told them what happened and that without a tie, I couldn't go in. Anne, being Anne, challenged the doorman who agreed to let me in 'as one of a party'. Anyone who knows me knows that I take after my Mum and refuse to accept social injustice silently. Once inside the club I spotted the manager at the bar and immediately told him what had happened. Not only did he apologise, he said he wouldn't employ anyone who was prejudiced in any way. No sooner had he said that, he went to the front door and told the doorman to collect his belongings and come back for his pay the following day. I'd never witnessed anything like that before or since.

So far, I've spoken about the socio-political aspects of the early 1980s for me, but how did I fair emotionally? As a thirty something disabled male I grew increasingly conscious of my status as an unattached person because apart from an ill-advised brief encounter with Nirit at University, I hadn't had a serious relationship for years. There had been several people I would've liked to have turned friendship into something else, but it hadn't happened for various reasons. Forming platonic relationships were often difficult enough for me, so engaging in romantic ones proved harder still. In an article for *Disability & Society*, Kirsty Liddiard (2014; 122) wrote:

> .... a common theme centred on informants residing in intimate relationships for reasons beyond (romantic) feelings for a partner, and exacerbated by a disabled identity within an ableist heteronormative sexual culture. For example, Robert, a 26-year-old wheelchair user with congenital impairment, said that 'having' or 'being with' an intimate partner was an important symbol to others: 'I've discussed with my [disabled] best friend, how we need a girlfriend to show 'Look a real girl likes me, I've sex with her and we're in love – I must be ok, world'.' (2014: 120)

An interesting point made by another Robert, but I'm still questioning whether feelings of loneliness might only be part of the issue and that the desire for social acceptance as a sexual partner might also feature? It's often said disabled men aren't very skilled at managing the boundaries between friendship and intimate relations and as a consequence misread the signs. The 'disabled identity' Kirsty speaks of is the imposed one which, through internalised oppression, demands the striving for 'acceptance'. I've already address this in a previous chapter at a theoretical level, but now I'm linking it directly to my own experience. Working in close proximity with Sarah, plus sharing a house with Anne, did lead to emotional trauma at different times; being candid about this isn't easy, but thankfully, my 'romantic turns' were rebuffed without ruining the existing friendships.

Working at Brockmoor became increasingly difficult; Anne and I witnessed some appalling mismanagement and bullying. The pamphlet I quoted from earlier gives us a flavour of the YOP Scheme via two quotations:

> One of the nicknames for Meredith, who likes to be known as a disciplinarian, is 'the Fuhrer'. (Johnson et al, 1984: 37)

One scheme at Coseley Youth Centre was allocated £920 from [the Silver Jubilee Fund administered by DVSC] towards building an adventure playground. All very commendable, except that Mr Meredith insisted that the work be done by YOP trainees as a condition of him releasing the grant. (Johnson et al, 1984: 36)

> We decided to join a trade union and recruit others via a meeting we held in a pub. Not surprisingly, Meredith sent a couple of spies along to see what our intentions were. He is quoted as saying of trade union organisations, '... whose permission you need before you can even turn over in bed.' (Johnson et al, 1984: 35)

Sheila and Anne had started roughly at the same time and were quite friendly with each other, so as a result, Sheila took Anne to one side and warned her to back away from the union idea. I'd different treatment which included a telling off for going to work wearing campaign badges. Then came the straw that broke the camel's back, I questioned a decision and was hauled into Sheila's office for another bollocking. Sitting there listening to her legitimising bullying was more than I was prepared to take. I told her I didn't accept her argument and therefore wasn't prepared to be as gutless as she was; and I quit. The rest of my team looked on in utter disbelief when I returned to the classroom and began packing my things before leaving.

Anne caught up with me later at home and we were discussing what had happened when a senior manager called Brian arrived on our doorstep. He was invited in; a nice man who had worked at Brockmoor when it was a steel plant. He shook my hand, saying he was sorry to see me go, but then added: 'Bob, I am ashamed; I wish I'd your guts and could tell Meredith where he could stick his job. Good on you.' Many felt the same way and Anne by now was among them. We'd been through a lot together, including Anne putting her life at risk when I was learning to drive a new mini my Mum helped me to buy. That wasn't the only time her life was at risk. One winter morning we walked to work in the snow arm-in-arm. Near the bottom of Adelaide Street, I slipped and kicked both of her feet him under her, thus ensuring we ended up on our backs in the middle of the snow -covered road.

Leaving Brierley Hill had been presented a number of problems because I was both homeless and jobless. A friend of mine called Fran allowed me to stay awhile till I'd secured a base. Fran and I'd met a few years earlier on a coach going down to a National Abortion Campaign march. She was an art therapist who worked in a large hospital in the north side of Birmingham with people who had learning difficulties. Fran and her colleague Anna were friends who were outside of my usual circle of friends. However, my friend Carlos and Fran went out together for a while which felt a little strange because it brought different relationships together for me. My stay at Fran's was always a stop gap because I knew how much she liked her own space but we both knew we could only tolerate each other for a short length of time.

One summer we had gone on a sightseeing tour of the Republic of Ireland together visiting places such as Limerick, Dundalk and Dublin. We did cross the border into the North and visited Newry. It was only after visiting Newry, did I really grasp the nature of

'Britishness' as viewed through the eyes of the Loyalist minority; although Newry has quite a unique history in terms of community politics. Roughing it in YMA hostels meant I was fairly reliant on Fran for support and felt comfortable with her understanding impairment related issues. Staying in a beautifully located hostel resulted in me writing a number of poems that eventually appeared in my second poetry pamphlet I published.

During my time staying at Fran's house I experienced a blatant form of employment discrimination. Given my interest in race and racism, I applied to become a Race Awareness Trainer with Thamesdown and District Council for Racial Equality, based in Swindon. It was a strange experience because after I arrived for my interview, I was informed that it wouldn't be going ahead as they hadn't realised that I'd a speech impairment and in their opinion the people they identified as requiring training wouldn't take someone like me seriously. I was far from happy with this appraisal and decided not to take this rebuff lying down. I could've left immediately, but decided that if all the other candidates were being taken out to lunch; why should I miss out? Besides, I wanted to make them feel uncomfortable by having to communicate with me. After I returned to Birmingham I wrote to the Minister of Disabled People, Tony Newton, and the shadow minister, Alf Morris, complaining about my treatment. Shortly before visiting Anne in Zimbabwe I received a copy of a letter Newton sent to Morris in which he wrote:

> I am, with their consent, enclosing a copy of their response since it seems to me to present a very full and frank explanation of their position.

Although I'd offered testimonies on my ability to train, the Minister accepted their justification for turning me down. A local newspaper reporter also sided with the Minister's point of view. It's important to remember that while

Newton had judged that I'd no grounds to complain of unjustifiable discrimination, we were still a decade away from disabled people having any legal redress in terms of challenging discrimination.

This was one of a number of incidents which brought home to me the fact that disabled people were in the same position they were in when I'd had my discussions with UPIAS; subjected to exclusion, marginalisation and discrimination. Taking about my frustrations to Paul Gilroy made me realise I'd little or no knowledge of what had happened with UPIAS and he suggested there was no point moaning about it if I wasn't prepared to do anything about it. I believe this was the trigger I needed to renew my interest in disability politics.

Being unemployed meant I'd quite a lot of time of my hands and some of this was spent doing research at the Birmingham Trade Union Resource Centre. A major influence on my future political direction was Steve Faulkner who was a Workers Educational Association tutor at the time. The last I heard about Steve, who has been a trade union activist for over forty years, was in relation to his role as a leader of the South African Municipal Workers Union in 2014. I regularly spoke to Steve after IMG meetings and after the debacle in Swindon he offered me a few hours co-training on a course helping unemployed people understand the benefits system and acquire improved social skills.

As our friendship grew, he introduced me to the people at 'Turk' – Birmingham Trade Union Resource Centre – and persuaded me to join his union branch of the Association of Scientific, Technical and Managerial Staffs (ASTMS) which was called Birmingham City 451 Branch. I remained in the Union, (which changed its name to Manufacturing, Science and Finance (MSF) in 1988,) for seventeen years. Through MSF I believe I helped make an important contribution to the development of disability politics within the trade union movement. I was aided by two tremendous disabled trade union activists called,

Mike Bramley and Caroline Gooding, both of whom are sadly no longer with us. In a later chapter I'll discuss how the three of us created the Trade Union Disability Alliance (TUDA). Through my Union I eventually became a delegate to Birmingham Trades Council and subsequently became a prominent figure within the local labour movement. A campaign body called, No One Is Illegal, published a pamphlet entitled, *Workers Control Not Immigration Controls*, in 2006 which reported:

> It's also now a legitimate trade union practice to support members under threat of deportation. For instance, UNISON and its forerunner NALGO, has consistently and actively campaigned against the deportation of its members since it successfully fought in the early 1980's the threatened deportation of Mohammed Idrish, a worker from Birmingham.

I was heavily involved in Mohammed's campaign and can remember a trip to Bristol with him on a cold Friday night in the back of a saloon. (*Socialist Challenge*, 1983; 11) My political activities changed significantly at the end of 1982 when the IMG changed its name to the Socialist League and begun the process of entrism in the Labour Party and this was followed up in March 1983 with the newspaper, *Socialist Challenge,* changing its name to *Socialist Action*.

During 1983 I shared a house in Small Heath with a fellow Socialist League member who was already a member of Sparkbrook Labour Party, so it made sense for me to join that Branch. It was an interesting period in my political education because Roy Hattersley was the local Member of Parliament and Sparkbrook Labour Party was well policed by an Irishman called John O'Keefe via a social club on the Stratford Road. One thing that struck me as strange was John's willingness to allow Birmingham Trades Council to use the Labour Club for its weekly Miners Support Meetings in 1984; perhaps it was the 'Irish connection' with Mick Rice the Trades Council's

Secretary and Mick Barr who was a Labour Party activist that paved the way. These meetings nevertheless made him feel uncomfortable as Paul Mackney recalls: 'O'Keefe got very upset when *Banner Theatre* sang a song which described AEU's General Secretary, Duffy as 'yellow and fluffy'!' I can also remember how John's eyes would narrow each time I made an intervention and I believe one night he came up to me after a meeting and said that he was watching me!

My association with Paul Mackney begun through the Birmingham Trades Council and he became another person who had a huge impact upon my political development. Paul was elected as the NATFHE representative to Birmingham Trades Council in the late 1970s, eventually becoming Vice-President and President. He pushed for establishment of the Birmingham Trade Union Resource Centre. Together we represented the Trades Council on the local Manpower Services Commission. He remains one of a number of longstanding political activists I remain in touch with.

As part of my political work during 1983 and into 1984, I became involved with the magazine, *Labour Briefing* at a national level. This I believe this is a fair description of how things were:

> While the magazine's followers often acted as a political faction, its internal politics were non-sectarian and open, ranging from democratic socialist backers of the former Labour MP Tony Benn to some of the Trotskyist groups. (Barberis et al., 2000; 284)

Perhaps a high spot for me came in 1984 when I was invited to chair a *Labour Briefing* meeting in Birmingham where Ken Livingstone and Tariq Ali spoke about their book, *Who's Afraid of Margaret Thatcher?: In Praise of Socialism*. Many on the political Left might be surprised to learn that the third speaker on the platform that night was

Margaret Beckett who has since travelled to the right within the Labour Party.

I want to return to my friendship within Anne briefly because I took a month out of my campaigning and research to pay her a visit. A few months after I left DVSC, Anne was offered a teaching post in Zimbabwe by the Catholic Institute for International Relations. It was agreed I'd spend Christmas and New Year in Harare with her and a small group of teachers and doctors at the central house owned by CIIR. I arranged a cheap flight with Balkan Airlines which meant a twenty three hour journey zigzagging across Europe and Africa. On the homeward journey the crew, well-built women, wouldn't let me off the plane in Libya, 'for my own safety' and neither would they serve me alcoholic drinks during the flight; given their demeanour, I wasn't going to argue! Well into the Outward trip I sat with a woman from Sierra Leone and shared a speechless joke when we looked at each other incredulously as the main meal we were being served was identical to the one we had been given the day before!

The month I spent in Zimbabwe was brim-full with incidents and a time I'll never forget. The people we stayed with were fantastic people, especially the three doctors, and I'd a whale of a time, for example: imagine eating Christmas Dinner on a veranda in the sunshine. I've spoken already about my experience as a disabled person living in Wivenhoe, but being out and about in Zimbabwe was unlike anything I've experienced in my life; the weight of oppression was generally speaking taken off my shoulders apart from two ugly incidents. In British repressed culture, the way the general public address visible signs of impairment, tends to be either to deny or shun its existence or to turn the person with the impairment into 'public property' by asking intrusive and often negatively laden questions. In Zimbabwe there was a different cultural approach in the sense that people would be more quizzical and direct rather than intrusive or judgmental – objective rather than subjective in terms of trying to understand who and what I was. People would simply ask: 'Why are you like that?' Once I'd said I was born this way, they would accept this in a matter-of-fact way and go on with their business. The exception to this rule was a middle aged white woman who decided to take the piss out of me in the centre of Woolworths; ironic don't you think?

Our trip to Victoria Falls was one of my lasting memories; the beauty was breath-taking, with millions of darting rainbows and showers from the spray cascading down, leaving us drenched one minute and dry to the bone next. This has to be contrasted with coming across a fatal accident where up to a dozen people were lying badly injured, dead or dying. The two doctors in the car with Anne and me immediately went into automatic mode and did what they could, but us pair of course had to remain sitting in the role of ghoulish bystanders. In another action-packed incident, I was mugged by a woman in a bar, however unknown to either the woman or her accomplice, there was an off duty policeman in the bar and he anticipated what was going down and was waiting to arrest them when they tried to escape. I was lucky to get my wallet back.

Being around Christmas and New Year, Anne dragged me off to a number of parties and before one of them she explained that she knew I'd only know her, but I could nevertheless chill by the pool. No sooner had we crossed the threshold, Anne was wishing she'd kept quiet because there was a chorus of: 'Hello Bob, what are you doing out here?' A party of Lefties what were the chances of knowing someone? With a smirk Anne said, 'Should've known better; can't take you anywhere without you knowing people; even in bloody Africa!' At another party we were among only a few white people there and it was a strange experience being a racial minority for a change. My feeling of liberation was heightened too because of a beautiful example of Zimbabwean hospitality which illustrates the point I was making earlier. Anne went off to the toilet leaving me alone to finish off a drink and no sooner had I done so, a woman from the other side of the room crossed over, picked a fresh bottle out of the create and replenished my glass, and returned to her seat. Only a smile was exchanged between us.

Talking of Zimbabwean hospitality, Anne also found it hilarious that on New Year's Eve when a group of us were having a drink in a Hotel bar before going onto a Thomas Mapfumo concert, (which lasted six hours), a young woman sat at the next table, kept inviting me to spend the evening with her. After my previous incident; I decided the best bet was to go to the concert! What a month that was and, not surprisingly, I'd tears in my eyes as the plane taxied on the runway. I was going from sunshine to the cold reality of a bleak future or, so I thought at the time.

I've no recollection of how I heard about a temporary research job, no memory of applying and thinking back, I'm amazed I managed to secure my first interview via completing an application form. Must have done something right because I was interviewed by a panel of three which was headed by Mrs Cynthia Lennard, who was the Director of Solihull Voluntary Service Council; a middle aged conservative lady. Once in post however everything slowly went downhill. It was my first adventure into full-time employment without back-up at the age of thirty and I was extremely naive if I'm honest. The post was a short-term research project investigating the needs and interests of young disabled people in the Solihull Borough. Why I thought I could do the job is lost in the midst of time, but what is interesting is that I must've thought my own 'personal' knowledge and empathy would carry me through and as a consequence it was to be my first faltering steps back into the world of disability. I do recall visiting various institutions trying to get a grasp of how the land lay in terms of existing services. My downfall however was the task of putting together a questionnaire to go out to young disabled people. It's impossible to know whether my first draft was crap or not; what was clear was Mrs Lennard had decided it wouldn't do.

Under her instruction I was to be supervised by a local college lecturer who was on the Council's committee. At first, he seemed okay, this nondisabled guy roughly my own age, but it soon became obvious he was a nasty snakehead intent on setting me up to fail so that he could covert the research project for himself. Each week he would set me tasks to do with the survey and I'd diligently carry them out to the letter, but during supervision he would move the goalposts and claim I hadn't listened or done it right. Two months into the project I was let go and I remember being told how disappointed everyone was. They told me that I secured the job because they thought that as a disabled person, I'd automatically know what young disabled people wanted and where they could be located. Any disappointment I was feeling was quickly subsumed under a mental image of me having some kind of invisible tracking antennae sticking out the top of my head! Disabled people communicate via telepathy or we all 'know' what each other are thinking, of course. Years later I was faced by a similar challenge, gathering and disseminating information from and to disabled people, however as we will see, I was slightly better equipped to deal with addressing the barriers that exist than I was back in 1983.

Despite this negative experience it was my first faltering steps towards getting involved in disability politics and was in many ways a watershed moment because I believe it marked a turning point in my life. I saw myself change from being a person with an impairment who was a political activist into becoming a leading disability rights activist over the next decade.

Part Three

More than a left foot

Chapter 13

I'm gonna try and change the world

> Never doubt that a small group of thoughtful, committed citizens can change the world. Indeed, it's the only thing that ever has.
>
> Margaret Mead

In the previous chapter I spoke about my conversation with Paul Gilroy in relation to the discrimination experienced by disabled people. It followed my awful treatment in Swindon and various other incidents I'd had including a stupid parking ticket I received during a visit to TURC. Since leaving Oakwood I'd had very little direct contact with many disabled people and had no knowledge of the emergence of the Disabled People's Movement. By a strange quirk of fate shortly after speaking with Paul I'd obtained a copy of *Disability Now* and within the advertisement section was a planned meeting in London organised by the Liberation Network of People with Disabilities to discuss setting up a Disability Resource Centre. I decided to go along and see what was being said by other disabled people. Alan Sutherland (2006; unpaged) I believe is right when he wrote:

The general political outlook of Network members was libertarian/left. One early member had trade union experience, I'd been part of the radical news collective People's News Service, and I think the late Chris Harrison had previously been a member of IMG, but on the whole we had little experience of conventional left politics. No-one came to Network meetings selling copies of 'The Next Step'.

Chris was the only person I knew in the Network, but that was to do with our association with the IMG. Attending this meeting was reminiscent of speaking with Paul Hunt; it was both new yet familiar at the same time. Part way through the meeting I realised I was with a group of people I could readily identify with; not simply because of the fact we all had impairments, but rather due to the shared experience of what I now call social oppression. It was the moment I rediscovered who I really was and wanted to be. The various forms of discrimination I experienced and going to the London meeting encouraged me to think again about how the State and society responded to the inequalities facing disabled people. It isn't going to be possible to do justice to the issues, people and events that surround the last third of my life as a disability rights activist, therefore I'm going to focus on recounting things that matter to me and the broader story I wish to tell.

Listening to people talking about creating a Disability Resource Centre in London made me reflect upon the type of groups and facilities that were available to disabled people in Birmingham. Further discussions and research revealed that very little beyond local authority and the voluntary sector existed. One organisation that did exist was the West Midlands Council for the Disabled (sic) which was based inside a hospital in Moseley. Was I simply trying to duplicate what they were doing? Although I was a relative newcomer to this field of political activity, I felt there was a world of difference

253

between what WMCD were doing and my vision of what a more radical approach would look like. Dr John Harrison (2002), a key player in establishing WMCD said:
Our mission statement in the first annual report was about acting as a liaison group, promoting education and information, and promoting (not providing) better services on the basis of our own experiences.

In Pete Millington's book, *Forward*, I am quoted as saying:

It was more geared around what I think we all know as the traditional building blocks: care, information, benefits. Very much the independency model of what we can do for the disabled people without actually analysing why disabled people would be excluded or marginalised within the mainstream sector. (2010; 33)

Without going into detail, what I was articulating here was the difference between the social democratic social welfare approach for example adopted by various charities under the umbrella organisation, the Royal Association for Disability and Rehabilitation (RADAR), as opposed to the more radical approach developed by UPIAS and then taken forward in the 1980s by the British Council of Organisations of Disabled People (BCODP). At this particular moment in time I still only had a rough and ready understanding of viewing disability as social oppression. At the time I wasn't aware that this was behind my disquiet, so it's enough for the time being to acknowledge that I felt there was something missing in the WMCD approach and I wanted to know if other disabled people agreed with me or not.

Following my initial contact with the Network I began writing a number of articles for them and local newsletters about discrimination and disabled people. Seeing the advert about the Network was the first of a number of pieces of good fortune. Within the local newspaper, *Birmingham Evening Mail*, there was a City Council call for applications for *Inner City Partnership Funding* and I mentioned this during a visit to TURC. A visitor there overheard me talking and told me that the partner of an associate of ours was one of the City Officers involved with ICCP grants and I should speak with her. The advisor was Marion Bowles and neither of us knew at the time that our first meeting would develop into a working relationship and friendship that would last for a number of years. I told Marion my plans and she was impressed, but the rub came when she asked about the 'organisation' I was representing. The blood visibly drained from my face; there wasn't one 'yet'. With a deadline fast approaching I had to take a gamble and have faith in my own ability to draw other disabled people into my project. This wasn't an ideal way to proceed, but sometimes needs require taking short cuts, and overnight the Birmingham Disability Rights Group was born. Assisted by Marion I wrote a constitution with broad aims and objectives.

As Millington writes:

> Bob managed to produce a leaflet about the group and a flyer which could be used to promote meetings. He booked the group's first meeting at Tindal Street School in Balsall Heath and began distributing the promotional flyers everywhere and to everyone he met. (2010; 34)

It was a disaster, no one came. I realised I was trying too hard to make things happen and a different method was required. I still used the leaflet but relied more and more on individual contact and word-of-mouth recruitment. Meetings were held with key members of WMCD, including their paid employee. Theresa and I'd a civil relationship over the years despite her becoming a Tory Councillor. I also believe the timing was right as Harrison (2002) recalled:

> .... in 1984-5 I was working on a national project on

NHS services for younger disabled people, which involved personal contact with a great many people in the disability movement in London and elsewhere. One or two who distrusted me being a medical professional. But overwhelmingly it was the experience in the WMCDP that gave me confidence in what was a fascinating, developing, national and international consensus and I made many friends.

I found John to be very supportive of my plans for BDRG. Perhaps it should also be noted that a number of WMCD members already knew of me because their Chairperson was Ted Marsland, the then Vice Chancellor of the University of Birmingham, and he had kept tabs on me when I was a student. Slowly the membership of BDRG grew from three close allies onto twelve and within eighteen months to two years we had recruited fifty people, both full members and nondisabled associates. This was only made possible because we had secured the ICP funding.

One of the earliest members of the BDRG was Maria Mleczko and when interviewed by Millington she recalled her initial involvement:

Originally it was just a monthly meeting and we talked about demonstrating, about public transport and whatever issue was around at the time. (2010; 35)

Away from politics and work, which was a form of political activity; my personal life was fairly routine for the most part and offered little excitement. Whilst I'd friends, including Steve who I shared a house with, I'd no personal relationships to speak of. A friend of Fran's and I would meet up for a chat on a regular basis, but it soon became clear that my approach to the relationship and the way she viewed it was vastly different. When I realised, I was being seen as a 'worthy cause' who needed entertaining, I ended the contact. Perhaps I'd become emotionally vulnerable since my days in Brierley Hill and was seeking safety. Whatever the truth as my career progressed so did my self-confidence and during a two-day weekend meeting of the Network, I got to know Claire Tregaskis who also has cerebral palsy. At the end of proceedings, we swapped details and soon after I invited Claire up to Birmingham for the weekend. Over the following months we would share time together at weekends in her flat. I recall visiting Claire's parents' house in Waddebridge and watched Band Aid before driving all the way back to Peterborough. Guess it was a reality check when she told me of her plans to join *Operation Raleigh* and go off to the Solomon Islands for six months.

Looking back, I realise Claire and I were at different stages in our lives and weren't looking at things from a shared perspective. It was an awkward parting of the ways but in recent years we've exchanged views on what took place, and both accept that period in our lives for what it was. I've followed her career over the years and there's no doubt it has been an impressive one. Being friends with Claire represented a good period in my life and I look back on it with fondness. Recently we've renewed our friendship which is good. While in reflective mode my relationship with the Liberation Network was of a similar nature; both at differing stages of political development. There were very few times of coming together face-to-face but over the last thirty three years I've had various degrees of contact with a core group of Network members who were, and some still are, quirky individuals who have made unique contributions to disabled people's struggle for liberation.

The majority of 1985 I spent much of my time working out of the front room at 33 Cyril Road in Sparkbrook trying to recruit members to the Group as well as developing and delivering what was then called Disability Awareness Training. As Kath Gillespie-Sells and Jane

Campbell (1991; 4) explained:

> Forms of .... [Disability Equality Training] have been
> organised and run by disabled people for over ten
> years, but it has developed a formalised structure
> only since 1985. Around that time emphasis began to
> be placed on equal opportunities policies and
> practices towards women, black and minority ethnic
> people and lesbians and gays. It seemed a natural
> extension to include disabled people under the same
> equal opportunities umbrella.

There are political issues involved here. By viewing
Disability Equality Training as an equal opportunities
issue there was a political compromise introduced which
shifted away from the radical analysis of UPIAS that saw
disablement intrinsically linked to the systems and
structures of capitalist society, towards an approach
which focused upon reducing or removing disabling
barriers. The rationale behind this is explained by
Gillespie-Sells and Jane Campbell (1991; 4) in the
following way:

> In order for people to understand why policies were
> necessary and why their work behaviour needed to
> change to accommodate good equal opportunities
> working practices, a range of training and education
> programmes was established. The area of disability
> was left until last so work around disability
> awareness (as it was then known) did not get off the
> ground until after racism and other awareness
> training. This worked in its favour, however, as
> disability awareness trainers learnt from the
> successes and mistakes of their colleagues working
> around the other issues.

I'd been training for a number of years before being
invited to join the group of trainers Kath and Jane worked

with and switched to calling it DET. I worked within the broad structure spoken of above however where possible I included a session on 'Disability History'. It was through undertaking DAT for a group of unemployed community volunteers that I met by first wife Brenda. In my opinion I must be the longest serving DE Trainer in the United Kingdom as I continued to train until I semi-retired in 2016.

I was tempted to leave out the fact that quite a lot of my time over a two year period was also spent on a flawed attempt to write a book called, *Coming to terms with Disability*, which was to be a political account of disabled people's issues. I obtained a £200 advance from Pluto Press, but I look back in embarrassment because I recognise now how naive I was in thinking I'd enough knowledge to begin such a project. Six or seven draft chapters are still lurking in my house somewhere on floppy disks! Perhaps I'm being slightly harsh on myself because during that period I did develop some theoretical arguments I continue to advocate.

By 1986 the committee of BDRG were keen to establish a proper office with a full-time worker and I insisted that the recruitment process was open, transparent and democratic. I resigned from the committee and applied for the post of Development Worker. Three people were interviewed, and I was offered the post. BDRG had four areas of work to focus on:

1. To bring together people with disabilities from across the City with the aim of organising to extend and promote their needs and rights.
2. To organise activities with and for people with disabilities, including those who remain at home or who cannot travel far. Our project will include investigating the feasibility of a Disability Centre run by and for people with disabilities.
3. To help build self-confidence and activity through the development and promotion of

Disability Awareness.
4. To ensure that the local communities are aware of
   the needs and interests of people with disabilities.
   This requires making links with organisations
   which serve those communities.

Pete Millington captures the situation when he wrote:

> Within a few months Bob and his growing team
> published *Building Bridges* the newsletter of BDRG.
> Produced in its early years on a very tight budget,
> sometimes two or three typed and photocopied A4
> paper held together by a staple in the top left hand
> corner, *Building Bridges* generally made up in content
> what it lacked in design impact. (2010; 37)

I remember proposing the name of the newsletter to the
Management Committee but Roy Benjamin, a visually
impaired Labour Councillor, wasn't too impressed and
suggested we used *Building Bridges* only until something
better was put forward. The name lasted as long as BDRG
did; going into the mid-1990s. Today I smile when I see
that Chelsea Football Club's equality programme is called,
Building Bridges.

BDRG influenced by me followed the Network's lead
of talking of 'people with disabilities' as opposed to
talking about 'disabled people'. In the early years there
were heated political debates among disabled people and
their organisations as to preferred terminology and over
time as BDRG worked closer with the British Council of
Organisations of Disabled People (BCODP) which led to
BDRG shifting our position on what was the most useful
term to use. I believe many of the debates that raged, and
still do in some quarters, fail to acknowledge that the
meaning of 'disability' is contested and struggled over
and as a result both terms are subjected to ideological
interpretations which means neither 'disabled people' nor
'people with disabilities' have singular meanings. Words

of course have different meanings and these change over time. The word 'disability' has its roots in legal and 'medical' contexts.

Why, for example, did John Stuart Mill talk about 'women with disabilities' in his essay, 'The subjugation of Women'? It's because of the legal definition of disenfranchisement is: .... the state of being deprived of a right or privilege, especially the right to vote. Unfortunately, perhaps, we usually see the focus on women not being allowed to own property or to vote, but this is a narrow interpretation. Looking at it in a broader context, 'the state of being deprived of a right' is understood to be a 'disability' e.g. a social restriction. This is how I defined 'people with disabilities' whilst at BGRG – those with impairments who were subjected to unequal and differential treatment which deprived them of specific rights.

There were quite a number of personal and political developments in 1986. I'd left Steve's house at the end of 1985 to share a flat with Brenda Hall who had two sons by a previous marriage and in March 1986 we were married. I've taken the decision not to write in any detail about either of my marriages beyond simple matter-of-fact statements and so at this point in time I just want to acknowledge that it was quite challenging at times finding one's self with a ready-made family. Brenda had already become an associate member of BDRG and was doing a lot of work behind the scenes. By a quirk of fate, we attended a Liberation Network meeting together at the end of the year and one of the first people we ran into was Claire.

For a short period, Maria Mleczko understudied me as a Disability Equality Trainer as I saw this as a good way to bring her out of her shell and build her self-confidence. Within two years she had grown to the point where she was able to become Chair of BDRG. Her replacement as a Trainer at BDRG was Alun Davies who was a visually impaired social work graduate. In a similar way to my recruiting of Maria, I'd gone out my way to draw in Alun. I'd spotted real potential in him however for quite a while he resisted my advances! It was good then that Alun and Maria went together to a national conference on Centres for Integrated Living as this was BDRG's first engagement with the Disabled People's Movement.

November 1986 was an important month for BDRG. Members of BDRG appeared on ITV's *LINK programme* to discuss the issue of language and disability and this was a follow up to a feature on BDRG I did earlier in the year. However, our priority was a lobby of Birmingham City Council with regards to having a Disability Resource Centre and disabled people having a representative voice in the City. This lobby took place following a face-to-face meeting between a BDRG delegation which I led, and a number of Councillors Roy had persuaded to meet us.

It was a long haul developing my idea for a Centre. We had gained some basic support, but it was decided to test the water with both organisations working with individual disabled people and individual disabled people themselves. It was still the era when the distinction between organisations for and of disabled people i.e. where mainly nondisabled people done *for* disabled people and self-organised groups *of* disabled people, hardly existed. Ironically perhaps, the first task I set myself was to design and send out a 'feasibility study questionnaire' in May 1987.

Not all the organisations responded and those that did offered mixed opinions. It was a real eye opener as some organisations reacted angrily to being 'associated with the disabled' (sic) and others were keen to protect their own power base whilst rejecting the very idea that disabled people could ever self-organise. The response from disabled people themselves was far more encouraging and so it was agreed to go one step further and organise a conference to discuss what a Disability Resource Centre might look like. Sometimes we forget what these early days of the emerging Disabled People's

Movement were like!

A major part of my life outside, but linked to BDRG, during this year was campaigning in support of two married disabled couples. One couple with learning difficulties were fighting Wolverhampton City Council over custody of their child and Brenda and I became their major emotional support. Their situation became a national story when the *Mail on Sunday* covered it, but this required the four of us to stay in a secret location in Yorkshire for a week to ensure no other media interest. Unfortunately, despite our best efforts, we lost the legal battle and the judge placed restrictions on what could be said in public. I was far from impressed by the couple's legal team who had an obnoxious 'do-gooder' as its front man; and I've chosen my description carefully. Things I witnessed demonstrated to what degree the legal system was and largely still is 'institutionally discriminatory' in terms of its ignorance of impairment reality and the system's own inability to address the oppressive nature of disablement within society.

The other couple was in a battle over the issue of buying their own adapted council house. Alun and I'd many reservations about getting involved in this issue because we were not in support of Thatcher's 'right to buy' policy in the first place, however, we also believed the policy of not having the right to purchase an adapted home placed disabled tenants in a less favourable position. On paper the reason for this less favourable treatment was to ensure the house could be passed onto other disabled people thus saving money on more adaptations in an unsuitable property. In reality, we knew adapted houses were often transformed back into ordinary housing by councils once disabled tenants died or moved, so we keen to expose this hypocrisy. The law hasn't changed with the introduction of either the Disability Discriminatory Act 1995 or the Equality Act 2010. BDRG had campaigns where the outcomes were negative, but we also had our share of victories as well.

Although Alun was recruited to be the Disability Equality Trainer it wasn't long before we were working more as a 'team' with regards to BDRG's campaigning efforts. Quite often though we would also co-train and I recall a particularly difficult session with civil servants who worked on State Benefits. There was complete resistance towards our social approach towards disability and some participants sought to provoke us into being 'unprofessional' and losing it with them. The chemistry between us was so good that almost without any signals we both adopted an identical set of responses which completely deflated our antagonists.

This chemistry also came into play after I'd had a raging row with a well-known local journalist whose description of disabled people was appalling even by the poor standards of the late 1980s. Foolishly, perhaps, I sought to engage her in a discussion of the language she was employing, however, not only did she reject what I was saying she also began to question my inability to 'accept that I was severely handicapped' (sic). The sheer arrogance that lay within her delivery became too much for me and, feeling like a rat trapped in a corner, I went for the throat and told her to – well, you can imagine the two words I used! Returning to the office I relayed to Alun what had happened, and we decided to employ a damage limitation exercise before alerting our Committee. Alun phoned her and apologised on behalf of BDRG but I'd to leave the room fearing that I'd burst out laughing at the condescending way he was speaking to her.

There are many stories I could share about Alun and me, but perhaps the most remarkable one was when we went together to greet Archbishop Desmond Tutu the South African civil rights campaigner. Surrounded by hundreds of well-wishers I was able to push through and also guide Alun to the front of the queue of people seeking to shake his hand. What unfolded I'm unable to explain even to this day. As Archbishop Tutu walked along hands were being thrust out from all directions, I'd managed to catch hold of his but immediately felt a pang of guilt as I watched Alun's hand dangling forlorn in mid-air; however, it was as if time had frozen still because suddenly the two men's hands found each other's. I'll never forget the look of sheer joy on Alun's face.

Apart from contact with the Liberation Network, BDRG had been fairly isolated from other disabled people's organisations. Our use of language also was a barrier to a degree, for example, Anne Rae from Manchester Coalition of Disabled People had a heated exchange with me in 1988 within GMCDP's magazine *Coalition*. A number of leading figures within the BCODP were very wary of us, but by 1989 they accepted our membership. Pete Millington's book charts many of our activities through the late 1980s and through interviews outlines how very talented disabled people swelled our ranks. Trying to gain funding for a DRC was a protracted affair and took more and more of my time as I worked with a number of City Council officers to identify a site and specifications.

Whilst the central focus of this chapter has been the development of BDRG and why I approached disability politics the way I did, I've seen little point me repeating the material found in Pete's book, although saying this, in Pete's book I do come over as being rather intimidating and forceful; somewhat of a real task master whereas others have called me charismatic and outspoken. Is that really how people saw me? Perhaps it not for me to say, but I'd argue the importance of the years building BDRG can't easily captured in a book, especially one by me. Many Birmingham disabled activists helped to shape the landscape of the Disabled People's Movement since the 1980s and I believe I assisted them by offering a platform and a vision. There are too many BDRG members to name individually, but similar to the Network, there are a number of people I associate closely with BDRG, but also have had long friendships with. Dave Nugent was a friend who we lost far too soon and was someone who did fill my shoes to a degree. I've also remained friends with Maria Mleczko, Mark Lynes, Robin and Tracy Surgeoner. The legacy left by BDRG and its DRC project hasn't had the prominence I believe it deserves; Pete has done more than most to put this right. I'm biased, but I believe Birmingham City Council and certain of its staff are guilty of underplaying this legacy not only within the City but nationally as well.

It's also important to recall that as Coordinator of Projects for BDRG I was involved in more than campaigning and training; for example, I represented BDRG on the National Council of BCODP and was a member of the Birmingham Community Care Special Action Project's Search Team. The CCSAP was run by Tessa Jowell who had been a social worker with extensive experience of child and community care work. Tessa moved on from Birmingham to lead the Joseph Rowntree Foundation's Community Care Programme (1990-92) before entering Parliament as a Labour MP. In the three years in charge of CCSAP Tessa and I'd many exchanges of opinion, but it was a healthy, combative relationship and I believe she, and Lorna Shaw who was part of the Social Services Inspectorate, both appreciated the radical perspective I brought with me. I worked closely on a number of projects with Lorna in her role of administrating *The Search Team* which was a forum of professionals, carers and service users acting in a scrutiny role. Towards the end of the life of the CCSAP, a new vacancy opened up inside the Birmingham Social Services Department and I was encouraged by one of its Assistant Directors to apply.

This was a huge decision to make. Could I really leave BDRG and go from poacher to gamekeeper? On a personal level I felt I could finally 'let go of my baby' and allow others to share the responsibility for BDRG. Part of me felt I'd taken BDRG and the DRC project as far as I could and perhaps a fresh pair of eyes and commitment might take things forward in ways that I couldn't. I was also ready for a fresh challenge myself and I liked the idea of assisting in the planning of services for 'people with physical disabilities' (sic). However, when I began reading the material written by the existing Planning Officer – a sincere nondisabled professional – I almost changed my mind because the ideas and culture were so dated in my opinion. Would I survive even five minutes in such a hostile and backward environment?

Terry Vincent had been a long standing friend of Brenda's and had experience of campaigning on women's issues. After talking to me about BDRG she became a member and it was no surprise to me when the time came Terry was interested in replacing me as Coordinator. Pete writes:

> Terry recalls feeling a mounting sense of disquiet at having to step into Bob's shoes and continue to meet the high expectations of the group, especially about having to be a very public spokesperson on controversial issues. Bob was going to be a hard act for anybody to follow. (2010; 50)

Talking about letting go of my baby, this was also the period in my life when Brenda and I discussed having a child of our own. Having gone through the limited choices we had, we finally approached Barnardo's about adoption and this became a steep learning curve for everyone involved. In the early days we were met with a degree of resistance, but over time with the support of a very good social worker called, Julia, we worked to overcome the barriers. During the early part of 1989 I found myself driving back from Norfolk with two and a half year old Dominic alongside Brenda in the back. Dominic also had cerebral palsy, so we had to learn about his support needs. It may seem bizarre but being a disabled person meant that the chances of Brenda and me adopting a non-impaired child were almost nil, therefore adopting a disabled child, was the only option. Apart from practical issues neither of us had a problem with bringing further 'disability issues' into our family. Looking back, it's clear that we had underestimated how difficult things would be for us and I can recall a time when Julia turned up at the front door just as I was heading in the opposite direction having flipped out! As things do, we finally found a routine and life went on.

As the 1980s closed the prospect of a bright 1990s for disabled people and I looked possible. There was an air of optimism, but as we shall see, looks can be deceiving because despite putting the building blocks in place things didn't quite go quite to plan at either the local or national level. The creation of BDRG and engaging in disability politics laid the foundations for the rest of my life. The majority of the 1980s was taken up by my deepening awareness and commitment to disability politics. I'd become part of a growing political movement. The self-organisation of disabled people beginning in the late 1970s and early 1980s gave rise to a new social movement – the Disabled People's Movement – which sought to end disabled people's experience of inequality and social oppression. Over time the dynamics within this new social movement saw it slowly shift away from the historical materialist radical overview of the need for a transformation of society. BCODP which was at the core of the Disabled People's Movement was an umbrella organisation for disabled people's organisations and it allowed its members to hold a variety of interpretations of what has become known as 'the social model of disability'. In reality these 'interpretations' created new social models based upon a spectrum of political opinion, but this wasn't necessarily a deliberate or a conscious act.

With hindsight I believe too little attention was paid to how *the* social model was being articulated by activists, trainers and others. The Disabled People's Movement therefore embraced disabled revolutionary Marxists like me through to Conservative thinkers such as Stephen Bradshaw who became Chair of the campaign group

Rights Now! Before looking at the massive upheavals in the 1990s, I want to end this chapter with a quotation from Andy Beaton who has had a long association with the DRC which began when he became the officer with responsibility for the DRC's service agreement on behalf of the Economic Development Unit of the City Council. Andy paid me the following tribute in Pete's book:

> The energy and enthusiasm of Bob Findlay is legend and he brought so much into it. Again he brought a very strong campaigning view to it, but a very overall understanding of managing an organisation. He was always a man to keep to his word and commitment to a particular issue. Again, I found Bob great to work with. (2010; 92)

Chapter 14

From both sides now

Both Sides, Now is, at first, a meditation on clouds, the whimsical way a child sees them, as 'ice-cream castles in the air,' but there are two sides to everything, and as we mature, we stop seeing clouds for their simple beauty, but as a sign of rain or bad weather. It's like that with all things that seem at first so simple and beautiful, such as love and life. We start out with such natural optimism as children, and then as adults we tend to learn a bitter pessimism or brutal honesty, seeing clouds/life/love for what they are.

Catherine MacLellan

The first half of the 1990s saw massive changes in my career, political activities and personal life. Being viewed as changing from poacher to gamekeeper raised all kinds of questions. At times I saw both sides of an argument which made life uncomfortable, especially when neither camp saw me as being one of them. Trying to be both a professional and an activist is never easy because the risk of unjustifiable compromise is always a whiff away.

Looking back, it was probably a mistake for me to take over as Chair of BDRG so soon after stepping down as its key worker, but we all thought it would provide both support for Terry and stability for BDRG for a short while. Campaigning for a DRC had taken almost half a decade and with hindsight I feel so much of my energy and that of others had gone into this, we had collectively neglected to build BDRG as a grass roots organisation. When the Disability Resource Centre was up and running, the relationship between BDRG and the DRC became problematic.

I wasn't convinced that the responsibility for both the day-to-day running of the DRC and the maintaining of BDRG as a campaigning organisation should fall upon the shoulders of a small management committee. There was the added problem that the funders would raise objections to money from the Council for service agreements ending up being used for political campaigning. At the BDRG Annual General Meeting it was agreed that the DRC would have its own autonomous committee, but a portion of its members would be elected from BDRG.

The new Co-ordinator of Projects, Terry Vincent, was a BDRG member but despite this fact BDRG members began to sense they were being marginalised within the new DRC. Robin Surgeoner, a leading member of BDRG is quoted as saying:

> It ended up with a board and a new set of employees. Even though the inception of the Resource Centre was BDRG's, the lead started to be dictated rather than being organic. If BDRG had been given the money, the management and had become the employer, that would have been a different story. I don't mean that in a sour grapes way, I just think that wasn't allowed to happen. It became the council's baby, it became the council's Disability Resource Centre. It lost that organic, that dynamism that came from BDRG. (2010; 68)

Whilst I don't fully agree with Robin's take, I do acknowledge there is a grain of truth in it. Pete's book notes for example that Derek Farr, as Treasurer and then Chair, moved the centre along the route of a service delivery model whilst acknowledging the need for a campaigning side of it. Over the next five years the change in personalities associated with the DRC did move it further and further away from the original vision that both I and BDRG had for it. I'm not sure how significant it was, but it wasn't too long before I stepped back from this role as well because I saw a conflict between being chair of BDRG and being an officer in the Birmingham Social Services Department. I believed at the time the best way I could serve BDRG and the Disabled People's Movement was to continue to be on the National Council of BCODP.

The two years I spent in Birmingham Social Services were very challenging. I saw the task as being similar to trying to turn a large oil tanker around because the culture was so alien. According to my letter of contract I'd become a Co-ordinator and Development Officer in Policy, Planning and Review however this wasn't the title employed. At the time there was no pressure in Birmingham to move away from the language of 'people first' therefore I was known as the Planning Officer for People with Physical Disabilities. I disliked the term because it continued the collapsing together of impairment and disability issues. Almost from the beginning I found myself having to address the power relations within the Department.

It wasn't simply a question of having to persuade people to accept my push for a cultural shift within the Department, there was the added problem of having to overcome how I was being viewed by my colleagues. The most graphic example of this was an early morning visit to meet the Manager of an Adult Training Centre. I walked up to the receptionist and said, 'Good morning, I – ', however with one movement she was out of her chair and sprinting to the door bellowing, 'Tom, Tom come quickly, I've a client in my office!'

Despite my appeals for her to stop and listen to me,

this bruiser called Tom, rushed in and attempted to drag me out by my arm. Within seconds the Manager arrived and didn't mince his words as the air turned blue. The last line he said was classic, 'Hope you realise you've just mishandled someone from Head Office!' The look on their faces was priceless. It wasn't uncommon for me to be seen as a 'service user upstart' rather than a fellow professional. Over time I did gain respect, especially from frontline managers I worked with, because I proved I was knowledgeable and wouldn't accept bullshit. My first meeting had set the tone because I quietly sat and listened to them talking about 'special needs this' and 'special needs that' for ten minutes and then I called the meeting to a halt. 'As the new kid on the block,' I said, 'perhaps one of you might like to explain this 'special needs' jargon to me.' All eyes dropped to the floor and there was silence. I explained my objections to this meaningless euphemism and informed them that unless they could define what it meant in concrete terms; I didn't want to hear it used in my company. This notion of 'special needs', as I suspected it would, had become just another oppressive label instead of a means of identifying disabling barriers.

A major Department wide initiative I was involved in featured developing a new assessment process under the recently introduced Community Care Act. I detailed how this project unfolded in a chapter entitled, *Community care and assessment: the Birmingham approach,* which appeared in: A challenge to change. In this chapter (1992; 77) I explained that:

> We wanted the people who were being assessed to help establish the agenda. The introduction to the section thus says: 'Do you have any needs or concerns arising from your daily living activities? These might include for example: needing someone to help you, the length of time it takes to do things, particular activities that are difficult, lack of

equipment, lack of opportunity to do certain things, unhappiness with existing help you have etc. Please give examples so we can have an overall picture.'

Despite the tremendous amount of work that went into the redesign of the assessment process and its radical approach, there was fierce opposition to its open-endedness from Occupational Therapists and Social Workers who preferred the traditional tick box approach to 'identifying needs'. It's somewhat ironical then that a major criticism of the new approach was that it: 'focused upon what people *can't* do.' The fact that the questions sought to tease out the negative interactions between the individual and their social environment was completely lost on these nondisabled professionals. The focus wasn't on what was *wrong* with the individual, but rather how living with impairments meant people encountered social restrictions and therefore their support needs should be around reducing or removing these barriers. I was drawing upon the concept of independent living developed in the United States where it was seen as being 'a living arrangement that maximizes independence and self-determination, especially of disabled persons living in a community instead of in a medical facility.' Perhaps as an aside I can express the opinion that twenty five years on, I believe Birmingham City Council remains utterly clueless when it comes to really understanding concepts such as self-determination and independent living.

One of the benefits of working for Birmingham City Council was that it encouraged people to attend training and conferences. BCODP were sending a sizeable delegation to the Disabled People's International World Congress III between 21-26 April1992 in Vancouver, British Columbia, Canada. Alongside the Congress was an Exposition on Disability called, *Independence '92*, and I made a case for going. I argued that this exposition would allow me to mingle with International experts in the field of disability and bring home a wealth of intelligence.

Phil Heard, Vice President of New Business Development, is quoted as saying:

> 'Our success will be measured by our ability to attract the right group of international delegates,' Phil explains. 'Our goal is to get these people to go back to their countries, cities and villages with the will and power, to make changes for the disabled community. We want to reach the decision makers.'

In one sense I believed I was pushing my luck and perhaps over yoking the egg, however, as it turned out it was one of the most rewarding events I've ever attended. Yes, I still have the tee-shirt to prove it!

Within the Book of Abstracts for *Independence '92* there were over a hundred presentations spanning the five days. The themes were: Community and Independent Living, Economic Independence, Education, Equality, Full Participation, Posters, Social Change Strategies and Technologies. I've listed these for a number of reasons, but essentially, I believe the topics give a clear insight into the central areas of disabled people's lives and how, in turn, these inform disability politics. I'm not in a position to recall all the sessions I attended however one stood out above all the rest.

As a disabled person and an activist, I was all too familiar with acts of discrimination and social exclusion, nevertheless the question of what has become known as 'disability hate crime' wasn't fully formed in my mind. Spending two hours listening to harrowing personal testimonies of people who had experience of 'disability hate crime' made me realise how important an issue it was for disabled people worldwide. I vowed to ensure the British Disabled People's Movement took the issue seriously.

One funny incident occurred on the final evening in Vancouver when we all went out for a delegation meal. I was sat next to a lanky fellow called John Speak who was from Preston. John had athetoid cerebral palsy which is characterized by involuntary movement and, as a result, this presented quite a challenge in the tight confines of a downtown Vancouver restaurant. His speech was also significantly affected which added to the difficulties of communicating in a crowded place. So, with spaghetti flying everywhere, John asked me what I did for a living. I'll never forget the look of horror on his face as he violently recoiled at the news that I worked for Birmingham Social Services. If we hadn't been so tightly seated, he would've fallen off his chair!

The week I spent in Vancouver was significant for a number of reasons not least of which was the time I spent with the BCODP delegation which included Lucille Lusk, co-chair of BCODP and its Chief Executive, Richard Wood. Not only did I develop a good working relationship with them, I also deepened our personal friendships. Lucille was a grass roots Scottish disabled activist who spoke with both passion and conviction. Unknown to me at the time, we were going to lose Lucille too soon and the friendship between Richard and I was going to be tested to the limit. Jane Campbell reminded me that:

> Lucille and I co-chaired for nearly 2 years but she became very unwell, so stood down and spent the last years of her short life with family, friends and her much adored caravan.

Jane and I both think she died of a heart attack end of 1994 or early 1995. Either way, disabled people lost a true champion. The week away also produced the first signs to show that I was becoming restless with both my career and life in general. Whilst my trip to Vancouver was a success and I returned with lots of useful information, the experience had nevertheless unsettled me.

The constant battle to develop positive policies and enact real social change was beginning to take its toll on me. On reflection I believe I'd grown isolated at work because many of the people who had supported the desired 'cultural shift' had left during my two years there and had been replaced by staid bureaucrats who sought to keep the status quo. It's hard to say how much progress I really made as the resistance to change was huge; but three policies in particular stand out. The largest of these was trying to radically transform the use of Day Centre provision. This process had been begun internally by the Centres managers, so through a service review I was simply trying to steer it further along the lines of using the Centres as a resource base instead of the traditional warehousing of people with physical impairments. The huge task of transforming the activities and culture of the four Day Centres for people with physical impairments was in the hands of their managers with me trying to ensure an overarching policy. The majority were willing to work with me and share ideas with the aim of arriving at a holistic approach; however, there was one manager who resented being 'told what to do' by a policy officer or perceived potential service user.

No doubt some disabled people, like for example John Speak, might've questioned why I of all people would be trying to transform Day Centres; why not just close the bloody things down? On paper this makes sense, disablement resulted in segregated provision therefore surely as a disabled activist, I ought to favour a policy that promoted inclusive practice? All things being equal, that would've been a logical position to take, however, segregation isn't just a physical phenomenon. Many of the service users had no or little experience of daily routines other than being warehoused, therefore as a result, they had no personal or collective vision of an alternative way of life because what they had was what they knew. In many ways it's like the prison system where many prisoners re-offend in order to have the security of the institution they had come to rely upon.

It was a learning curve for me because I'd to face

ideological conflicts; did I really want to 'improve' segregated provision? I quickly realised that idealistic desires rarely matched material reality. Would closing the Day Centres really benefit disabled people who had become institutionalised over many years? I saw people who would be isolated at home if some organised community activities weren't available. Issues such as Independent Living were still in their infancy. De-institutionalisation can't be a quick fix where people are dumped into 'their communities' and expected to cope with little or no support. Ending the social oppression of disabled people can't be achieved simply by introducing measures to integrate them into existing structures or practices because too often these approaches set disabled people up to fail. What I sought to do is borrow the philosophy I adopted with the DRC and work towards moving Day Centres into being a gateway into communities.

With the support of the managers I drafted my Adult Day Centre review, but it immediately hit a snag when an Assistant Director went ballistic at the proposal to completely overhaul how the in-house transport system worked. There were set times for picking up and returning home – the idea of having a more flexible system was deemed unthinkable not to mention unmanageable given the cost factors. Over the last twenty five years we have seen the shift from Community Care to Social Care which coincided with the marketisation of services through the adoption of neoliberal policies. With hindsight I was on the cusp of this ideological and managerial shift in thinking and practice. It's interesting to note how the website for Birmingham Adult Social Care speaks of its day services for people with physical impairments in 2017:

> Day Centres provide a range of activities, a chance to socialise and meet friends and have a hot meal. They are usually open all day and staff and volunteers

organise different activities to suit and entertain the people who go there.

There are many day services that can be accessed independently, many services do not require an assessment and can be found here in our marketplace.

In terms of the review of Adult Day Centres, the changes that took place were cosmetic rather than transformative and as this dawned on me, I started to question to what degree I'd be in a position to bring about effective change. The two other pieces of policy development I pushed forward provided me with an answer.

It's necessary to provide some background information on the second radical policy area I sought to develop. As the second city, Birmingham had the National Exhibition Centre on its outskirts and it had just opened the International Convention Centre in the heart of the city, but while both were fairly accessible venues, they were very expensive and prohibited to many disabled people's organisations and the voluntary sector. At the time, and even today, there are very few venues around England that can adequately cater for large numbers of disabled people with adjacent accommodation at affordable prices. Historically, this has proved a major headache and I can't tell you the number of conferences, meetings and events I've attended where disabled people have felt excluded, marginalised or poorly treated. We're of course talking about a time prior to any legal duties to provide access but the truth is that very little has changed in Birmingham over these twenty five or so years and fully accessible meeting places in the city are still few and far between.

While this may be a concern for a disabled activist, how could this be turned into a policy issue for a Birmingham Social Services Planning Officer? Indirectly I'd become interested in the issue of respite care both as a professional and as a parent. Respite care, for those who don't know, is planned or emergency temporary care provision provided to give a break to the main persons caring for a child or supporting an adult. There are various models of respite care however the central purpose is to create some space and look after each party's well-being. Respite can be within a person's own home or they go to a facility to be 'cared for' (sic). Within Birmingham Social Services the emphasis was on providing respite care for carers of people with learning difficulties, which was understandable, but after a while I began thinking that other groups of disabled people and their families might benefit from 'short breaks' apart.

My emphasis was on disabled adults with significant physical impairments as that was my remit. I wanted them to have a 'meaningful break' away from the usual relationships that they had and to avoid them being upset by the experience or made to feel a burden. If respite care was needed, could it be delivered without the medicalisation of disabled people's lives? I thought I could offer a dual propose solution. Why couldn't there be a purpose built hotel/conference centre with enough accommodation space to allow disabled adults with significant physical impairments short breaks. The venue would have trained staff capable of providing personal as well as conference/leisure support. This would be an accessible mainstream facility and not some flash new 'Crip ghetto' or a second lavish DRC.

To be able to sell my idea, I needed to be realistic in my approach. I knew my proposal would be immediately knocked back if I presented it as a high cost project for Birmingham City Council, therefore I confess, I took a market orientated approach and decided to 'sell' my idea as being a partnership between the Council and the private sector. I still believe it's a viable project even today. The policy I wrote outlined the case as I've outlined above and all I was seeking was a similar pattern to the DRC, namely to commission a feasibility study and investigate partnerships. My line-manager approved my paper for it to go before the Birmingham Social Services Committee which was mainly made up of City Councillors. I presented my paper and felt it had a reasonable reception until a Conservative, Councillor Green, launched a fierce attack upon the proposal which he saw as 'costly, idealistic nonsense', and of course, this managed to kill it dead on the spot. I felt really gutted however, typical of the Department, neither my line-manager nor anyone else, mentioned the paper again.

It's perhaps ironical that my third area of policy development was successful to a degree, but nevertheless resulted in a number of slaps in the face for me. In 1992, like most local authorities, Birmingham City Council believed 'equal opportunities' only extended to the issues of race and gender. I realised my efforts to bring culture change to Birmingham Social Services were wasted if the rest of Birmingham City Council had no or little exposure to 'disability politics' or what I saw at the time as 'the social model of disability'. The key question was how could the social approach towards disability be embedded into the life of the Council? There was no umbrella Equalities Department at the time, so race and gender issues were addressed by separate Units. On my return from Canada I wrote a detailed paper, none of which I can now recall, which made the case for a Disability Issues Unit. Much to my delight this went through all the committees it was presented at and it was agreed that such a unit would be established. I'm not going to pretend that a part of me saw this as an exit strategy; I did have the desire to lead the Disability Issues Unit, why not? Very quickly I was told that this was the Council's project now and my involvement in it had ended. Once the Unit had been established, I was able to work with it, but mainly from the outside.

Despite this set back I'd managed to persuade Birmingham City Council to support the inaugural celebration of the International Day of Disabled Persons and I worked with Sharon Lee who led the Disability

Issues Unit to co-ordinate the first of many annual city-wide events. So, I'm proud of that achievement. On the UN website it explains that:

The UN International Day of Persons with Disabilities (December 3) is an international observance promoted by the United Nations since 1992. It has been celebrated with varying degrees of success around the planet. The observance of the Day aims to promote an understanding of disability issues and mobilize support for the dignity, rights and well-being of persons with disabilities. It also seeks to increase awareness of gains to be derived from the integration of persons with disabilities in every aspect of political, social, economic and cultural life. It was originally called 'International Day of Disabled Persons' until 2007. (UN, 2018; unpaged)

As you can see in the United Kingdom, we've maintained the original name for the reasons given at the beginning of this book. In terms of my tenure at the Council, the final straw which led to my resignation might appear as something quite petty, but to me it was a point of principle: I wasn't prepared to collude with ageism. My line-manager wanted me to re-write the criteria for bathroom adaptations, but to insert a clause which placed an age limit on people who could have baths replaced by showers. I wanted to be clear as to the rationale behind this, though I was certain I knew already, but it was still a shock to hear it so crudely expressed, 'The conversions cost a lot of money and old people have a habit of dying.' So, you get to a certain age and Birmingham Social Services had you already earmarked for the grave. I point blank refused. Think I'd had enough by that stage.

Before I move on, at risk of being accused of sour grapes, I want to put on record my belief that Birmingham City Council, through various officers, councillors and official documentation, have unfortunately buried large chunks of Birmingham disabled people's history in relation to the Council, and as a result, they've produced a distorted and incomplete version of events. I'm not going to name names, but here's an example of what I mean. Mike Oliver (2004; 30) wrote in:

> In 1996, Birmingham City Council adopted the social model as a guide to service provision for disabled people. However like many organisations that claim to endorse the social model, when it was reviewed five years later nothing much had happened.

I'm not challenging the statement that 'Birmingham City Council adopted the social model as a guide to service provision for disabled people' in 1996 by accepting a paper from the Equalities Department; what I'm inferring is that this account leaves out the fact Birmingham City Council had actually taken a decision to employ the social model four years earlier. Just like the 1996 attempt, the policy I put forward was never fully implemented, but that doesn't mean it never existed.

There are other examples I could give which seem to imply that no 'disability politics' took place prior to the mid-1990s and as a result of this deliberate 'revisionism' the hard work of Birmingham disabled people has been ignored and disregarded by 'outsiders' who parachuted into the city looking for fame and fortune whilst seeking to teach us natives how to do things properly. I'm aware that local disabled activists like Sandra Daniels believe there were other factors involved such as the desire of activists to distance themselves from the rightward drift of the DRC, but I stand by the broad point I'm making regarding the de-politicisation of disability issues within Birmingham.

As a Planning Officer I regularly attended meetings to represent the Department or my section of it. One of these regular meetings was to do with dissemination of information across the public and voluntary sectors and the focus was on what was called 'disability information'. Britain has had a long history of providing advice services however the 1970s saw the first one that was aimed at disabled people.

In the book, *Access To Information*, which was the final report of the National Disability Project team, Nick Moore (1995; 6) provides some historical context when he wrote:

> The Disablement Information and Advice Line (DIAL) services were one of a number of services that developed from the Independent Living movement in Derbyshire. ... They were controlled by disabled people. ..... In 1977 the then existing DIALs came together to form DIAL UK to provide common services and to represent the local interests at national level.

The history of 'disability information' therefore begins within the embryonic Disabled People's Movement however like so many other concepts and ideas grounded in disability politics 'disability information' found itself transformed within the mainstream culture and depoliticised over time. (Williams-Findlay, 2015) Coopers and Lybrand, management consultants, were called in by the Department of Health and Social Security in 1988 to 'examine and report on the basic information needs of disabled people, their carers, and service providers'. Moore acknowledges however that while Coopers and Lybrand consulted with DIAL UK, the report they produced failed to make any reference to 'specialist services' such as those provided by DIAL UK which led him to conclude there was no understanding of the nature and role of advice services. (Moore,1995; 25) Call me cynical, but I read more into this than that.

Over the years I've come to see this 'not understanding the issues' as being a recurring theme in terms of the relationships between the State and disabled people's organisations. In my opinion it has become a successful way to suppress radical ideas articulated by disabled people over the last forty years. Whether I'm right or wrong, the fact remains, the Coopers and Lybrand report altered the way 'disability information' was being addressed by the Disabled People's Movement.

Key members of Birmingham Social Services who provided information and information technology were greatly influenced by the Coopers and Lybrand Report and quickly established the Birmingham Information Federation as a result. In its first three years it existed on 'in kind' support from Birmingham City Council departments but it was able to develop further when it applied for funding from the National Disability Information Project which was established to pilot projects testing the findings from the Coopers and Lybrand Report. BIF was one of twelve 'information providers' funded by NDIP and I believe it's important to situate both BIF and NDIP in their historical context:

> The National Disability Information Project ran for three years from the autumn of 1991. .... The conditions that brought NDIP into being were the product of three separate but related developments: the growth of advice services; the moves towards equal opportunities for disabled people; and a new interpretation of the concept of citizenship. (Moore, 1:1995)

With hindsight I recognise that there were undercurrents involved in how and why these developments were able to come together and their influence on how the national project unfolded; however, at the time I was focused on my own role at both a national and local level. In its funding application to NDIP, BIF had outlined five objectives:

- To create an extensive network throughout the city of Birmingham of relevant organisations and individuals so that information can be shared more effectively.
- To actively include black and minority ethnic organisations in that network.

- To experiment with using technology to network organisations.
- To be consumer led.
- To research the information needs of disabled people and carers within the city.

I believed I'd enough experience in four of these areas to manage this project and the panel agreed. My initial contract as Director for Birmingham Information Federation ran between 14 July 1993 and March 1994 however this was extended for six months. Perhaps the most ironic thing about moving from Birmingham Social Services to the Birmingham Information Federation was the fact the project had, with my help, secured space at the DRC. BIF had a small team initially of three staff members. George was responsible for the training and development around the use of technology; Sarah was our administrative worker who was also charged with updating the information directory and, of course, the trio was completed with me having policy and management responsibilities. Nick Moore (1995; 38) notes in his book that:

> Following the appointment of a new director, BIF sought to establish methods which ensure a greater degree of participation by and accountability to disabled people. The federation has also tried to develop a broader range of services. These include disability equality training and community development work.

My aim was to shift 'disability information' back under the control and accountability of disabled people. One project started shortly after my appointment was a pilot signposting information service called Disability Link Line which sought to direct enquirers to the most appropriate agency. The DLL was sponsored by a local company and in truth had little success because it was beset by all the usual difficulties facing services aimed at disabled people.

Disablement is about how society's structures and systems exclude and marginalise disabled people, therefore a paradox exists; any service seeking to assist in removing barriers will nevertheless encounter those barriers. It's almost a catch twenty two situation. Disabled people need 'disability information' because they're excluded and marginalised, but often they don't know how or where to obtain this information from because of the barriers they encounter. Being director of BIF meant I was also involved in the National Disability Information Project itself and sought to inject wherever possible the influence of disability politics.

In a NDIP Newsletter I wrote an article called *Disability information or misinformation?* which was about what constituted disability information as a means of raising key political questions. Alison Sheldon in her PhD entitled, *Disabled People and Communication Systems in the Twenty First Century*, wrote:

> Furthermore, there is a lack of clarity over what actually constitutes 'disability information'.... Most of the information services funded to provide so called disability information are controlled by non-disabled people who subscribe to the medical rather than the social model of disability, with vast amounts of public money being given by central government to charities and voluntary organisations .... (2001; 193)

Alison supports this with reference to my article:

> As Bob Findlay (1994: 1) explains *disability information* has come to represent a patronising attempt to help disabled people overcome their problems - the problems caused by having impairments and not being able to access information because of those

impairments. And of course, their needs and interest are *special*.

Whilst there is of course a place for impairment information, especially at 'crisis points' such as receipt of a medical diagnosis, according to Findlay, disability information should first and foremost address the unmet needs of those who experience disability oppression, looking for example at 'the consequences of living in a disabling society' and facilitating those with impairments to overcome social barriers. (2001; 194)

By raising these types of political questions within both NDIP and BIF I obviously ruffled a few feathers. Many nondisabled people, especially professionals, are happy to talk about empowering disabled people, but at the same time resent having power taken from them. With the power and culture changing with BIF, a number of its founders made excuses to leave. Funding became an issue and with DLL failing to secure a second year of sponsorship we had to let Richard go. George also left to join another project at the DRC and wasn't replaced. Sarah, meanwhile, went on long-term sick leave. The majority of the last year of the NDIP project saw me singlehandedly run BIF with the support of its new Chair, Mary Smith.

The early 1990s saw both dramatic highs and lows for me, but somehow, I survived. These years had produced dreams, schemes and other things as I'll now go on to elaborate.

Chapter 15

Dreams, schemes and other things

Every great dream begins with a dreamer. Always remember, you have within you the strength, the patience, and the passion to reach for the stars to change the world.

Harriet Tubman

In the previous chapter I stated the early relations between BDRG and BCODP were tense and full of distrust on both sides. During early meetings I attended I was convinced Rachel Hurst, a leading member of BCODP, looked at me as if I'd two heads! Over time by working with people like Rachel on the National Council and later as part of the Executive Committee I managed to establish myself as a credible activist in the Movement.

My main political activity during these years was being involved in BCODP and so I was very much involved in what has become known as the campaign for anti-discrimination legislation (ADL). It isn't possible to do justice to the complexities surrounding disability politics, so my aim is simply outline my involvement and the key questions that were raised. This particular period in the history of the British Disabled People's Movement remains subject to fierce political debate therefore before discussing my involvement I want to offer a broad outline for the ADL campaign.

John Evans a former chairperson of BCODP gave a speech entitled, *The U.K. Civil Rights Campaign and the Disability Discrimination Act,* in Vienna during 1996 to the European Network for Independent Living in which he gives his account of the campaign. Whilst there are elements of John's speech, I'd take issue with, I still believe it offers an interesting perspective on what took place. John explained that:

> Since the early 1980s there have been 14 attempts to get anti-discrimination [legislation] for disabled peoplenon the Statute books of British Law, all of which have failed. (Evans, 1996: 1)

These attempts were through Private Members Bills and there's a discussion to be had about the understanding and content of most of these Bills. Many of the Bills were in response to evidence showing the type of discrimination faced by disabled people. Colin Barnes in his book, *Disabled People in Britain and Discrimination: A case for anti-discrimination legislation,* points to two studies into social restriction:

> [T]he Silver Jubilee Access Committee (SJAC) report *Can Disabled People Go Where You Go?* (1979) and the report of the Committee on Restrictions against Disabled People (CORAD, 1982), the first because it drew attention to a 'number of blatant acts of discrimination against disabled people', and caused the then Labour Government to set up CORAD under the chairmanship of Peter Large, himself a disabled person, who had chaired the SJAC. (Barnes, 1991:1)

Not surprisingly perhaps, Thatcher's government rejected

the CORAD Report and as a result a succession of Private Members Bills followed. Each Bill, with one or two exceptions, was accompanied by half-hearted campaigns led primarily by the disability charities and the voluntary sector. A march around Parliament on a Friday as MPs debated what was once called, 'the goodwill towards 'the disabled' (sic)', and this became a frustrating annual ritual.

In 1990 BCODP decided to take matters into their own hands and they commissioned a disabled academic, Colin Barnes, to undertake a fresh comprehensive study of discrimination which was published a year later. Colin's book certainly raised the profile of the case for anti-discrimination legislation however the BCODP's Executive took the view of that the method of campaigning had fallen into a bit of a rut and too much power was invested in the hands of the large disability charities. The fact BCODP made the struggle for ADL their main campaign has been debated off and on within the Disabled People's Movement ever since and it's an issue that continues to divide opinion. It's important to acknowledge that at the time I was fully behind the ADL campaign, though with hindsight I can see that huge mistakes were made.

The organising body behind campaigning for ADL, which had been going since the mid-eighties, was called Voluntary Organisations for Anti-Discrimination Legislation (VOADL), and not to put a too finer point on it, neither flowed off the tongue nor had the zest to inspire. Rachel Hurst and I argued it was time for a more vibrant and eye-catching campaign capable of enthusing people. Together we said this new campaign needed a direct, no nonsense name, and we suggested *Rights Now!* Rachel was charged with taking our proposal to VODAL and it wasn't seriously resisted, so the Rights Now campaign was launched in 1992 to organise and co-ordinate events around campaigning, promoting and publicising the need for anti-discrimination legislation.

John Evans again broadly captures the period between 1992 and 1994 when he writes:

> Direct action no doubt heightened the profile for the need for civil rights legislation in the eyes of the general public and did a lot to shake up the politicians' complacency on the issue but it could never be enough by itself. Without the lobbying of parliament and meetings with politicians putting forward constructive arguments based on available evidence of discrimination   and seeking their support the cause would have been lost. Any changes in the law have to be done through Parliament so you have to get some politicians fighting for your cause. At the same time disabled experts and lawyers have to work alongside other lawyers and politicians in writing up the Bill. (Evans, 1996: 3)

The first test for the new wave militancy and Parliamentary campaigning came when Roger Berry tried to push through the Civil Rights (Disabled Persons) Bill. Ian Parker, in an article called 'Spitting On Charity' which appeared in the Independent, wrote:

> In May 1994, however, a private member's bill, the Civil Rights (Disabled Persons) Bill, was killed messily by the Government, and the minister for disabled people, Nicholas Scott, eventually had to resign. (Parker, 2011: unpaged)

This caused a public outcry and put the ADL campaign into mainstream politics. It was becoming increasingly obvious that it was only a matter of time before Parliament had to pass legislation to outlaw forms of discrimination against disabled people, but the Tories and big business weren't going to be prepared to see the Civil Rights (Disabled Persons) Bill go through because it was a comprehensive approach and not individualistically focused on impairment based discrimination. As Lorraine Gradwell stated:

....the Tory government were so concerned about the increasing popularity of anti-discrimination legislation that they brought forward this fudge of a compromise'. (2015)

Their only course of action was to head off our Bill by introducing the weaker Disability Discrimination Bill led by William Hague, the new Minister for Disabled People. What followed was a two-horse handicapped chase. Harry Barnes in February 1995 picked up the gauntlet and re-introduced the Civil Rights Bill, but Hague had the advantage of proposing a Bill supported by John Major's Conservative government. The rotten piecemeal Bill was eventually passed into law as the Disability Discrimination Act (DDA). In the eyes of the more radical disabled activists the passing of the DDA was a significant political defeat for disabled people and the struggle against social oppression.

I want to continue to discuss the campaign for ADL however this time from a different perspective. BCODP was made up of disabled people's organisations however the Disabled People's Movement included activists who worked in other campaigns and bodies outside of BCODP and our disabled people's led organisations. During my time at Social Services I'd joined the National Association of Local Government Officers (NALGO) whilst also maintaining my membership of the Manufacturing, Science and Finance Union (MSF). Within an earlier chapter I briefly mentioned that Mike Bramley, Caroline Gooding and I were instrumental in establishing the Trade Union Disability Alliance and so now I plan to explain how this came about. Mike was a fellow member of the BCODP National Council representing the Derbyshire Coalition of Disabled People and a fellow member of MSF. Mike and I became close friends and often discussed how to take the politics of the Disabled People's Movement forward and I believe we were successful in doing that in three specific ways.

Our overall aim was to take disability politics into the Trade Union Movement through educating union members via the self-organisation of disabled trade unionists. The first project we begun involved contacting Anne Gibson, now Baroness Gibson, who was the National Officer for MSF and floated the idea of having an MSF Disabled Members Committee similar to a body that existed in NALGO. We worked closely with Anne to set this up and later a Regional Officer called Ken Orme, who identified as a disabled person, became the committee's secretary. Mike and I were the driving force behind the committee as Ken had a scant understanding of disability politics if the truth was told. We were fortunate to be joined on the committee by Caroline Gooding, a trained lawyer, who was working for the Royal Association for Disability and Rehabilitation (Radar), now Disability Rights UK, at the time.

Mike and I were a little cagey with Caroline to begin with because of the somewhat fractious relationship between BCODP and Radar, but we soon became a close-knit triad of disabled trade union activists. We were later joined by Dave Cook who was on the MSF National Committee and he became chair of the Disabled Members Committee. Our first major project was launched through an article written by Mike and me on the Case for Anti-Discrimination Legislation which appeared in the MSF Equality Bulletin. Our meetings had a regular attendance of around twenty disabled members.

Our second project involved joining forces with other disabled trade unionists belonging to various unions. Key to assisting us was Lesley Child, from NALGO, Dave Lupton, from NUJ, and Jenny Cook. We decided to launch a new disabled people's organisation called the Trade Union Disability Alliance [TUDA]. The first AGM was held on 6 June 1993 and agreed the Constitution's objects which were:

- To coordinate the voice of disabled people in the trade union movement.
- To relieve the disability of people with physical, mental, or sensory impairments and further their independence and full participation in the workplace and wider community.

It's a little ironic that I'm writing about TUDA at the beginning of the week in which it will be marking its 24th anniversary. Today's aims are roughly in keeping with our original ones, namely, to:

- Co-ordinate the perspective of Disabled people in the Trade Union movement;
- Bridge the gap between the Trade Union and Disability movements;
- Work within, and lobby, Trade Unions to ensure they make their own services accessible and relevant to Disabled Members;
- Ensure that Trade Unions support our continuing campaign for full civil rights;
- Promote understanding of disability as an equalities issues, giving talks and training to Trade Unions;
- Work with Disabled people to persuade them of the benefits of Trade Union membership and activity.

We recognised that the only way we were going to set about the task of bridging the gap between the Trade Unions and disabled people's movement was to not only work within the individual unions through our members but also attempt to influence the Trade Union Congress. Once again, we turned to Anne Gibson who was a member of the TUC General Council to make the case for the TUC to work with TUDA in order to set up a Disability Committee. Mike had a wonderful sense of humour and thought it was really hilarious that we had to work with a TUC official called Owen Tudor who is still employed by them. Richard Exell, a Senior Policy Officer until he retired, was another close ally we developed within the TUC and his association with the Disabled People's Movement was for almost twenty years.

In 2014 a poster was produced on Disability History by the University and College Union (UCU) in which it was claimed that the first TUC Disability Conference wasn't held till 2002! Whilst accepting it's hard to access records to chart the history of the TUC's engagement with sections of the Disabled People's Movement, especially TUDA, I was surprised that the author was unaware of the conference that was held in the bowels of Congress House twenty years before her poster. There were regular Disability Forums held in the TUC's Chamber as well.

At the 1994 Trade Union Congress I successfully moved an MSF motion outlining proposed policy on disability issues. Funnily enough, I lost a forfeit in 1995 because I foolishly bet that I wouldn't speak during that year's Congress however when the MSF delegation met Hilary Benn, an MSF officer at the time, put my name forward as a possible speaker on any disability related motion. Roger Lyons, general secretary of MSF, wasn't satisfied with this proposal and argued that MSF should seek a composite motion on ADL with other unions with motions on that topic and that I should take the lead, including moving it. When I spoke the previous year, Rodney Bickerstaff general secretary of Unison, had come over and congratulated me on my speech, but this time around I was collared by Anthony Booth who was an Equity delegate. It was such an honour to speak to the actor who had played the Bolshie Mike Rawlins in the TV series, *Death Us Do Part*. He talked quite candidly about his mental health issues and his support for disabled people's rights.

Looking back now it's quite ironic that he had gone out of his way to speak to me about anti-discrimination legislation, whereas his son-in-law, Prime Minister Tony Blair, refused to meet with me to discuss anti-discrimination legislation when I became Chair of BCODP.

Other areas of disability politics came to the fore in the early 1990s which were linked to civil rights. The Campaign for Accessible Transport became the first campaign to see a more militant face to disabled people's politics. CAT ran a sustained campaign of direct action which involved demonstrations outside transport providers' buildings, blockades of major roads in, for example, central London which often involved disabled people chaining themselves to buses and there were also other symbolic stunts. It needs remembering that it was virtually impossible for wheelchair users and others with significant mobility impairments to use public transport. For the most part I watched these activities from the wings because the BCODP's Executive had taken the position due to the fact officers were called upon to negotiate with government departments, we couldn't be actively involved in 'direct action' where arrests could be made. I did however take part in a famous protest in Manchester during a BCODP Conference – much to the disapproval of Jane Campbell and Richard Wood who kept their distance – and a similar event organised with BDRG in Birmingham where Dominic came with me.

The other major campaign was called *Block Telethon* and most activists were involved with one or both of these protests. The ITV Telethons were three charity events organised and televised in the United Kingdom by the ITV network. They took place alternate years from 1988. Each lasted for 27 hours and all were hosted by Michael Aspel. Disabled people weren't sure what to expect in 1988 but were soon angered by the negative portrayals of disabled people used by the Telethon. Two of the main organisers of *Block Telethon* were Barbara Lisicki and Alan Holdsworth, (also known as Johnny Crescendo), the singer and songwriter who penned the song 'Choices and

Rights' which became the anthem for the Disabled People's Movement during the 1990s and at the time they regularly visited Birmingham to do Disability Equality Training. Brenda would babysit for them, so we were fully briefed on *Block Telethon*. Barbara explained in an interview given to the charity Scope:

> With two weeks to go before [the] 1990 Telethon, a few young disabled people from Ealing in West London met me and Alan….These young people told us: 'We cannot sit through another assault on our senses, our identity and our dignity for another year. This is what Telethon does to us and we want to do something'. So we did something. Within two weeks, we had printed t-shirts and leaflets, and mobilised up to 200 disabled people outside Telethon. We got coverage, satisfaction, and reaction, but not enough. (2015, unpaged)

Block Telethon 1992 saw disabled people and their allies better organised and prepared. Personally, I can't separate the two protests in my own mind, but there are loads of excellent photographs around marking the second protest where 2,000 campaigners turned up. Barbara captures the moment perfectly when she wrote:

> The streets were jammed; we had banners and placards, and proudly wore black t-shirts with 'Piss on Pity' in shocking pink. The police were unimpressed, calling the language offensive and demanding we took them off. I was willing, but told them that I wasn't wearing anything underneath! (2015, unpaged)

This wasn't just a mob of angry disabled people converging on ITV's studios. What we were witnessing was disabled adults and children, performers and speakers, sign language interpreters and support workers, all freely gave their time, all to support disabled people to reclaim our dignity. It's important to place *Block Telethon* in its historical context. There were two aspects to our protests; firstly, was our opposition to the patronising imagery often employed by charities to exploit the public's emotions. These images more often than not misrepresented the real lives and issues of disabled people. The second aspect is explained here by Barbara:

> Our argument was simple: the only time disabled people appeared on TV was in tragic and needy roles, begging for money. Why? And what damage did this do? What employer watching – and probably donating to Telethon or allowing staff to organise a fundraising event – would hire 'poor creatures'? (2015, unpaged)

Twenty five years on and the representation of disabled people's real lives and issues within the mass media has hardly improved at all. There is a slight increase in the number of disabled characters or shows featuring disabled people, but progress is painfully slow.

One of my own vivid memories is having an *EastEnders* star wind down the window of her chauffeur driven limousine and shouting, 'Fuck off!' in my face. Shame on those of us who weren't being silently accepting of being hidden from view or for refusing to be forever grateful to celebrities for 'doing their bit' for charity. Shame on those of us who were saying we had had enough of situations where other people were using their power and ignorance in ways which ultimately oppressed disabled people.

Mike Oliver, disabled academic and activist, perhaps best describes what *Block Telethon* was about during a speech to the crowd. He said:

> Today, this is the only place in the entire country where you can feel proud you're a disabled person.

(2015, unpaged)

Barbara Lisicki captures the mood of disabled activism during the early 1990s when she wrote:

> Rights Not Charity!' was the disabled people's movement's early call to arms. .... We were sick of traditional solutions to the 'problems' of disabled people and demanded an end to discrimination. Two thousand disabled people – all proud, angry, and strong – chanted, sang, and brandished banners. Celebrating our difference and challenging negative stereotypes, we stopped Telethon. (2015, unpaged)

Even today disabled people are still discussing *Block Telethon* on social media. Perhaps one of the most ironical things about ITV's Telethons is that they offered a sharp contrast to the Central TV's flagship disability programme, *Link*. Two key disabled activists associated with this project were Vic Finkelstein and Rosalie Wilkins, now a Baroness. Vic explains:

> A long time ago the Sunday morning Link programme started on television. It was wholly concerned with disability and was presented by Rosalie Wilkins. .... I was fortunate in attending some of those discussions. At one of these consultative meetings I argued that instead of having a programme with an occupational therapist presenting aids, equipment and discussing current legislation relevant to disabled people – that sort of thing – we ought to do much more: explore the nature of disability (what It's really all about). The programme ought also to look at important key issue for us – e.g. that society is disabling us and therefore it's society that has to change, not disabled people. (Finkelstein, 2001; unpaged)

I remember watching *Link* and getting frustrated with listening to the occupational therapist presenting on aids and equipment when I wanted to hear more about the social and political aspects of being a disabled person. Vic went on to discuss how challenging the mass media and professionals find our perspective. He wrote:

> I remember at one meeting a person who had been involved for some time in the so-called disability world, the professional world, protesting 'But what you're saying is revolutionary. It'll never happen. People will never regard disability as something that is created by society. Disability is something you're born with or when you have an accident. It's part of you and people need to intervene to help you. You need professional services.' (Finkelstein, 2001; unpaged)

Rosalie Wilkins had spent most of her career prior to entering the House of Lords in the media where she was involved in bringing about better coverage of disability issues. She was a freelance video and documentary producer between 1988 and 1996, and presenter and co-producer of the pioneering Central TV's Link Programme from 1975 to 1988.

There was something about Rosalie I really liked, so when I was trying to establish BDRG, I decided to make contact and we met up in Birmingham. The first thing I realised about her was the fact her use of a wheelchair couldn't mask how tall she was! We hit it off straight away and she invited me to do a segment on *Link* about BDRG. Over the next few years, I appeared on the programme a number of times including a debate involving Vic Finkelstein and I believe my contributions tried to push the programme in the direction Vic favoured.

Link wasn't the only TV programme I occasionally appears on as there were also specialist programmes like the BBC's *One in Four* and *Same Difference* on Channel 4. The programme *Same Difference* gave me two new experiences. On one programme it featured me doing a stand-up routine and then the Producer also commissioned me to research a piece on the Spastics Society and its then CEO Ken Young. I'll admit I was out of my depth; so, when the piece did go to air late 1989, it was nothing like I'd researched! I was nevertheless still interviewed as part of the item although I'd proved a fairly useless researcher for the mass media.

This book has focused upon my life as a person with an impairment in terms of personal experience, career choices and my politics. In passing I've mentioned the fact that I'm a poet, but in the context of my life I've haven't so far said a great deal about this. On reflection many of my poem alluded to my experiences, however, it wasn't until I became involved in disability politics did my poetry began to take more of an overt political turn. This development I believe was true of many disabled people of my generation. Allan Sutherland, for example, has commented that:

> I don't think disability arts would have been possible without disability politics coming first.... Our politics teach us that we are oppressed, not inferior .... Our politics have given us self-esteem. They have taught us, not simply to value ourselves, but to value ourselves as disabled people. (Sutherland, 1989; unpaged)

Colin Cameron reminds us that the Disability Arts Movement emerged from the mid-1980s onwards as disabled people began to develop their own voices and perspectives rooted in an understanding illuminated by the social model. (Cameron, 2009) A key figure in the Disability Arts Movement during this period was Paddy Masefield, and he explained Disability Arts as being:

.... are art forms, art works and arts productions created by disabled people to be shared with, and to inform other disabled people, by focusing on the truth of disability experience. (Masefield 2006, p. 22)

Given the limited opportunities to engage in cultural and art activities due to other commitments, I'd a peripheral role within the Disability Arts Movement which was really just writing an occasional article within the Magazine, *Disability Arts in London* and the odd gig. As a performer my contribution to Disability Arts wasn't so much my poetry at the time but rather the occasional stand-up routine put together, for example, for events as celebrating the International Day of Disabled People. I've always seen my stand-up routines as being a little bit of fun that I do now and then and I certainly wouldn't compare myself with people such as Laurence Clark, Francesca Martinez or Liz Carr who are professional disabled comedians. Knowing and watching Barbara Lisicki and Alan Holdsworth perform as Wanda Barbara and Johnny Crescendo was enough to tempt me into getting up and having a go.

Barbara was the first female disabled political stand-up comic in the UK. She was a co-founder along with Alan and folk singer Ian Stanton, of The Tragic but Brave Show, a touring company of Disabled Poets, Dancers, Musicians and Comics which toured internationally for five years. I was never invited to perform with The Tragic but Brave Show, but for the 2016 International Day of Disabled People, actor and comedian Liz Carr, organised an event to relive past performances at a famous Disability Arts venue, *The Workhouse*. Barbara and I were both on stage that night.

The early half of the 1990s were hectic years of both hope and despair. During the first couple of years it could be said that I'd the type of life anyone might want to dream of, yet by the middle of 1993 it was lying shattered and I'm not being untruthful when I say I don't fully understand what went wrong. Out of respect to Brenda and my sons I've decided not to go into too much detail. There wasn't one single reason that put our marriage under strain; a number of things contributed to the eventual split including the death of my mother, the pressure of trying to be a father, partner, professional and an activist all took its toll. Somehow, I'd lost my way and lost my moral compass in the process.

It was a terrible shock when Brenda said she wanted to end our marriage and whilst I was devastated, I could understand why she felt we had gone to the point of no return. I eventually moved out into a single bedroom flat and sought to pick up the pieces of my life. Mike Bramley was a great support in the early stages of my marriage break up, so it was a real hammer blow when one morning Ken Davies, a long-standing disability activist in Derbyshire, phoned to say Mike had collapsed and died.

I'd look after Dominic for a few hours each week and he would come and stay with me for a weekend in my newly acquired one bedroom flat. Sadly, over time, as he got heavier looking after him became more difficult and dangerous and I began to question the wisdom of trying to maintain our relationship. The emotional side of things increased as well as we both struggled with our time together. Painful though it was, I concluded that seeing him was doing more harm than good and I felt I couldn't provide the care he needed on my own; so, the visits stopped. Words can't express how low I felt at this moment in my life. Brenda suggested I got counselling and I did, but the non-judgemental approach the counsellor took did nothing to ease the guilt, pain and disappointment I was feeling. Looking back, I believe both my paid work and political activities kept me from going under.

Chapter 16

Make your mind up

There comes a time in life when you know what you like and have to make up your mind to like what you know, or at least have begun to know. In other words, you must determine in what direction your knowledge is leading, thus far.

Vincent Price

The middle of the 1990s proved a struggle for me as I tried to adapt to my new life in a flat I didn't particularly like. It wasn't easy as I had to cope with being alone after living so many years with other people. The Treasurer of the DRC, Derek Farr, was supportive of me and arranged for one of his neighbour's daughters to act as a part-time personal assistant for me, particularly when Dominic was still coming to stay. Derek wasn't that political and if anything, he was rather conservative, however, having become a disabled person later in life, he believed in the right of disabled people to lead active lives. Despite many differences in our outlooks, I considered him a friend. It's strange how easy it's to lose friends when a marriage ends, and people feel the need to be judgemental based on little or no information.

My membership of BDRG had continued but I'd taken a back seat since joining Social Services, but I was still a major link for them with regards to the Disabled People's Movement and BCODP in particular. I remained an ear for committee members and for a while I socialised with an activist called Lois who had moved to Birmingham. Many members of BDRG found Lois difficult to relate to and this upset her; however, being an older activist, I think she appreciated coming under my wing; besides we both had a wicked sense of humour. Sadly, I didn't get a real opportunity to know her because we lost both Dave and Lois in a relatively short space of time.

Through BDRG's membership of BCODP I was able to maintain my role as Vice Chairperson and be on both the Executive and National Committees. In November 1993 Rachel Hurst, who was Chair of DPI-Europe, asked me to co-ordinated the UN International Day of Disabled Persons in the UK which meant helping to organise the publicity, ensuring events followed the guidelines set and recruiting a representative delegation to the First European Parliament of Disabled People. Although I helped to co-ordinate the Birmingham event, I wasn't able to attend because I flew to Brussels to be the British Delegation leader.

The Report on the First European Disabled People's Parliament informs us that it was held in the 'Hemicycle Of The European Parliament Brussels, Belgium, on Friday 3 December 1993'. It reported my speech in the following manner:

British Delegation leader: Bob Findlay

This is the first European Disabled People's Parliament, said Bob Findlay. Speaking for all those present, he said: 'We're proud; proud of who we're; proud of our experience. We're here to give warning to those who have historically denied us; marginalised us outside mainstream social activities.'

Disabled people were attending the Parliament, said Mr. Findlay, to lay down a marker. Each 3 December, disabled people will hold to account those who have oppressed them - to see what they have done in the previous year. Here, in this institution of power, he said, disabled people are opening the floodgates for social change: 'Our power will not be denied. Our voice will not be silenced. Our dignity will not be rubbished. We're here to say: nothing about us without us.' Mr. Findlay said it was time to stop talking about rehabilitation and to start talking about self-determination; time to stop talking about being aware and to start talking about legislation.

The strategy for social change, explained Mr. Findlay, must include full participation in every institution that takes decisions about disabled people's lives. 'Equal[ity] is about being there; making choices; exercising power. We cannot afford to be invisible.' Too many people, said Mr. Findlay, are waiting to thrust disabled people back into obscurity. 3 December must not be a token. For 365 days a year, our message, voice and power must be seen and felt. We all have a duty, said Mr. Findlay, not just to talk about what is wrong and to say that we're angry, but to say what we will do about it. How are we, as organisations at the European level, to shift power at the European Parliament. We must question what programmes mean; they must be more than fine words on paper but a living reality to us, in every village, town and city across Europe. Today is just the beginning, concluded Mr. Findlay, we must fight those who work against us.

Mr. Findlay's statement was met with warm applause.

This was really my first public stage for representing BCODP outside the confines of the Movement. The second followed quite quickly. As Vice Chair of BCODP I prepared the written evidence submitted to the House of Commons Employment Committee who were looking at 'The Operation of the Disabled Persons (Employment) Act 1944' and on 8 March 1994 I gave oral evidence to the Committee. Thornton and Lunt (1995; 44) reported that:

> What may be required is a mechanism for ensuring that employers keep records of the proportion of disabled employees, so that the incentive effect imputed to the quota system is not lost. That might be policed as part of a statutory code of practice, or by an Equal Opportunities Commission with rights of investigation.

A major problem with the old quota system was that it wasn't adequately policed and was based upon a ratio of employer numbers which failed to address a wide range of issues such as the nature of work of a given company and the skill base required. In my opinion it encouraged employers to 'find' existing employees who had some kind of impairment and then register them as 'disabled' or to place disabled people into low skilled and therefore low paid jobs. What BCODP put forward was the idea of a more robust system. Thornton and Lunt go on to explain that:

> ....Companies over a certain size would have an obligation to register their equal opportunities policies and monitor their practices. A proposal for such a scheme was submitted by BCODP as written evidence to the House of Commons Employment Committee Inquiry, 1994 (pp. 50-51). An annual statement might include targets for recruitment and retention. Difficulties should be noted so that advice can be given. Such a legal document would be open to public scrutiny. Employment equity programmes have the added appeal of, in theory at least,

promoting the employment of sub-groups, such as people with learning difficulties. How employment equity programmes are enforced is another question. The BCODP evidence suggested withdrawal of permission to register and a period for improvement. Failing that, the company would be fined and publicly de-registered.

The register was my idea based on material I obtained during my visit to Canada and after discussions with Caroline Gooding. Caroline was working close with me on a number of fronts at this moment in time as we were TUDA officers, members of the MSF disability committee and we did research work for the Rights Now Campaign.

In the previous chapter I presented a brief overview of the campaign for civil rights and now I wish to say more about my own role. A personal problem for me was that the Rights Now steering group meetings took place in London and with BCODP not wishing to flood them or have unnecessary travel costs, I was an infrequent attendee. Nevertheless, I was involved with the campaign in other ways. When the Disability Discrimination Bill was going through its committee stages I wrote a briefing paper for the opposition parties on the definition of disability and the social model.

On 9 July 1994 the Rights Now! Campaign held a Rally for Disabled People's Civil Rights in Trafalgar Square and I spoke on behalf of TUDA. In the pamphlet produced for the Rally there was a brief outline of the campaign for the Civil Rights Bill and the dirty tricks, which were mentioned in a previous chapter, the Conservative government had used to defeat the Bill.

I'm speaking about this again here because there's a poignant comment that I believe acknowledge an event that had huge political significance for the British Disabled People's Movement and for me personally as well as we'll see. The pamphlet recalls:

On 20 May, despite the valiant efforts of its many parliamentary supporters, the Bill ran out of time, with the Minister talking for over an hour and a Conservative backbencher calling for a quorum vote, knowing that most of the Bill's supporters would be at John Smith's funeral.

The Bill was buried on the same day as John Smith who had been the leader of the Labour Party, however, I believe also buried that day was any real hope of passing a comprehensive piece of legislation granting disabled people civil rights. The reason I believe this is because there was about to be a huge political shift. Smith had been fully behind the Civil Rights Bill and in discussions with BCODP, he had promised to bring it in as a Labour Party policy when they gained power and if this particular Bill was lost. His death however led to Tony Blair becoming the new party leader and this resulted in a complete break with the traditional, if somewhat paternalistic, relationship that had historically existed between Labour and the Disabled People's Movement. Blair had little time for BCODP and as a result this increased the influence of the major disability charities with regards to government policies when New Labour came in. Within the context of my own role in the campaign for anti-discrimination legislation I'd an unexpected invite.

At its annual conference in November1994 the Confederation of British Industry asked me to debate the Disability Discrimination Bill with William Hague which was an interesting experience. It's a little ironic that despite our political differences Hague treated me with a certain degree of dignity and respect, unlike two New Labour Ministers of Disabled People who followed in his footsteps. Away from national disability politics the end of 1994 brought a new person into my life via the DRC.

On the morning of 5 September 1994 for some reason I can't now recall, I was eager to speak with Elaine Giles who was Sector Co-ordinator for the Birmingham Training and Enterprise Council. I do know I was already in the reception at the DRC when Elaine arrived with a young woman who was about to start work as the new Disability Training Co-ordinator for a project called Disability Training Services which later became Enable (Birmingham) Ltd which was based like BIF at the DRC. The project was funded by TEC and supported by Birmingham City Council's Economic Development Department. George, who had worked for BIF, was responsible for an equipment pool to support training providers and the role of the Disability Training Co-ordinator had been to raise disability issues with the same group of people.

While the new worker was signing in, I managed to collar Elaine, but I was distracted by the woman's need to swing her long hair out of her way in order to bend down to put her face close to the signing in book. When I eventually finished my business with Elaine I was introduced to Cindy Williams. Cindy had a visual impairment and was in her early 20s. It was a good ten days after our first meeting that I'd an opportunity to spend any time talking to her; this was partly due to the fact she was being taken around to meet training providers and I was away at the TUC Congress. When we did get to speak, we hit if off well and I was particularly interested in knowing more about how she was going to undertake her role as disability equality training was still my area of expertise. For a week I watched Cindy come and go before using the feeble excuse of a headache to go and ask if she had any Paracetamol tablets. (I rarely took tablets in those days!)

A couple days later I dropped by Enable's office and explained to Cindy that I'd two questions and that one of them was technical. She offered to answer them, if she could. 'First of all,' I said, 'is George around?' Having told me he wasn't, she then hesitated before asking me what the technical question was. I smiled and said, 'What I need to know is, do you like curries?' Fortunately for me, she did. On our first date, not that either of us called it that, I did ask her a lot about training and the social model. Months later she told me she thought it was 'just the founder of the Centre checking her out to see if she was worthy of working there'. The comedian in me would say that was half true.

I attended the BCODP Annual Conference in October along with Irene Wright who was on the DRC Board of Directors. I'd first met Irene many years earlier when I spoke at her Banking, Insurance and Finance Union branch meeting. That night I'd persuaded her to get involved in BDRG. Being a close friend who knew Brenda through BDRG, I was able to spend some time with her on the Saturday night of Conference talking about how things were. Irene liked Cindy, so I was able to confide in her that I was growing fond of her, but I was hesitating because of the twenty year age gap between us and I wasn't keen to rush into anything. She gave me sound advice that night and as a result I took at number of bold decisions.

At the time I was still a member of the Labour Party and was supported by my branch to put myself forward for selection as a candidate in the next year's local elections. I can remember pacing up and down in my flat two hours before the meeting trying to decide what to do. I'd reached the conclusion that if I were chosen as a candidate that there would be little time for much else and any hope of getting to know Cindy better would be out the window. I eventually decided not to go.

One of the things I'd insisted on when planning the DRC was that it had to have a trainee kitchen and restaurant. The majority of trainees were learning disabled people and two in particular, Joyce and Christine, would be waitresses in the Strawberry Studio restaurant. These two would argue over which one would serve me. I regularly had my main meals in there and when possible Cindy, sometimes along with George, would join me. One lunch time I told Cindy that BCODP were sending a delegation to the Disabled People's International's World Congress in Sydney, Australia. BCODP's Chair, Jane Campbell, was unable to go therefore as the next senior officer I'd lead the delegation along with Rachel. I asked Cindy if she wanted the opportunity to attend an International Conference and also double as my personal assistant. I'd met her parents a couple of times and they knew she'd stayed over at my flat, but I believe it was only a couple of months after we returned from Australia, did they realise we were starting a serious relationship.

The plan was to attend the Congress and spend a week relaxing afterwards however things didn't work out that way. Organising travel proved a nightmare as Cindy and I were able to travel out together but we had to return separately. The event went well and then we started to visit various attractions in Sydney including Bondi Beach however Cindy started to feel unwell and we spent an anxious seven hours at the Hospital where she was eventually diagnosed with Glandular Fever. This put an abrupt end to our first adventure together and the next month and a half proved difficult because we had no contact.

My contract as Director was only for the duration of the NDIP project and there was a period of uncertainty as things drew to a close. Mary Smith was on the Board at the DRC before becoming Chair of both Disability West Midlands and BIF, and it soon became clear that DWM as a major provider of 'disability information' had designs on BIF. Nick Moore (1995: 38) summed what came next this way:

> BIF has obtained funding for three years from joint finance, albeit at a lower level than previously. The funds are not sufficient to cover the full cost of running an office. Instead, a contract has been issued to Disability West Midlands for the provision of services to the federation members.

I was never going to be part of the new service agreement and in some ways the end of my directorship came as a bit of a relief. Mary was an ex-nurse and a well-meaning person, however, politically we were chalk and cheese which meant the weekly 'catch up' regarding my task list became quite gruelling since she insisted on holding the meetings at four o'clock on a Friday afternoon six and a half miles from the DRC at Birmingham Airport! Painfully going over everything I was doing under micro management was far from fun. My original contract was due to finish at the end of March 1994, but it was extended by six months so by the end of the year I was closing down the BIF office and looking at ways of stepping up my disability equality training activities once again.

In reality I'd never given up being a Disability Equality Trainer because from 1989 until 2004 I'd periodically deliver training for a company called *Equal Ability* which was run by Sue Maynard-Campbell who was a trained solicitor and a fellow trainer. Sue and I were friends over many years and when I wasn't in full-time work, I'd do training for her. Rather than depend entirely on Sue for work, I established by own company called Birmingham Action on Disability (BAD) which I ran for around six months until I placed it in mothballs. Over this period, I did very little local training or consultancy work and things weren't helped by the fact I was squatting in BDRG's office because I couldn't face the prospect of being in my flat all the time. My presence in the BDRG office didn't go down well with the DRC Manager as tensions were growing between the two organisations, so in an attempt to ease the situation, I applied for a full-time position with a training agency known as ENTA (Employment Needs Training Agency) as a Project Co-ordinator.

I'd heard about the post through Cindy, and Elaine Giles wasn't hostile to me applying either although it did prove a little awkward as both were to part of the panel alongside the two managers of ENTA. The project was to oversee the management of the training of disabled people to deliver National Vocational Qualification courses and Disability Equality Training. Despite a few hiccups I was appointed to the post however I felt at a disadvantage because two of the other appointed trainers had trained together at another agency and had obtained their City and Guilds 7323 Foundation Certificate in Teaching, Training and Development whereas I hadn't. It was agreed I'd complete my training in-house for the 7323 and run the *Three Ts* (Training the Trainers) course. It was far from ideal.

The fact ENTA had two managers made things interesting because they were like chalk and cheese. I really liked one of them, but all too often he'd sit on the fence and bottle supporting me when the chips were down. The other one was very forthright and, despite being in my union, we rarely saw eye to eye. We clashed more than once. It's hard now looking back to accept that I was criticised and accused of having discriminatory attitudes because I questioned the smoking policy of the company. There were quite a number of trainees with mental ill health who liked to smoke heavily, and it was deemed okay that this could happen in a communal area for both staff and trainees next to the entrance to the workplace. What this meant for me as someone who has shallow breathing is that each morning I'd struggle to breathe when I entered the building and had to limit the time I could stand being in the communal area. It was suggested I wanted to put my needs ahead of people with different needs which, of course, wasn't the case. At no time did this manager address any of my support needs and he would insist I kept 'factory' hours even though this presented personal difficulties for me and had no impact upon my ability to meet my contractual agreement.

The other staff members were really nice people however I always felt they kept their heads down and made sure no boats were rocked. The culture reminded me of my days in Brierley Hill. Once the *Three Ts* course had been established I made a case for running the course at the DRC because facilitates were better there for my trainees and this meant two days in a nicer environment. By end of the year the majority of trainees had gained their qualification and it was time for me to move on again. I'd decided to have a break from working for an organisation and go back to doing freelance training and consultancy work. By this time Cindy and I'd become engaged but with no immediate plans to marry. We spend most of time divided between staying in my flat and living with her parents. I recall one incident at Cindy's where she decided to wash some of my clothes but had forgotten to check the pockets. My car fob was stuck in a cycle, so we had to make a mad dash to the train station to get to work in Birmingham albeit an hour or so late!

In terms of my working career three major projects came along over the following five years. I resumed my working relationship with Sue and became a Senior Consultant with *Equal Ability* alongside Fran Brandfield. Fran and I were the major trainers for the *Department of Employment*'s 'Disability in Employment' course aimed at their Disability Employment Advisors which we ran for quite a number of years. This was a stiff test for both of us, especially for me, as we were not always accepted either because of the course content which was based upon the social model or because they objected to me because of my speech. Both Sue and Fran defended my ability to be the trainer and eventually we redesigned the course to include an in-house trainer and this silenced our critics. We ran a two day course over a residential three day period from Wednesday lunchtime to Friday lunchtime and my waistline expanded as a result of this monthly activity. Other contracts I worked for *Equal Ability* included 'Disability Equality Training' for *Transport for London*, 'Disability and Personnel' for *Sheffield College* and 'A Powerful Change' for *Oldham Social Services*.

In 1997 I worked as a Consultant in my own name

supporting the Disability Working Group which had been set up by the Sparkbrook, Sparkhill and Tyseley Regeneration Team. I recall very little of the work apart from writing up a report. The same year saw the start of a five year part-time post with the West Mercia District Workers Educational Association as their Disability Issues Co-ordinator. My main role to raise the awareness of the tutors in relation to the Disability Discrimination Act 1995, which I always found ironic as I was seriously critical of it, and ensure policies, procedures and practice could be as inclusive as possible.

The second half of the 1990s saw political turmoil within the Disabled People's Movement and I still have heated debates over what took place. In this chapter I'll keep to the facts as I saw them at the time and how, with hindsight, I see things now. My starting point is to argue that there remains reluctance amongst people from oppressed sections of society to reveal internal differences and there's always pressure to close ranks and avoid washing 'dirty linen in public'. One of the many things I admired about Vic Finkelstein was his willingness to have open public debates about differences of opinion.

Another thorny issue is where does one draw the line between the personal and the political? The unfolding politics of the late 1990s were driven by disabled people's organisations and individuals within them. I'm not going to go into great depth about 'who did what and why' however I feel it's necessary to outline some of the things that took place in order to explain my own role in history and disability politics. I'll begin with some background starting with the political defeat I believed the Disability Discrimination Act was for the disabled people.

Tensions existed prior to and after the defeat of the Civil Rights Bill and the passing of the Disability Discrimination Act (DDA). Vic Finkelstein (2007) who helped establish the Disabled People's Movement believed there was a too narrow focus on obtaining 'anti-discrimination legislation' whilst others concluded that the DDA was in fact a victory for disabled people – which goes against all the evidence that existed then or since. The differing positions taken on the DDA was the first indication of a fundamental split within the Disabled People's Movement and it resulted in a tendency emerging with a focus solely on protecting and extending 'disability rights'. Here was a clear division between those that stood for radical political action to promote change and a revision of the politics of disability which offered a reformist agenda. Although the actual division is clear, the forces who make up the two camps isn't necessary obvious. Some disabled people's organisations and individuals moved away from radical interpretations of social oppression and began to open a dialogue with traditional disability charities such as Scope and Leonard Cheshire Disability who were 'using the right language' (sic).

Jane Campbell stepped down as Chair of BCODP and later became a Co-Director the National Centre for Independent Living (NCIL) that was established in 1996. It was a project set up by the BCODP Independent Living Committee in order to promote and develop Direct Payments. In the same year the Community Care (Direct Payments) Act 1996 was passed to enable local authorities to provide direct payments to disabled people to allow them to commission their own services. I must admit that as someone who had next to no support from social services, I felt it was more appropriate that those who were directly involved in the Independent Living Movement should lead this work within BCODP and as Vice Chair I'd simply take a watching brief. With hindsight I now regret not taking a greater interest in this area because I believe huge errors were made and I wasn't educated enough to address them.

I'm not exactly sure when I became Chair of BCODP but by 1997 I was in the thick of it. There was divided opinion on how the Disabled People's Movement should respond to the Disability Discrimination Act. Both Greater

Manchester Coalition of Disabled People and TUDA argued that we should campaign around the demand to 'Repeal and Replace the DDA'. While I shared the desire to do this, I wasn't convinced it was a sensible political position to take at that moment in time. We'd no idea what the Labour Party would do if they won the General Election and it was unlikely that the trade unions or general public would understand why we'd want to replace a new law that 'appeared' to give disabled people legal protection against discrimination. I was of the opinion that we had to take a more cautious approach and expose the weaknesses within the DDA and use the evidence to then call for its replacement. Some forces saw my position as an act of betrayal and started to plot against me. The situation was further complicated when New Labour finally came to power.

The new Labour Government recognised weaknesses within the Act and established a Task Force to carry out a review of civil rights legislation for disabled people. Alan Howarth, who was Minister for Disabled People, announced the membership of the Task Force on 3 December 1997. I'd prior knowledge of some of the suggested names from our Movement however whilst respecting all of them, I wasn't convinced there was anyone among them capable of offering a radical perspective or would be strong enough to stand up to being compromised. I personally approached Howarth at a conference to see if the current Chair of BCODP could be considered. One has to admire his honesty when he said, 'Oh, come on Bob, no one with your type of politics is ever going to be put on an official body.' Despite one or two further attempts down the years, his statement has proved true.

The Task Force consisted of 24 members drawn from the disability field, business, trades union and local authorities. It was chaired by Margaret Hodge, the then Minister for Disabled People, for the majority of its life (having been chaired initially by Howarth). Halfway

319

through the life of the Task Force it became obvious to the Left within the Movement that the disabled people involved weren't being accountable and standing up for crucial changes we wanted. Blair was only willing to tinker with the DDA and so we requested a withdrawal of BCODP representatives, but they refused. This, I believe signalled the first nail in the Disabled People's Movement's coffin and led to visible splits in its ranks. In December 1999 the Task Force produced a report which, among other things recommended a number of changes to the DDA 1995 but none of these change the *nature* of the Act or made it comprehensive in terms of the areas it covered.

There was a great deal of acrimony within BCODP and I'd come aware that my leadership was going to be called into question and a challenge made. Rightly or wrongly, I didn't believe it would benefit BCODP to have extra internal conflict with so many other cracks appearing, therefore I stood aside and let Anne Rae take over as Chair and I simply sat on the National Council. Within a year or so I'd had a request to return to the Management Committee and its Personal Sub-Committee as major problems had been developing and a group on the Executive felt my knowledge and expertise was urgently needed. Things had clearly gone drastically wrong, but it wasn't until I was involved in the discussions, did I fully grasp how toxic the situation was.

It would be both unprofessional and inappropriate for me to go into the ins and outs of the situation because some of the people are not able to challenge what would be my account of things; however, I believe I've a right and need to explain my own actions. Over the last decade I've heard different versions of went on, so for the main part, I'll present here what I believe is already known in a variety of circles and then add a few things which until now haven't been spoken about by those involved.

My starting point is that I see BCODP to be like many other voluntary sector organisations of that era. The decision -making bodies were full of volunteers who had various levels of management skills and often they had to work at arms lengths. Most of the Chairs felt the communication and information passages that existed were inadequate and therefore as the numbers of staff grew, the more unsatisfactory the internal culture was. Anne Rae in February 1999 made a statement in which she said, '... most of the staff have expressed distress with their working conditions at various times, but did not wish to make their concerns official .... which made it almost impossible for the Man Com to deal with them.'

Here then was the first major headache; much of what was talked about was both undocumented and 'hearsay'. I fully understood why the Chair sought Management Committee support to bring in a consultant to conduct an organisational review, however, as Anne went on to say in her statement:

> Whilst this review did not receive wholehearted approval, it certainly did provide many useful signposts for where consideration of change was needed.

The review did offer some 'useful signposts' however a sizeable percentage of the Committee felt these were over shadowed by too much subjective opinion and unsupported allegations which made the review and its recommendations unsafe. Those who were content with the recommendations wanted to press ahead with them as soon as possible. Hence the reason I was thrown in at the deep end. Once I became familiar with the material and arguments, I voiced alarm at some of the text and recommendations because no one had put the correct procedures in place or had respected the rights of specific members of staff which I saw as making the review a ticking time bomb. I called for the review document to be put on ice until the Committee had obtained independent advice from ACAS. As I suspected they held the view that if the review were to become 'public' the allegations alone would be enough grounds for a case of unfair dismissal by a senior staff member. The Management Committee agreed a new course of action to achieve the desired outcomes.

This issue wasn't going to go away. I believe one or two disabled people's organisations weren't happy with the decision not to publish the original review and one National Council member kept writing to me demanding to see it although I'd explained it had been commissioned by Anne, but the Committee had voted to reject it in that form and it was their property. Two other internal projects were in trouble and I tried to disentangle the 'personal from the political'. The most serious was the secret plot to separate NCIL from the BCODP's IL Committee and to establish it as an independent body in London was underway. There are differences of opinion as to when this became an open issue within BCODP however I believe BCODP's CEO and I stood up to this potential threat to break NCIL by writing a document offering a new framework which acknowledged the IL Committee as NCIL's governing body which was taken to the National Council for approval. Unfortunately, the same clique who had undermined me over the debate on the DDA, sought to stir things with the organisational review was now siding with those who favoured a split.

Where Anne Rae and I both agree is that there was a lack of courage by the then Council members to make difficult decisions. I stand by the course of action I took as it wasn't the failure of leadership that resulted in BCODP losing NCIL, but the underhand tactics used against those working in the best interests of the organisation. My action prevented legal action against BCODP and I had negotiated a settlement where all sides had been happy with the outcome. I'd laid down a platform for changing the culture inside the Headquarters of BCODP while maintaining its functioning over a very difficult period. Despite all of this, on the morning of our AGM I discovered that a secret motion of no confidence in me as a Chair was going to be tabled. This placed me in an impossible position because the CEO was off on long term sick leave and because the motion was against me, I couldn't rule it as unconstitutional. The delegates were being asked to vote on a motion they hadn't seen let alone discussed in their organisations.

Unfortunately, the Management Committee met and felt pressured to the extent that they agreed to add it to the agenda. This went against our procedures in relation to meet people's access needs in meetings. It was a farce as I was given ten minutes to defend myself against the tabled allegations. I was unable to deal with the main issues as this would mean breaking the law or staff confidentiality. I bitterly complained about the undemocratic nature of the proceedings but to no avail; I was a condemned man. When I challenged a longstanding activist and supposed friend as to why she wasn't going to defend me against the censor motion, I was told the motion was being moved by a woman and women activists never tell a lie! BCODP staff members were devastated by the decision as they knew what had really taken place. I agreed to stay on as Chair until a new one had been elected and so with my resignation, I begun a decade outside national politics having become totally disillusioned by what had taken place.

Chapter 17

The wilderness years

But how could you forget such a time? And if life has a purpose, what is the purpose of wilderness years?

Samira Ahmed

A number of important things took place in my life that weren't directly related to either my work or politics at the end of the 1990s and into the new century. Since school, where I was involved in the pantomimes, I've always enjoyed watching performances and been drawn to the writing and directing of scripts. Christopher Fry's *The Lady's Not for Burning* held me spellbound because I'd seen two very different productions of it and that intrigued me.

Being involved to a degree with the Disability Arts Movement I got to know people such as Nabil Shaban, a disabled actor who was central to forming the Graeae Theatre Company, and Sarah Scott who has had over thirty years' experience of working within D/deaf and disability arts as a performer, producer and development officer. Over the years I've seen a number of Graeae productions however one in particular stands out. In 1993 they put on *Soft Vengeance* by April de Angelis, which was adapted from the book, *The Soft Vengeance of a Freedom*

Fighter by Albie Sachs. The cast included Sarah, Ray Harrison-Graham, Debbie Wilkinson and Ewan Marshall, most of whom I've known over many years. The background being that n 7 April 1988, Albie Sachs, an activist South African lawyer and a leading member of the ANC, was car-bombed in Maputo, capital of Mozambique, by agents of South Africa's security forces. The play is very much about his struggle to be part of a rising new South Africa.Playwrights such as Bertolt Brecht and David Edgar, who I met first through his partner Eve Brook, influenced my decision to try and become a playwright. Over the years I'd written a few very short scripts for training videos on behalf of Equality Ability. It began when the Co-operative Insurance Society commissioned Equality Ability to produce a DVD called, *It's Good For Business'*, which outlined how the company was complying with the DDA 1995. I was asked to check the proposed training scenario scripts and found them wanting, so offered to re-write them.

A few years later a Solihull company called Configure approach Sue with regards assisting making an interactive training package around the Goods and Services section of the Act and I was hired as a Consultant. I wrote the scripts for the four training clips and advised for the dos and don'ts, but had little acknowledgement of my work. Awhile later I discovered the package had been sold on to the disability charity, Scope, which didn't please me at all. Ironically, Sue's sister Alice was the Chair of Scope at the time, so I requested a copy of the package.

How I came to know about the launch Disabled Writers Mentoring Scheme has been lost in the midst of time. The New Playwrights Trust, known also as WritersNet, along with the Graeae Theatre Company, worked in association with New Writing North to set up the Scheme in March 1999. Jonathan Meth (2004; unpaged) explained in an interview that:

> Our partnership with Graeae Theatre Company has enabled us to fill the gaps in provision for disabled

playwrights, but also to bring that practice to other organizations (like Soho Theatre and Ty Newydd).

I decided to apply to be a mentee and was interviewed by Jonathan Meth from WritersNet and Jenny Sealey from the Graeae Theatre Company. Nine mentees were selected, and I was allocated Kaite O'Reilly, who had been born in Birmingham, to be my mentor. Working with Kaite was really enjoyable and she gave me real encouragement because I was a complete novice. What we were tasked to do is draft a full-length play. Looking back, it's quite embarrassing to realise that I was trying to put everything into my first draft, including the kitchen sink. I started out attempting to write a play called, *The Catalyst* however over many, many drafts and tantrums, it finally became *Creating Ripples.*

During the Sociology and Literature MA course I begun at Essex, I considered doing my dissertation on something relating to the writer Franz Kafka. I was particularly drawn to his short story called *Metamorphosis* because like many of his stories it's allegorical but for me there was other issues contained within its ambiguity.

Many writers have written about the theme of alienation within modern society that features in many of Kafka's stories, his abusive relationship with his father and his own self-image as a man with increasingly poor health. In my eyes I first saw *Metamorphosis* as a symbolic representation of the individual tragedy approach towards disability. The less human he became the more he experienced rejection and isolation until the only logical outcome was death.

I was reminded of Le Court and the book, *A Life Apart;* but while the sociologists were focused upon 'social death', as was Kafka, the residents of Le Court used this oppressive narrative to launch a liberation struggle. Why not take some of the themes and angst within *Metamorphosis* and both subvert and transform them in a play which challenges both actual death and social death?

Creating Ripples has gone through countless re-drafts over an eighteen year labour of love, not to mention a name change, but I'm finally happy with the final product. Although I've not realised my ambition of seeing the play performed, I haven't abandoned hope that someday I might. The synopsis reads like this:

> Greg is a working class lad who finds himself in a coma. Having had an awful childhood, the prospect of death doesn't seem that bad. Deep down, his inner or other voice has different ideas. Greg's journey from expecting death through to his acceptance of himself as a Disabled person is spiked with inner conflicts, the fear of the unknown and legacies from the past. Trixy, an outspoken Disability Rights campaigner, challenges Greg and his relationship with his family.

Creating Ripples remains my only full length play however I've written several other shorter plays although only two have seen full production; one of which was a radio play. Radio *Five Live* ran a short sports play competition where you had to write a five minute radio play on a sporting event and I entered, *One The Last Day,* which centred upon West Bromwich Albion's 'great escape' from Premier League relegation in the 2004-2005 season. Each BBC region had a regional winner and I won the West Midlands prize and had my play recorded for Radio WM. It was an interesting experience sitting in one how a radio play is produced. Other plays of mine called, *Passing the Buck, Perfect Strangers, Poppy* and *Another Anne Robinson,* have had public rehearsed readings. *Passing the Buck* is about a family where two brothers have left their sister to be the sole carer of their mother. *Perfect Strangers* is a two-character drama set in a café. But the short comedy called, *Another Anne Robinson,* concerns murder and mistaken identities. *Poppy* isn't really a play; it is an educational dialogue centred around the First World War.

To assist my development as a playwright I joined *New City Playwrights* which was a small group of playwrights and actors in the Wolverhampton who met monthly at Bantock Park. We would bring along pieces of work to be read and critiqued or set ourselves small projects. The Wolverhampton Art Gallery commissioned the *New City Playwrights* to write, produce and perform ten playlets based on the venue's new Pop Art Gallery, for its opening day. I chose *Jackie* by Andy Warhol and wrote a play entitled, *'But then you start learning the details.'*

It's fair to say I don't believe I'd a fair rub of the green in terms of support because a number of promises have been made by theatre companies however, they have failed to materialise. I've also had a bizarre situation where I applied for a BBC mentoring scheme but was turned down on the grounds that I was still being supported by Graeae, which certainly was news to me! Despite these knock backs and disappointments, I still write scripts.

It's slightly ironic that despite my political opposition to the DDA 1995 I found myself being employed on a consultancy basis to support a range of companies and agencies to comply with it. In 2002 because of my work with the West Mercia Workers Educational Association I was approached to be a part-time Consultant with the WEA's National Inclusivity Working Group to assist them to review their policies, procedures and practice. I enjoyed working within adult education because it threw up a host of challenges given the unique culture it had. Many of the tutors had delivered their subject area for a countless number of years and suddenly found themselves being asked to consider if the approaches they took were 'inclusive' or not. Perhaps it should go without saying that not for the first time and certainly not the last, I occasionally encountered stiff resistance to change, although I must give full credit to the members of the National Inclusivity Working Group who were totally committed to enact a cultural shift.

I'd stepped back from involvement in national politics in an organised sense, but I hadn't abandoned disability politics altogether. In 2003 Michael Turner, Phil Brough and myself were appointed as project workers for a new project called, *'Our voice in our future,'* which was funded by the Joseph Rowntree Foundation and run by the Shaping Our Lives National User Network which is an independent user-controlled organisation, think tank and network. Starting out as a research and development project, it developed into an independent organisation in 2002. The organisation works with a wide and diverse range of service users which include:

- people with physical and/or sensory impairments
- people with learning difficulties
- users and survivors of mental health service
- young people with experience of being 'looked after'
- people living with HIV/AIDS
- people with life limiting illnesses
- older people
- people with experience of alcohol and drug services
- homeless people

My overall role as a project worker was to assist the local disabled people's organisation to organise and run a conference as well as approaching disabled people from across the City about their experience as service users. This latter task included a remarkable meeting with a group of disabled Somali refugees. My particular project was called, 'INFLUENCING OUR FUTURE IN SHEFFIELD' and part of the remit was the writing up the project with a conference report. When the Joseph Rowntree Foundation published, *'Our voice in our future,'* my section of the report had been edited without my knowledge. Those involved in developing the conference had been encouraged by me to write a number of sketches on the experiences of being a service user. I wrote one called, A BOYS' NIGHT OUT, deliberately focusing on males in order to challenge a number of stereotypes within the comedy.

When JRF published the whole 'A Voice in the Future' Report I discovered the sketch I'd written and performed at the Conference had been re-written and was called, A GIRLS' NIGHT OUT. I never discovered exactly who took this decision, it's could have been Mike as the main project worker, but I suspect it was someone higher in the organisation. Whoever it was I'd like to suggest the decision was a foolish one. The original script sought to challenge stereotypes about 'care roles' and male 'bonding' and as a result of the re-draft, the script that was published merely offered a comic status quo take on the relationship between a female care staff member and female service user. The other sketches had women characters, so it wasn't as if only a male perspective was being put across. Besides, my aim was to confront assumptions; so, I'm still baffled by the decision to publish a politically correct 'gender' shift. No one had questioned the original script on the day or in the project steering group, so I felt the final report had re-written not only my sketch but also history.

At the conference Mike Higgins, a disability activist and musician, performed a number of songs including, *the same old story in a different disguise*, which we co-wrote. Despite the incident with the sketch, I continued my association with *Shaping Our Lives*, so when its Director, Fran Branfield who had been my fellow Senior Consultant at *Equal Ability*, informed me that they were looking for a Research and Development Worker who would work from home, I declared an interest. With hindsight this was a mistake because I didn't really understand the philosophy put forward by Peter Beresford who was the *Shaping Our Lives'* Chairperson. I thought I understood the focus on what made effective service user involvement, namely, user networking and knowledge, but once in the job I struggled with Peter's conceptualisation of 'knowledge' because it wasn't adequately explained but assumed to be 'common sense'. If, for example, we look at the work of Michael Foucault, we can see that power and knowledge are not seen as independent entities but are inextricably related; in other words, knowledge is always an exercise of power and power always a function of knowledge. Therefore, from Foucault's perspective Power/knowledge not only limits what we can do, but also opens up new ways of acting and thinking about ourselves.

My difficulty was moving from this abstract theory to developing a methodology that was capable of capturing and making sense of what *Shaping Our Lives* referred to as 'service users' knowledge'. In the publication, '*Making user involvement work – Supporting service user networking and knowledge*', this view was put forward:

> Increasing political and policy interest in 'evidence' or 'knowledge' based policy and practice has highlighted issues relating to knowledge and different knowledge sources, including service users' experiential knowledge. Service users see themselves as having a particular role to play in the production of knowledge for health and social care, as 'experts in their own experience' and because of the experiential nature of their knowledge. Both individual service users and service user organisations feel that they have difficulties impacting on health and social care policy and provision effectively. (Branfield and Beresford, 2006; unpaged)

As the Research and Development Worker the expectation was for me to find ways of getting service users to articulate the 'experiential nature of their knowledge'. My own 'knowledge' comes from being a disabled person, professional and an academic among other things, therefore the point raised by Leonard about dominant ideology in relation to disability influenced how I approached this project. He wrote:

> One result of this powerful external definition of their situation is that it tends to suggest that people with disabilities cannot live worthwhile, active lives and that their capacities can only be *defined through medical and social expertise, for their own definitions are bound to be 'subjective'.* [Emphasis added] (Leonard, 1984; 188)

Most of my professional career in one guise or other I'd worked with users of services and had promoted and offered training around user involvement, empowerment and self-determination. My time at Social Services taught me a great deal about how many professionals relate to disabled people and other service users. The attitude of: 'we know best' was often supported by subtle, but nevertheless still coercive, methods of maintaining the imbalance of power within decision making.

In my opinion service user involvement in service delivery and planning always raised red flags for me because of the power inequality that existed between the professionals and service users. I've lost count as to number of consultations I've witnessed where they simply acted to rubber stamp the outcomes desired by the professional or where service users' views were seen as 'unrealistic' and 'not representative' enough.

Years later I came back to this issue when I explored how Health and Social Care sold 'Personalisation' to service users. The language of both the Disabled People's Movement and Service Users' Movement was used to promote co-production of services under the banner of 'choice and control', but in reality, it was a shift towards the marketisation of services, greater commodification and individuals being expected to manage their own 'care packages' in an age of austerity and cutbacks. The work of Sarah Carr traces this development, as cited in Williams-Findlay (2016). This isn't the time or place for this discussion however I must admit I'd a number of sleepless nights questioning my own grasp of what was being asked of me and those I was expected to talk to.

The point I'm trying to make is that the issue or difficulty for me wasn't that I questioned the validity of service users' experience, because subjectivity isn't a problem in itself; it was more a question of me not being confident in the belief that people were fully conscious of 'the knowledge' they had. The initial work I did on user knowledge tried to bring this to the fore with the compiling of a questionnaire for both individuals and organisations which can be found in the Appendix of 'Making user involvement work' along with an analysis of the findings.

Where I found myself struggling was finding appropriate ways of holding interviews or discussion groups with service users around 'their knowledge' as this seemed problematic without first establishing a framework and I was being discouraged from doing that. So, I wasn't convinced people would know what I was seeking from them. In my opinion this section from part three of the Report captures the difficulties I felt I was experiencing:

> We have preferred to use the term 'knowledge' in our discussion because it does not take for granted the complexities of how what people know comes (or doesn't come) to be seen as evidence underpinning or justifying something. There is now much more discussion about knowledge in health and social care. It has raised issues about what knowledge is, whose knowledge we're talking about, how we come to know things, whether different approaches to finding things out result in different knowledge and so on. These are big, often complex issues and frequently they are discussed in ways which are themselves complicated and difficult to understand, using big words and professional jargon. (Branfield and

Beresford, 2006; 26)

This is why I felt caught between the rock and the hard place. What I didn't want to do is create conditions which replicated the status quo as described in the report:

> This has frequently meant that such discussions have excluded long-term users of health and social care or been very difficult for them to engage in on equal terms. We know that many people with learning difficulties, disabled people and mental health service users have had limited and inferior educational opportunities. (Branfield and Beresford, 2006; 26)

Unlike me, both Peter and Fran held the view that service users understood their own needs and also could articulate what worked and didn't work for them and this view is reflected in the project report:

> Significantly, while the concept of 'knowledge' can be a complex one, the majority of service users who took part in this project did not need the idea of 'service user knowledge' explaining to them. They readily related to the term. The general feeling seemed to be a taken-for-granted assumption that service users were 'experts by experience' or, as a service user put it: 'Of course, I am an expert on the services I receive. I've received services all my life, of one sort or another and you just get to be an expert. It's like you have to otherwise you don't get what you want. Not that I often get what I want but if I wasn't an expert it would be even worse. I mean you talk to anyone who has just started using services.' (Branfield and Beresford, 2006; 30)

Again, I fully accepted that knowing one's way around the system or looking after one's best interests is something many service users learn to do by experience and I certainly wasn't questioning that experience, however, what I did question was how far this personal experience as 'knowledge' was being employed and made sense of in terms of influencing or developing service delivery. I also believed different groups of service users had particular relations with professionals which impacted upon their ability to use their 'knowledge' productively. There developed a communication breakdown between *Shaping Our Lives* and myself due to differing opinions on what was needed to progress the project. There were no bad feelings because each side acknowledged the differences were too large to overcome, therefore we agreed to go our separate ways. Even now the meaning of 'service user knowledge' remains troublingly problematic for me.

In Wolverhampton where I lived there was a disabled people's organisation called, *One Voice*, that was until recently funded by the local authority. Due to both personal and political reasons I never felt able to join them as they were more consumer-facing group than a campaigning organisation. I nevertheless had a cordial relationship with their worker and attended various meetings they organised or were involved in. At one such meeting I met Sarah Bidwell who I'd met several times over the years because she was an equality officer with Wolverhampton City Council. During our conversation Sarah mentioned she was about to have a new role at the Council and her old post would be advertised. Having left *Shaping Our Lives* and been unsuccessful at obtaining a similar post in Birmingham years before, I was keen to have a shot at this job.

Despite suffering from food poisoning on the day of the interview I managed to secure the position of Senior Equality & Policy Officer primarily around Disability Equality at Wolverhampton City Council in 2006. My role was both internal and external facing; assisting in developing and advising on policy. Chief among my tasks was supporting my team in relation to the Equality

Standard for local government in England which was established in 2001.

The year I joined the Council the Standard was extended to address six equality strands: age, disability, gender, race, religion / belief and sexual orientation. The Standard worked alongside new public sector duties that were introduced for race, disability and gender. The aim of these public sector duties was to promote excellence in the management of equality outcomes. While I supported my colleagues Val and Delva on producing Equality Schemes for race and gender, my own responsibility was to develop one on disability. I'm quite proud of the work I did around the Wolverhampton City Council Disability Equality Scheme 2006 – 2009 even though in the final analysis it was shelved by the Council's Chief Executive. Before revealing what happened it's necessary to provide some context.

My time at Birmingham City Council taught me how difficult it was to enact a cultural shift and in Wolverhampton I'd a battle on two fronts. Sarah Bidwell had established a Deaf People's Forum and a colleague called Will, who was an officer in Social Services, and I took over the running of it. We were both met with suspicion and encountered resistance in the early days and after conversions with Sarah and others I quickly realised there was much distrust between the Deaf community and the Council. Will only stayed a few months, so I became solely responsible for the Forum and I made it perfectly clear that the way Sarah ran things and my approach would be completely different. To demonstrate this, I organised a discussion about disability politics and Deaf culture and I don't think they knew how to view me after that! I began to understand their frustration with the Council and in the time that I was there I tried to remove some of the barriers which won me lasting respect in the Deaf community. My role also involved setting up the Council's British Sign Language Interpretation Service and managing it.

When it came to developing the Disability Equality Scheme, I used a number of methods to obtain data and engage in consultation with users of our services. The Deaf People's Forum was one avenue, but I also established a DES steering group of disabled users and staff to give the Scheme its shape and focus. This was established after I worked with the Council's Participation Officer to hold a City-wide consultation event to map out key areas for addressing inequality within the City.

The steering group met regularly and held meeting with representatives of the various departments to discuss the possible priorities in each area in relation to the information gathered from the event. I wrote several drafts of the Scheme and shared them not only with the steering group, but the also the departments where the Scheme would list actions and outcomes for the next three years.

Cindy had been developing her own Disability Equality Scheme for the University of Wolverhampton and we agreed a joint launch. The Equality and Human Rights Commission requested copies of all DES produced by public sector bodies for a review and my Scheme was positively received by them. Over the following twelve months I sought to get the action plans operational and was met with stiff resistance. Charged with writing an annual review of the Scheme I pulled no punches; as a result, the senior management team pulled my report and instructed that it be written. I was hauled before the Chief Executive and asked why I'd developed a Scheme with the expectation that 'the Council would *do things*'? In other words, I was being scapegoated for producing an 'unrealistic' Scheme people had signed up to. There was nothing unrealistic or costly involved; the truth is the desire to change the culture just wasn't there.

An example of this entrenched attitude at the Council was to be found in the unwillingness to consider how to provide Council information to the Deaf community. The historical excuse was that the Council's server was too old to support video clips with BSL. I'd provided evidence of how this could be overcome via an external host, but no one wanted to know. There are a number of other examples I could cite to support the general point I'm making which is simply the fact equality wasn't a priority and I was rocking the boat.

While this might sound very depressing and perhaps all too familiar to many people who've been employed in local authorities, there were also elements of my job I enjoyed. Among the organisations I worked with was the Wolverhampton Network Consortium which led to the creation of the Wolverhampton Disability Network which sought to bring new disabled people into community building and to ensure disability related issues were more visible within mainstream social and political activity.

This project was always going to be a struggle due to the passive nature of disabled communities within Wolverhampton and the historical role played by *One Voice*. Despite the willingness of everyone involved the barriers protecting the status quo were too great to overcome and as a result *One Voice* took control of it until it petered out. I nevertheless met some good people as a consequence of being Chair of the Wolverhampton Disability Network.

I also had a good working relationship with many other council officers including Ruth Wilson who was an equality consultant with the Quality and Improvement section. I supported Ruth in a workshop called *Getting Started* aimed at promoting disability equality in schools and fed into her own Disability Equality Scheme. Through partnership working I managed to get disability related issues more visible within the Council itself and other public sector bodies.

Once again, I'd a career decision to make. I wasn't being forced out of the Council but my ability to carry forward the disability equality agenda had been badly compromised, and I couldn't see myself sat idle behind a desk or churning out pointless policy directives until the axe fell on me. I was considering my options when Sue Maynard Campbell phoned Cindy and hearing I might be available again was keen to meet and discuss possibilities however Sue shortly afterwards had a heart attack which brought our long fruitful association to an abrupt and terribly sad end. I was utterly devastated to lose such a close friend and ally.

Leaving the Council was a blessing in many ways as it gave me an opportunity to recharge my batteries and take stock of the world around me. There was also an additional factor which worked in my favour. Colin Barnes established the Centre for Disability Studies as the *British Council of Organisations of Disabled People's* Disability Research Unit in the School of Sociology and Social Policy in 1990 at the University of Leeds and was its Director until 2008 and, of course, I'd known him all of this time. He had periodically tried to get me to enrol on the Disability Studies MA course and as this was his final year, I finally agreed to do the two year distance learning course. I was still at the Council until the December, so the first essay I wrote was a struggle as I sought to balance work with studying.

Much of the material was already well known to me, so the biggest headache was remembering how to write essays and format them, especially how to present quotations! My essays covered such topics as:

1. How valid is Mike Oliver's (1990) contention that the 19th century provided both the 'ideological' and a 'practical' solution to the problem of disability?
2. Explore the contention that within contemporary western societies, campaigns for anti-discrimination legislation and human rights laws for disabled people can only partially address the problem of disability.
3. Critically explore the role of 'disability culture' in the empowerment of disabled people.

4. Explore the claim that simulation exercises in disability awareness training sessions reinforce rather than expose the limitations of conventional individualistic approaches to disability.

Writing these essays didn't simply enable me to demonstrate that I'd understood the subject areas or done the reading, I felt the course provided me with the first academic space to fully express my own experience, knowledge and interpretations of the issues. It gave me the confidence to write about theory and not simply to promote disability politics. The second year was taken up by writing an essay on research methodology which I found tough going. Then the bulk of the year was taken up with writing a dissertation. My dissertation advisor was Alison Sheldon who I didn't know until I joined the course. Distant learning can contain some communication difficulties, which meant that from time to time Alison and I were frustrated by each other responses or lack of them.

Deciding the topic of my dissertation wasn't too difficult because I wanted to return to an old interest of mine. I didn't manage to look at how 'race' was covered in the media during my time at CCCS, so here was an opportunity to consider how 'disability' was reported upon. I was familiar with studies that had taken place in both the USA and the UK, therefore, I took the opportunity to use their methodological framework for part of my exploration. My dissertation was entitled, 'Is there evidence to support the view that the language and subject matter selected by the Times and the Guardian in relation to disabled people has changed over the last twenty years', and while Alison and I were happy with it, Colin complained bitterly about its length! A copy is still available on the Centre for Disability Studies' website.

I obtained my MA with Merit and attended the Graduation Ceremony on a bitterly cold December day in 2009, aged fifty eight. Personally, I thought that was quite an achievement, but within weeks this was to be surpassed. One of the Graduation photographs has Cindy looking glowing in it and at the time I put that down to the weather; however, on Christmas Eve having felt a little strange for a few weeks, Cindy took a pregnancy test. Shocked by the result she immediately made a doctor's appointment, and, after two further tests, she discovered that 2010 was going to transform our lives.

Chapter 18

Into the light

Long is the way and hard, that out of Hell leads up to light.

John Milton

While I hadn't been active for a while in national politics, I still kept up-to-date with New Labour's Neoliberal reforms and how they had side-lined radical disability politics. I coined the term 'Janus politics' which refers to looking back to the disability politics of the 1980s and the concepts that were developed, such as the social model of disability and independent living, whilst emptying them of their original meanings and transforming them into ideas fostering the notion that inclusion was possible via legal rights and responsibility. Blair helped develop a new market facing 'Disability Movement' which was a hybrid of traditional charities alongside certain disabled people's organisations who were keen hone their entrepreneurial skills in the service delivery sector. Employing language taken from the Disabled People's Movement, these organisations pushed messages associated with 'citizenship', 'social cohesion' and 'inclusion', and this is best typified by what was called, *Equality 2025*.

Equality 2025 was a non-departmental public body of publicly appointed disabled people which was established in December 2006. The group's role was to offer strategic, confidential advice to Government on issues that affect disabled people. This advice included participation in the very early stages of policy development and in-depth examination of existing policy. The group worked with Ministers and senior officials across government. The government closed it down in 2013. Several experienced disability activists, included me, attempted to get appointed but were 'overlooked' for what was euphemistically called, 'not the usual suspects'. The 1990s and through the 2000s we had seen the demise of the Disabled People's Movement and many of the old guard feared the worse.

On 26 April 2009, David Cameron gave us a chilling warning as to what was about to come crashing down upon us. Cameron spoke of entering an age of austerity which demanded what we referred to as 'responsible politics' which actually meant an ideological and organisational assault on the Welfare State and local government. He said:

> Over the next few years, we will have to take some incredibly tough decisions on taxation, spending, borrowing – things that really affect people's lives. Getting through those difficult decisions will mean sticking together as a country – government and people.

A general election took place on Thursday, 6 May 2010, however none of the parties achieved the 326 seats needed for an overall majority. David Cameron's Conservative Party won the largest number of votes and seats, but still fell 20 seats short which resulted in a hung parliament. The inability to form a government led Cameron to set up a coalition government with Nick Clegg's Liberal Democrats. This was the first coalition in British history to emerge directly from an election outcome. Both parties were committed to an austerity agenda. Many of us who were politically aware knew only too well what that was going to mean in reality; while at the same time, understanding that disabled people were ill-equipped to deal with the onslaught that was bound to come our way. This period in recent history is well documented from several differing perspectives. (Williams-Findlay, 2011; Briant et al, 2013; Deeming, 2015)

Shortly before the Conservative Party held its first annual conference in Birmingham since the election, a small group of disabled people led by Linda Burnip met to discuss organising a protest. Linda, who also has a disabled son, had like spent much of her life campaigning for rights and change. In her early years she had been a Nupe shop steward in a very militant union branch and was an active campaigner throughout the Thatcher period. I'd only just met Linda through the BDRC but was keen to join the small collective who met in a Bebo's café in the centre of Birmingham.

The original plan was to establish a disabled people's protest in Chamberlain Square in the heart of the city and then join in with the march organised by the TUC. On a soggy October Sunday morning a handful of us arrived at the Square however it quickly became clear to us that a sizeable number of disabled people were going straight to the march and where we were would attract little or no attention, so we decided to meet the march on route.

The TUC let disabled people lead it and that made it easy for us to filter in. We had come together under the banner of 'the disabled people's protest' however during the planning stage it was agreed that a permanent campaigning group would be established, with Linda coming up with the name: Disabled People Against Cuts (DPAC). Perhaps the context of an email I sent Linda foresaw the relationship I was to have with DPAC and the other co-founders:

I think everyone, especially you, deserves a huge slap on the back for Sunday. I'm sorry, but I've to admit that I was a little lax in keeping up with the pre-demo info on various sites, so I know on Friday I cut across proposals already made - apologies for that.

When you get to know me, which I hope you will, you'll discover 3 things about me: first, I'm a pushy bastard, second, I say what I believe needs saying, and third, my bark is worse that my bite ... This often gets me into trouble because it's misread - people think I crave power, etc. The truth is, I've the drive, commitment and passion which means I set the bar high for myself and expect others to be like me. I'm saying all this because I've already been criticised by someone for taking the Crippen blog on the logo onto Ouch - to me, our Movement has to be both open and democratic - we've no time to waste on prima donnas or those who want to see themselves as 'an elite' - Nothing About Us Without Us is what motivates me. I'm a foot soldier with experience, that's how I see myself and I'm willing to put my experience behind this fight - irrespective of who is leading it. I'll of course continue to kick ass if I think things aren't moving quickly enough! Keep me posted re: DPAC.

As a co-founder of DPAC I became part of the Steering Group and remained centrally involved over the following three years writing articles, speaking on platforms on behalf of DPAC and, when I could, taking part in activities. My engagement was difficult having a small child and this was something not always acknowledged by other activists.

It was quite distressing to hear oneself spoken as an 'armchair activist' or that people were only real activists if they were 'on the streets'. Impairment reality was often understood as a reason for not being able to participate, but awareness of other equality issues seemed lacking.

There were from time to time also political

disagreements. While most of the Steering Group were centre-left leaning, very few had been in Left groups and as a result, my approach clashed with others who were more individualistic in their approach and weren't too concerned with collective accountability.

DPAC also followed to some extent in the footsteps of the Direct Action Network, which used various forms of 'direct action' e.g. the occupation of buildings and blockading of roads, as a central part of their campaigning. I've always viewed 'direct action' as a useful tactic however cautioned against turning it into a campaigning fetish because this would weaken its effectiveness. Holding such an opinion didn't go down well in some quarters and lead to me being characterised as 'outdated'.

Following a series of incidents which I felt under-minded my credibility and misrepresented my activism, I decided to step down from the steering group. I've remained involved with DPAC mainly through the setting up of the regional DPAC West Midlands which I co-ordinate along with another longstanding activist called Sandra Daniels. Before moving on from my involvement with DPAC I want to acknowledge what's on their website states:

> DPAC co-founders are the original Disabled Peoples' Protest organisers. Leading coordinator Linda Burnip was instrumental in getting disabled peoples' voices heard and disabled people represented at the protest, along with, Sam Brackenbury, Bob Williams-Findlay, Tina Hogg, Debbie Jolly, Eleanor Lisney, Pete Millington, Dave Lupton, and most important of all: all those that marched in the pouring rain on October the 3rd, all those that joined the virtual protest, and all those that supported us with email campaigns and messages when the march was threatened: all made DPAC a reality.

My time in DPAC led me to re-evaluate the nature of disability politics during the second decade of the twenty first century. BCODP had transformed into the United Kingdom Disabled People's Council however by 2012 it had become ineffectual. Debbie Jolly recognised as I did, that DPAC was the legacy of the old Disabled People's Movement, however it wasn't in a position where it could substitute for that Movement. In a joint paper we presented to the Leeds Disability Studies Centre, we stated our view that three crucial issues underpinned DPAC's approach:

- Began because we were tired of waiting for DPOs to raise issues of what was predicted to happen to disabled people under Coalition.
- Feel DPOs missed vital clues when New Labour were in power – many 'reforms' now are versions of previous New Labour 'reforms'
- As DPAC grew we realised that many disabled people did not know what DPOs were and they also felt Big Disability Charities would support disabled people well

Building upon this understanding I tried to initiate a discussion around setting up a new project in a paper entitled, 'Building a social movement within the politics of resistance: The New Challenge'. In the paper I argued that we must start to address the immediate question: what do disability politics look like in a time of capitalist crisis? This requires disabled people to understand the need to build a new social moment around aims that correspond to defending the existing interests of disabled people – the need to develop within disability politics a specific type of 'politics of resistance'. As well as being anti-cuts I believed the United Nations Convention on the Rights of Disabled People needs to be central to any new social movement, especially Article Nineteen.

I acknowledged that the immediate and central focus

had to be on opposing the ideological and material attacks from the Government and other policy makers / administrators and at the same time putting into place the mechanism whereby this new movement could make a firm defence of disability politics by 're-claiming' the ground secured by the original Disabled People's Movement. I recognised, as I thought others would, that this was a huge task especially when our resources were so depleted. What I was proposing was the creation of a new social movement with a radical political practice which drew upon the work undertaken by the old Disabled People's Movement but will seek to be more 'directional' in its approach. The numbers involved wouldn't be huge, but we had seen an upsurge in political activity.

This received lukewarm reception both within DPAC and the wider audience of disabled activists. It took a further five years before any type of discussion took place along these lines and little progress has been made. Alongside trying to get an organisational response, I continued to develop a critique of the implications of the shift from Social Democratic welfare policies of the 1980s to the anti-welfare state policies of Neoliberalism as seen through a social approach to disability.

Mike Oliver and I spoke about the historical materialist basis of his social model and to what extent there was a need for a new socio-economic analysis which captured the present form of disablism encountered in the UK and more globally. On the ground there remains a reluctance to engage in theoretical debate, especially around the social model which has come to be viewed as a safety blanket, therefore disability politics for the time being are reduced to focusing on the resistance to cuts, services and Rights. (Oliver and Barnes, 2012).

My life from 2010 wasn't just about politics. The University of Wolverhampton and Wolverhampton City Council sought an Equality Training Officer in 2012 and being out of work since leaving the DRC I applied, but narrowly missed being appointed. Sadly, the person who was successful died shortly after taking up the post and I was then invited to take up the position. This was once again an odd position to be in as I worked two days under the direction of my former colleague, Delva Campbell, and two days for Cindy.

Both public bodies had different cultures which impacted upon how I was expected to deliver the training around the Equality Act 2010. This was an enjoyable challenge however I was fully aware the post was time limited due to the Council's funding restrictions. Perhaps the biggest challenge was keeping equality issues on the agenda during the age of austerity.

Corners were being cut, not to mention services, which meant staff were resistant to having to consider the impact of equality issues within both policy development areas and service delivery. Similarly, within the University the resistance to culture change largely came from the academic staff, many of whom had taught the same way for decades! There were times when I achieved small victories which were rewarding.

Between 2013 and 2015 I worked full-time as the University of Wolverhampton's Equality Training Officer and played a more supportive role within the Equality and Diversity Unit. In addition to my on-going training role I took over the role of co-ordinating the Disabled Staff Network which ran a series of events including presentations on 'What is 'Disability History'?', 'Disability and the Holocaust', 'War and Impairment: The Social Consequences of Disablement' and one relating to my dissertation entitled, 'The Politicisation of Disability Images'. My main task was to run a series of training events around the following topics:

- Equality Checks Workshops
- Introduction to Equality Checks

- Introduction to the Equality Act 2010
- Dignity at Work
- Avoiding Disabling Practice
- Exploring Unconscious Bias
- Disability Issues in the Workplace: Introduction to key issues for supporting disabled employees

The most interesting courses were around the subject of 'Dignity at Work' because the topic stemmed from a discreet piece of work I was commissioned to do by a specific workforce within the University. I decided a straight forward training course would probably go down like a lead balloon, so we hired an actor to play in a narrative I wrote called, 'The University of Impropriety'. Within this unfolding story I'd included a series of scenarios which portrayed incorrect behaviour at work.

After each video clip we'd produced, we'd get the attendees to discuss what they saw and what the appropriate action would've been. Most of these sessions were well attended and provoked a great deal of discussion, however, this didn't go down with the senior management team who felt I'd poked a hornet's nest. Just as the City Council had done, the University begun to demand a less hands on approach to addressing equality issues and both Cindy and I saw the writing on the wall for both of us. I was the first to leave as my contract wasn't renewed. Cindy left the following year.

I'd been inactive in mainstream politics since the late 1990s however in 2013 film director Ken Loach appealed for a new party to replace the Labour Party which Ken rightly claimed had failed to oppose austerity and had shifted towards Neoliberalism. I found most of what was said by Ken and the early members of Left Unity to my liking and so I became a member. On 9 October 2013 along with eight others I signed the following statement:

> We have been feeling excited and proud of how well
> Left Unity has done up 'til now in bringing in

disabled people, but there is so much to be done. That is why we have set up a disabled people's caucus within Left Unity. To us, the severity of the current government's assault on us and the growing solidarity between different disability groups in response, make the importance of our having a strong voice within Left Unity absolutely vital. It will make Left Unity stand out from all other parties if we can be seen to be a powerhouse within it from as early as possible.

In 2014, the party had 2,000 members and 70 branches across Britain however the election of Jeremy Corbyn as leader of the Labour Party in 2015 changed the political landscape and many members of Left Unity re-joined the Labour Party to support Corbyn whilst remaining sympathetic to Left Unity's policies and its openness to politics. The organisation although much smaller than it was, remains affiliated to the Party of the European Left, and offers a radical programme which I remain firmly committed to. At the time of writing this chapter I'm a member of Left Unity's National Council and co-ordinator of the Disabled Members Caucus.

At roughly the same time as I joined Left Unity, Robert Punton, Sandra Daniels and I met to celebrate Robert's Birthday. They had both been members of BDRG and so I'd known them for over twenty years, but we had rarely socialised together. We'd discussed the current situation within DPAC and disability politics, especially within Birmingham and across the West Midlands and decided that perhaps the way forward would be to establish a region wide DPAC. While we haven't been that prolific in our activities across the West Midlands, I believe we've had an influence in many anti-austerity activities locally and nationally.

Disabled People Against Cuts West Midlands organised a street protest on 3 October 2016 during the Conservative Party Conference. The theme of the protest was: *No more 'Cinderella' Role – We Will Go To The Ball!* DPAC WM sought to highlight how disabled people continued to be socially excluded from or marginalised within mainstream activities – inadequate access arrangements, disabling barriers to travelling, cuts to services available and savage reductions in social support. The local Metro line running through the centre of Birmingham was brought to a halt.

The last few years have thrown up contradictions and proved extremely challenging. I'm busier and more engaged in political activity than I've ever been and far more confident in my own ability, but this has come at a price. Having both family and political commitments isn't been easy to manage; and my health has been poor in recent years therefore the stress and strain, financially and emotionally, over the last decade has taken its toll. Where things go from here is hard to say because the world is in a different place to where it was when I realised my own personal journey couldn't be viewed in isolation.

My realisation was that I wasn't just a person living with a significant impairment, this fact had social and political implications that went well beyond me as an individual. I reject the view that disability politics is a form of 'identity politics' because the definition of identity politics is that they 'tend to promote their own specific interests or concerns without regard to the interests or concerns of any larger political group.' In my opinion, disability politics are about changing social relations in order to facilitate people with impairments engagement with larger political and social groups. Disablism, rather than 'specific interests or concerns', maintain disabled people's social exclusion and marginalisation. The desire for inclusion isn't wrong or idealistic, provided there's an understanding of what needs to be done to make the world a home for all,

What I've come to understand is that the personal is political. I therefore embrace the political identity of being a disabled person and all the implications I've spoken about during the writing of this book. Am I more than a disabled socialist? I believe I am, but my individuality has always been informed by both who, and what I am. Who knows what kind of life I may have lived, if my birth had been uncomplicated? I do know I would've been a different person to whom I became because my lived experiences would've been very different. There's been much darkness in my life, most of it underpinned by the need to struggle to survive, but through determination and the love and support of others, I believe I've come into the light and I hope people will see me for whom I really am. This has been my journey to date and I hope *More Than A Left Foot* has provided an insight into an array of historical events, socio-political issues and personal narratives worthy of your time.

References

Abberley, P., (1991), 'Handicapped by numbers: a critique of the OPCS disability surveys.' *Occasional Papers in Sociology*, 9, Bristol Polytechnic: Department of Economics and Social Science.

Abberley, P., (1997a), 'The Concept of Oppression and the Development of a Social Theory of Disability' in *Disability Studies: Past Present and Future* edited by Len Barton and Mike Oliver; Leeds: The Disability Press, pp. 160 – 178.

Abberley, P., (1997b), 'The Limits of Classical Social Theory in the Analysis and Transformation of Disablement' in *Disability Studies: Past Present and Future* edited by Len Barton and Mike Oliver; Leeds: The Disability Press, pp. 25 – 44.

About Wivenhoe, http://wivencyclopedia.org/About_Wivenhoe/about_wivenhoe.htm.

Ahmed, Sarah, (2004), The Cultural Politics of Emotion (Edinburgh: Edinburgh University Press).

Annan, N., (1975), *Report of the Annan Enquiry 1974*: University of Essex.

Barberis, P., McHugh, J., Tyldesley, M., (2000), *Encyclopaedia of British and Irish Political Organizations: Parties, Groups and Movements of the 20th Century*. A&C Black. P. 284.

Barile, M., (2003), 'Globalization and ICF Eugenics: Historical coincidence or connection? The More Things Change the More They Stay the Same', *Disability Studies Quarterly*, Spring, Vol. 23, No. 2, pp. 208-223, www.cds.hawaii.edu/dsq.

Barnes C., (1991), *Disabled People in Britain and Discrimination: A Case for Anti-Discrimination Legislation*, London, C. Hurst and Co. Ltd, p. 264.

Barnes C, Mercer G, *Disability*, Oxford: Polity Press, 2003, iv, p. 186.

Birmingham City Council, (2017) 'Birmingham Adult Social Care' https://www.birmingham.gov.uk/info/20018/adult_soci al_care_and_health/1522/day_opportunities_for_adults_i n_birmingham_-_vision_and_strategy.

Bickenbach, J. et al., (1999), 'Models of disablement, universalism and the international classification of impairments, disabilities and handicaps,' *Social Science and Medicine*, 48, pp. 1173–1187.

Biggs-Davison, J. https://www.revolvy.com/topic/John%20Biggs-Davison&item_type=topic.

Borsay, A. (2005) *Disability and Social Policy in Britain Since 1750: A History of Exclusion*, Basingstoke: Palgrave Macmillan.

Branfield, F. Beresford, P., (2006), *Making user involvement work: supporting service user networking and knowledge*, Joseph Rowntree Foundation, Bristol. https://www.jrf.org.uk/report/making-user-involvement-work-supporting-service-user-networking-and-knowledge.

Briant, E. Watson N. & Philo G., (2013), Reporting disability in the age of austerity: the changing face of media representation of disability and disabled people in the United Kingdom and the creation of new 'folk devils', *Disability & Society*, 28:6, pp. 874-889.

Brown, W., (1995), *States of Injury: Power and Freedom in Late Modernity* (New Jersey: Princeton University Press).

Callinicos, A. and Turner, S., (1975), 'The Student Movement Today', *International Socialism* (February).

Cherry, K., (2018), 'What Is Self-Concept and How Does It Form?', *very well mind*, https://www.verywellmind.com/what-is-self-concept-2795865.

Connell, K., (2014), Centre for Contemporary Cultural Studies, Transcripts of interviews with Hazel Chowcat, Michael O'Shaughnessy and Errol Lawrence, https://www.birmingham.ac.uk/schools/historycultures/departments/history/research/projects/cccs/interviews/index.aspx.

Connell, K., (2014), Interviewing Bob Findlay as part of the Centre for Contemporary Cultural Studies project, https://www.youtube.com/watch?v=AYGF088Mk0I.

Campbell, F. K., (2008), 'Exploring internalised Ableism using critical race theory', *Disability & Society*, 23 (2): 151 – 162.

Cameron-Smith, C., (2004), 'The story of the self: a grounded theory perspective', Thesis (D. Litt. et Phil.), Rand Afrikaans University, (2004) Bibliographical references: leaves 250-283. Available at: https://core.ac.uk/display/18215609

Carnie, H. J., (undated), 'Talking to the Centre: Different Voices in the Intellectual History of 'The Centre for Contemporary Cultural Studies' (CCCS)', http://homepage.usask.ca/~jgz816/archive21.html.

Clapton, J. & Fitzgerald, J., (1997), The History of Disability: A History of 'Otherness', *New Renaissance magazine:* Vol. 7, No. 1. http://www.ru.org/artother.html.

Crow, L., (1996), Including All Of Our Lives: Renewing The Social Model Of Disability, in *Exploring the Divide,* edited by Barnes and Mercer, Leeds: The Disability Press, pp. 55 – 72.

Csordas, T. (1999) 'Embodiment and cultural phenomenology', in Weiss, G. & Haber, H. F. (eds.), *Perspectives on Embodiment: The Intersections of Nature and Culture,* London: Routledge. pp. 143 – 62.

Deeming, C. (2015) 'Foundations of the Workfare State – Reflections on the Political Transformation of the Welfare State in Britain', *Social Policy & Administration,* Vol. 49, No.7, pp. 862 - 886

Dene Park College (1986). BBC Domesday Reloaded http://www.bbc.co.uk/history/domesday/dblock/GB-556000-150000/page/17

Dimbleby, R. (1964) *Every Eight Hours. The story of The Spastics Society,* London: Hodder.

Dunn, D. S., & Burcaw, S. (2013) Disability identity: Exploring narrative accounts of disability. Rehabilitation Psychology, Vol. 58, issue 2.

Engels, F. (1892) *The Condition of the Working Class in England in 1844,* London, Sonnenschein & Co.

Engelund, S. R., (2012), 'Other and Othering', *Multicultural Literature at the University of Oslo*, Blog, WordPress.

Evans, J. (1996), The U.K. Civil Rights Campaign and The Disability Discrimination Act – speech made in Vienna, 1/2 November 1996.

Farrar, M., (2009), 'Who We Were', *Big Flame 1970 – 1984* https://bigflameuk.wordpress.com/about/

Fielding, S., (2008), 'Political History', *Making History* http://www.history.ac.uk/makinghistory/resources/arti cles/political_history.html

Findlay, B., (1993), 'Community care and assessment: the Birmingham approach' (72 – 82) in *A Challenge To Change*, (eds) Beresford, P., Harding, T., London: National Institute for Social Work.

Findlay, B., (1994) 'Quality and Equality in Education: The Denial of Disability Culture'. In *Improving Education*, Ribbins, P. & Burridge, E. (eds); London: Cassell Publishers. 126 – 140.

Findlay, B., (1994), 'Disability information or misinformation?' *NDIP Newsletter*, No. 9: 1.

Finkelstein, V., (1980), *Attitudes and Disabled People*, New York, World Rehabilitation Fund.

Finkelstein, V., (1981), 'Disability and the Helper/Helped Relationship: An Historical View', in Brechin, A., Liddiard, P., and Swain, J. (eds) *Handicap in a Social World*, Sevenoaks, Hodder and Stoughton in Association with the Open University, pp. 58 – 62.

Finkelstein, V., (1990), *Experience And Consciousness*, Notes from Talk to Liverpool Housing Authority.

Finkelstein, V., (2001), 'The Social Model Repossessed', presented to Manchester Coalition Of Disabled People – 1 December 2001 https://disability-studies.leeds.ac.uk/wp-content/uploads/sites/40/library/finkelstein-soc-mod-repossessed.pdf.

Finkelstein, V., (2007), 'The 'Social Model of Disability' and the Disability Movement', Coalition, (March) http://pf7d7vi404s1dxh27mla5569.wpengine.netdna-cdn.com/files/library/finkelstein-The-Social-Model-of-Disability-and-the-Disability-Movement.pdf.

Foucault, M., (1977), *Discipline and Punish: The Birth of the Prison*, Translated by Alan Sheridan, London, Allen Lane, Penguin.

Fromm, E., (1961), *Marx's Concept of Man*, Frederick Ungar Publishing, New York, 1961. pp. 1 – 85.

Gearty, C., (2015), 'Beware the Extremists', *London Review of Books*, https://www.lrb.co.uk/v37/n04/conor-gearty/beware-the-extremists.

Gillespie-Sells, K., Campbell, J., (1991), *Disability Equality Training the Trainers' Guide*, LBDRT, London: CCETSW.

Gilroy, P. et al., (1982), *The Empire Strikes Back: Race and Racism in '70s Britain*, London: Hutchinson in association with the Centre for Contemporary Cultural Studies.

Gleeson, B. J., (1997), 'Disability Studies: a historical materialist view', *Disability and Society*, 12 (2), pp. 179-202.

Grover, C. and Soldatic, K., (2012), 'Neoliberal restructuring, disabled people and social (in) security in

Australia and Britain', *Scandinavian Journal of Disability Research*, Vol. 15, Issue 3.

Gunnarsson, T., (2008)., 'Au Pairs Interview', *Penny Black Music*, http://www.pennyblackmusic.co.uk/MagSitePages/Arti cle/4558/Au-Pairs.

Hall, S., Roberts, B., Clarke, J., Jefferson, T., Critcher, C., (1978), *Policing the Crisis: Mugging, the State, and Law and Order*, London, Palgrave Macmilan.

Hall, S., (1992), 'Cultural Studies and its Theoretical Legacies,' in *Cultural Studies*, ed. Grossberg, L.; Nelson, C.; and Treichler, P.; New York: Routledge, p. 278, http://grad.usask.ca/gateway/archive21.html.

Harrison, J., (2002), *The early history of West Midlands Council of Disabled People* – A presentation at the 25th Anniversary of Disability West Midlands, http://www.disability.co.uk/sites/default/files/resource s/John%20Harrison%20%20the%20early%20history%20of %20West%20Midlands%20Council%20of%20Disabled%20 People.pdf.

House Of Commons Employment Committee, (1994), *The Operation of the Disabled Persons (Employment) Act 1944*, Minutes of Evidence Tuesday 8 March 1994, 281-i, London: HMSO.

Ikäheimo, H., (2009), 'Personhood and the social inclusion of people with disabilities: a recognition-theoretical approach', in *Arguing about Disability: Philosophical Perspectives*, edited by: Kristiansen K., Vehmas S., Shakespeare T., London: Routledge.
Available at: http://hdl.handle.net/1959.14/87043.

Imrie, R., (2004), 'Demystifying disability: a review of the International Classification of Functioning, Disability and Health' *Sociology of Health & Illness*, 26: pp. 287–305.

Jobbins, D., (2013), *UK higher education since Robbins – A timeline*, University World News, http://www.universityworldnews.com/article.php?story =20131028123008296.

John Greenwood Shipman; Source updated: 2017-06-28T23: http://en.wikipedia.org/wiki/John_Greenwood_Shipman

Johnson, A., Kline, R. and Poxon, G., (1984), *Dudley Council Ltd.*, Birmingham: Lookonit Publishing.

Jolly, D., (2013), 'A Tale of Two Models', Disabled People Against Cuts.

Keith, M., (2014), 'How did the empire strike back? Lessons for today from The Empire Strikes Back: Race and Racism in 70s' Britain', *Ethnic and Racial Studies*, Vol. 37, Issue 10.

Leonard, P., (1984), *Personality and Ideology: Towards a Materialist Understanding of the Individual*, London, Macmillan.

Liddiard, K., (2014) 'The work of disabled identities in intimate relationships', *Disability & Society*, Issue 1, pp. 115 – 128.

Mandal, A., (2018), 'What are movement disorders?' *News Medical*, https://www.news-medical.net/health/What-are-movement-disorders.aspx.

Marks, D., (1999), *Disability: Controversial Debates and Psychosocial Perspectives*, London: Routledge.

Mason, M., (1990), 'Internalized Oppression', *Disability Equality in Education*, Reiser, R. and Mason, M., (eds), London: ILEA).

Maude, A, (1971), 'The Enemy Within', *Sunday Express.*

Millington, P., Wood, H., (2010), *Forward: The History of Birmingham Disability Resource Centre*, Birmingham: BDRG.

Miller, E. J. and Gwynne, G. V., (1972), *A Life Apart*, London: Tavistock Publications.

Moore, N., (1995), *Access To Information*, London: Policy Studies Institute.

National Union of Students (Undated), *Our History*, https://www.nus.org.uk/en/who-we-are/our-history/.

Naudin, A., (2014), *Back in CCCS*, https://backinthecccs.wordpress.com/author/annettena udin/.

Nelson, L. H., (1993), 'Epistemological Communities' in L. Alcoff and E. Potter (eds.), Feminist Epistemologies (London: Routledge), pp. 121-59.

No One Is Illegal, (2006), *Workers Control Not Immigration Controls*, https://www.yumpu.com/en/document/view/5201209 6/workers-control-not-immigration-controls-no-one-is-illegal

Oliver, M., (1990), *The Politics of Disablement*, London: Macmillan.

Oliver, M., (1996), 'Defining Impairment And Disability: Issues At Stake' in *Exploring the Divide*, edited by Colin Barnes and Geoff Mercer, Leeds: The Disability Press, pp. 29 -54.

Oliver, M., (2004), 'The Social Model in Action: if I had a hammer', in *Implementing the Social Model of Disability: Theory and Research*, (eds) Barnes, C., and Mercer, G.; Leeds: The Disability Press, pp. 18-31).

Oliver, M. & Barnes, C., *Disability Politics: Where did it all go wrong*, Coalition 2006, pp. 8-13, http://pf7d7vi404s1dxh27mla5569.wpengine.netdna-cdn.com/files/library/Barnes-Coalition-disability-politics-paper.pdf.

Oliver, M. & Barnes, C. (2012), *The New Politics of Disablement*, 2nd ed., Basingstoke, Palgrave Macmillan.

Pfeiffer, D., (1992), 'Disabling definitions: Is the World Health Organization normal?' *New England Journal of Human Services*, 11, pp. 4-9.

Positive Psychology Program, (2017), *Self-Actualization: Definition & Examples*, https://positivepsychologyprogram.com/self-actualization/.

Ramsay, R., (1996), 'The influence of intelligence services on the British left', *Lobster*, https://www.lobster-magazine.co.uk/articles/rrtalk.htm.

Reeve, D., (2014), 'Psycho-emotional disablism and internalised oppression', in J. Swain, S. French, C. Barnes and C. Thomas (eds) *Disabling Barriers – Enabling Environments*, 3rd Edition, London: Sage, pp. 92-98.

Revolutionary Marxist Current [RMC], posted by archivearchie on 19 November 2009, https://bigflameuk.wordpress.com/2009/11/19/revolutionary-marxist-current/.

Russell, M. and Malhotra, R., (2002), 'The political economy of disablement: advances and contradictions', Socialist Register, York University.

Sapey, B., (2110), 'Disability Policy: a model based on individual autonomy', [English language version of: Politique du handicap: un modèle basé sur l'autonomie des personnes, *Informations Sociales*, 159, pp. 128-137.], http://eprints.lancs.ac.uk/35506/2/Disability_Policy_a_model_based_on_individual_autonomy.pdf.

Scheer, J. and Groce, N. (1988) 'Impairment as a Human Constant: Cross-Cultural and Historical Perspectives on Variation', *Journal of Social Issues*, 44 (1), pp. 23-37.

Sheldon, A. (2001) 'Disabled People and Communication Systems in the Twenty First Century', PhD thesis, University of Leeds.

Solomon, E. S., (1993), 'Women with a physical disability: A review of literature and suggestions for intervention' In Willmuth, M. and Holcomb, L., eds. *Women with Disabilities: Found Voices*, New York: Harrington Press.

Stone, D., (1985), *The Disabled State*, London, Macmillan.

Socialist Challenge, (1983), 'Bristol campaign against deportations continues', *Socialist Challenge*, no. 280, February, p.11.

Sutcliffe-Braithwaite, F., (2013), 'Margaret Thatcher, individualism and the welfare state', *Opinion Articles*, History & Policy.

Sutherland, A., (1989), 'Disability Arts, Disability Politics', *DAIL magazine*, September.

Sutherland, A., (2006), 'The Other Tradition: from personal politics to disability arts' – transcript of an interview,
http://disability-studies.leeds.ac.uk/files/library/Sutherland-The-Other-Tradition.pdf.

Swain, J. and Cameron, C., (1999), unless otherwise stated: 'Discourses of Labelling and Identity', in Corker, M. and French, S. (eds), *Disability Discourse*, Buckingham: Open University Press.

Symeonidou, S., (2014), 'New policies, old ideas: the question of disability assessment systems and social policy', *Disability & Society*, Vol. 29, Issue 8,

Tartakovsky, M., (2016), 'Self-Esteem Struggles and Strategies That Can Help',
https://psychcentral.com/lib/self-esteem-struggles-and-strategies-that-can-help/

The Royal College of Pathology, (2018) *What is pathology?*
https://www.rcpath.org/discover-pathology/what-is-pathology.html

Thomas, C., (2004), 'Developing the Social Relational in the Social Model of Disability: a theoretical agenda' in Barnes, C. and Mercer, G. (eds), *Implementing The Social Model of Disability: Theory and Research*, Leeds: Disability Press.

Thornton, P. and Lunt, N., (1996), *Employment for Disabled People: social obligation or individual responsibility?* University of York, Social Policy Research Unit

Townsend, P., (2004), *The Fortunes of Sociology at Essex 1963-1982*. This paper was given: 11 November 2004, Department of Sociology, University of Essex, 40th anniversary,
https://essexsociologyalumni.com/memories/peter-townsend-the-fortunes-of-sociology-at-essex-1963-1982/

Voigt, R. J., (2009), 'Who Me? Self-Esteem for People with Disabilities',
https://psychcentral.com/lib/self-esteem-struggles-and-strategies-that-can-help/

Voluntary Action History Society, (2013.), *'Margaret Thatcher and the Voluntary Sector'*, Voluntary Action History Society,
http://www.vahs.org.uk/2013/04/margaret-thatcher-and-the-voluntary-sector/

Warren, D., (2007), *The Key to My Cell*, Living History Library.

Weinreich, P. and Saunderson, W., (2003), Analysing Identity: Cross-Cultural, Societal and Clinical Contexts, London: Routledge.

Wikipedia (2009), John Biggs-Davison,
https://en.wikipedia.org/wiki/John_Biggs-Davison.

Williams-Findlay, R, (2009), 'Is there evidence to support the view that the language and subject matter selected by the Times and the Guardian in relation to disabled people has changed over the last twenty years',
https://disability-studies.leeds.ac.uk/wp-content/uploads/sites/40/library/williams-findlay-RWilliams-DisabilityDissertation-200372855-3.pdf

Williams-Findlay, B., (2011), *Lifting the Lid on Disabled People Against Cuts,* http://disability-studies.leeds.ac.uk/files/library/williams-findlay-Lifting-the-Lid-on-Disabled-People-Against-Cuts-D-S-final.pdf 2011.

Williams-Findlay, B., (2015), 'Personalisation and self-determination: the same difference?', *Critical and Radical Social Work,* Vol. 3 (1) pp. 67 – 87, Policy Press.

Wolf, S. & Mann, M., (1975), *The Troubles at Essex: A Case Study of Student Unrest* (Unpublished), https://essexsociologyalumni.com/memories/notable-events/.

World Health Organisation, (2001), *International Classification of Functioning, Disability and Health (ICF),* Geneva, http://www.who.int/classifications/icf/en/.

Wood, P. (1980) *International Classification of Impairments, Disabilities and Handicaps,* Geneva: World Health Organisation.

Yaa de Villiers, P., (2006), 'Phillippa Yaa de Villiers – Biography', *Boarder Crossing 3,* Trans Cultural Writing, British Council, http://www.transculturalwriting.com/radiophonics/contents/magazine/issue3/index.html.

Zarb, G., Oliver, M., (1992), *Ageing with a disability: what do they expect after all these years?* University of Greenwich, London.

Zevallos, Z., (2011), 'What is Otherness?' *Other Sociologist,* https://othersociologist.com/otherness-resources/.

About Resistance Books

Resistance Books is the publishing arm of Socialist Resistance. We publish books independently, and also jointly with Merlin Press (London) and the International Institute for Research and Education (Amsterdam). Further information about Resistance Books, including a full list of titles available and how to order them, can be obtained at www.resistancebooks.org.

Resistance Books:
  info@resistancebooks.org
  www.resistancebooks.org
  PO Box 62732, London, SW2 9GQ.

Socialist Resistance is a revolutionary Marxist, internationalist, ecosocialist and feminist political network. You can read analysis and news from *Socialist Resistance* at www.socialistresistance.org.

Socialist Resistance collaborates with the Fourth International. Its online magazine, *International Viewpoint*, is at www.internationalviewpoint.org

Lightning Source UK Ltd.
Milton Keynes UK
UKHW011921060520
362881UK00001B/2